MW01178941

RURAL TRANSFORMATIONS AND RURAL CRIME

Research in Rural Crime series

Series editors: **Alistair Harkness**, University of New England in New South Wales, Australia and **Matt Bowden**, Technological University Dublin, Ireland

---

The Research in Rural Crime series reflects the multi-faceted nature of rural crime and provides an outlet for original, cutting-edge research in this emergent criminological subfield. Truly international in nature, it leads the way for new thinking on a wide range of rural crime topics, rural transgressions, security and justice.

Forthcoming in the series:

Gender-based Violence and Rurality in the 21st Century
Ziwei Qi, April Terry and Tamara Lynn (Editors), March 2023

Farm Crime: A Rural Criminology Perspective
Kyle Mulrooney and Alistair Harkness, May 2024

Dark Tourism and Rural Crime: Crime and Punishment in Rural Australia
Jenny Wise, November 2024

Chinese Rural Criminology: The Impact of Chinese Social Economic Structure
Qingli Meng, January 2026

Find out more at
bristoluniversitypress.co.uk/research–in–rural–crime

RURAL TRANSFORMATIONS AND RURAL CRIME

International Critical Perspectives in
Rural Criminology

Edited by
Matt Bowden and
Alistair Harkness

BRISTOL
UNIVERSITY
PRESS

First published in Great Britain in 2022 by

Bristol University Press
University of Bristol
1–9 Old Park Hill
Bristol
BS2 8BB
UK
t: +44 (0)117 374 6645
e: bup-info@bristol.ac.uk

Details of international sales and distribution partners are available at bristoluniversitypress.co.uk

British Library Cataloguing in Publication Data
A catalogue record for this book is available from the British Library

ISBN 978-1-5292-1775-9 hardcover
ISBN 978-1-5292-1776-6 ePub
ISBN 978-1-5292-1777-3 ePdf

Cover design: Liam Roberts
Front cover image: Stas Kulesh

This book is dedicated to the late Maura Bowden (née Hicks), 1937–2020

Contents

Notes on Contributors

Matt Bowden is Senior Lecturer in sociology and Head of Research at the Faculty of Arts and Humanities at Technological University Dublin, Ireland, and Adjunct Senior Lecturer at the University of New England in New South Wales, Australia. His research interests are in the politics and everyday realities of security, plural policing and crime prevention, and he is currently researching on rural security/safety, security consumption, police culture and police habitus.

Vania Ceccato is Professor at KTH Royal Institute of Technology, Stockholm, Sweden. Her research includes the geography of crime and fear in urban and rural environments. She wrote the open access book *Rural Crime and Community Safety* (Routledge, 2016) and she is coordinator of the Safe Places network, a partner of the UN–Habitat Safer Cities programme.

Walter S. DeKeseredy is Anna Deane Carlson Endowed Chair of Social Sciences, Director of the Research Center on Violence, and Professor of Sociology at West Virginia University. He has published 27 books, over 120 scientific journal articles and 90 scholarly book chapters on violence against women and other social problems.

Joseph F. Donnermeyer is Professor Emeritus / Academy Professor in the School of Environment and Natural Resources at The Ohio State University, and Adjunct Professor at both the Research Center on Violence at West Virginia University and the Centre for Rural Criminology, University of New England, Australia. He is the author or co-author of over 100 peer reviewed publications issues related to rural crime and rural societies. He was the editor of *Routledge International Handbook of Rural Criminology* (2016).

Rachel Hale is an independent researcher and Research Associate with the Centre for Rural Criminology at the University of New England in New South Wales, Australia, and a member of the International Society for the Study of Rural Crime's executive. Her critical, feminist research promotes decarceration, prevention and access to justice.

Alistair Harkness is Senior Lecturer in criminology and co-director of the Centre for Rural Criminology at the University of New England, and is treasurer of the International Society for the Study of Rural Crime. His primary research interests are in rural acquisitive crime, with a particular emphasis on crime prevention, policing responses and community partnerships.

Kyle Mulrooney is Senior Lecturer in criminology and co-director of the Centre for Rural Criminology at the University of New England, and is Vice President of the International Society for the Study of Rural Crime. His primary field of research is the sociology of punishment in which he has examined issues ranging from the nexus between penal populism and political culture to drug policy, and rural crime more broadly.

Artur Pytlarz is a doctoral student in the School of Languages, Law and Social Sciences at the Technological University Dublin, and an Irish Research Council Government of Ireland Scholar. He holds an MA in Sociology from Wroclaw University and an MA in Criminology from the Dublin Institute of Technology. His research interests include rural security and safety production and role of rural communities; rapid social changes, typical of the late-modern landscape; and rural resilience.

Susanne Stenbacka is Professor in human geography at Uppsala University. Her research revolves around regional development and rural transformation with a specific focus on provision of welfare services, gender relations and migration. Her current studies deal with rural transformation in the aftermath of police withdrawal, refugee migration to rural areas and rural experiences of disability.

Rob White is Emeritus Distinguished Professor of Criminology at the University of Tasmania, Australia. Among his recent books are *Theorising Green Criminology* (Routledge, 2022), *Crossroads of Rural Crime* (edited with Alistair Harkness, Emerald, 2021), *Critical Forensic Studies* (with Roberta Julian and Loene Howes, Routledge, 2022) and *The Extinction Curve* (with John van der Velden, Emerald, 2021).

James Windle is Lecturer in criminology at University College Cork, Ireland. His research has focused on drug markets and policy, gangs, opium farming, organised crime and agricultural theft. He is author of *Suppressing Illicit Opium production: Successful Intervention in Asia and the Middle East* (Bloomsbury, 2016) and co-editor of *Historical Perspectives on Organized Crime and Terrorism* (Routledge, 2018) and *Giving Voice to Diversity in Criminological Research: 'Nothing About Us Without Us'* (Policy Press, 2021).

Andrew Wooff is Associate Professor of criminology at Edinburgh Napier University. His research focuses on a number of areas, recently including the policing of COVID-19 in rural communities. He has published on rural policing, police custody, vulnerability, police education and the special constabulary. He is a member of the Scottish Institute for Policing Research.

Acknowledgements

This book contains significant contributions that enrich our theoretical understanding of the social, political, economic and cultural aspects of crime in rural society. The authors consider the rural as a particular socio-spatiality, identifying contemporary theoretical, empirical and practical issues in respect of crime and the environment. We gratefully acknowledge authors of chapters in the text for their contributions – not just to this volume but for the advancement of rural criminological thought, too.

The kernel of an idea for this first book in the Bristol University Press Research in Rural Crime series, for which we are co-editors, originated in Reds, a small bar in San Francisco's Chinatown. We acknowledge Ashley who supplied liquid refreshments as ideas similarly flowed. The rough notes taken on serviettes there in November 2019 became a book proposal.

To this end, we are also gratefully indebted to our commissioning editor, Rebecca Tomlinson, for her input, patience, support, cheeriness and constant sage guidance. With Rebecca's stewardship and the support of the Bristol team, this series has a very bright future.

Finally, and more broadly, many thanks to the many colleagues – members of the academy both established and emerging, and students and practitioners as well – who have stepped forward in recent years to join the rural criminology journey.

Matt Bowden and Alistair Harkness
April 2022

Series Preface

Matt Bowden and Alistair Harkness

Contemporary criminology grew out of mass transformations in society during the twentieth century – a period that witnessed the formation and consolidation of cities through migration, and the restructuring of 'the urban' following the emergence of the information age. Considerable debate, research and scholarly theory has been formed primarily within the urban domain in this regard: witness, for example, the influence of the Chicago School and its influence on the rise of urban ecology-based approaches to crime prevention.

Rural areas themselves are currently being transformed by the new patterns of global flows as societies undergo transitions within. Nevertheless, myths about peaceful, crime-free areas beyond the cityscape persist, when in fact rural crime is multi-faceted – raising new policy predicaments about policing and security governance. With approximately 45 per cent of the global population living in rural areas, a focus on rural crime in these diverse communities is critical. The series provides a space for new research and writing on a wide range of rural crime topics, rural transgressions, security and justice.

The *Research in Rural Crime* series has emerged to fill an important gap; to provide an outlet for mid-length monographs which focus on rural crime and responses to rural crime – providing an opportunity for original, cutting-edge monograph-length research in the criminological subfield of rural criminology. Truly international in nature, it welcomes and produces titles that are jurisdictional specific or related to themes that transcend political and juridical boundaries, and presents outlooks on contemporary theory, research and pressing public policy issues.

In essence, this series provides a formalised space for voices hitherto overlooked or without a venue for longer length exploration of rural crime, policing, security and other issues. It allows for the consolidation of intellectual thoughtfulness in monograph form, either from sole- or joint-authored volumes, or from groups of colleagues in edited collections.

Importantly, too, it provides an opportunity for the combination of academic scholarship and empirical research with contemporary application.

Contributors to this series provide cutting-edge interdisciplinary and comparative rural criminological perspectives. Titles will be theoretically and conceptually driven, empirical or adopting mixed-methods approaches, and topics will focus on regional, rural and remote parts of the globe that are often overlooked in criminological works.

This book – the first in a new series – is edited by the series' editors. It seeks to redress the balance in theorising rural criminology and research in this emerging sub-discipline with a collection of scholarly essays that focus on critical contemporary perspectives on the rural. It offers state-of-the-art scholarship from across the globe, and considers the future agenda for the discipline.

What are the theoretical and conceptual framings of rural criminology across the world? Thinking creatively about the challenges of rural crime and policing, in this stimulating collection of essays experts in this emerging field draw from theories of modernity, feminism, climate change, left realism and globalisation.

In this text, we have chosen to focus primarily upon weaving conceptual arguments and theoretical issues through a series of critical essays. Contributors were briefed to refrain from the particularities of locale in favour of conceptual framing, and to avoid jurisdictional specificity, instead giving priority to in-depth discussions of the conceptual challenges now presenting to this sub discipline within criminology. This is not to suggest that contributions in their endeavour to articulate theoretical issues eschew empirical research. Instead, contributions build and explore these conceptual spaces with references to empirical work that they have access to. We are particularly mindful of the power of theoretical cases and have encouraged contributors to draw on national and transnational cases to highlight the arguments they make.

The individual contributions discuss crime and rural socio-spatiality against classical and contemporary theories on transitions. They discuss, *inter alia*, how rural areas are transformed by the information age through greater connectivity and the comingling of urban/rural spaces (the so-called 'rurban'). Recognising our common understanding of rural as 'remote' and 'peripheral', contributors consider the withdrawal of police services as a collapse of the modern 'solid' institutions that once held rural communities together. Peripheralisation implies an edge between different states of being and acting, or as resulting from the space between different sets of social relations.

Contributors explore these themes in respect to policing, welfare, crime prevention and punishment, reflecting on themes of spatial inequality and spatial justice. Moreover, as we stand at the edge of a new geological epoch – the Anthropocene – contributors theorise these new challenges in terms of peripherality and remoteness. Peripherality contains many hidden areas, where the panoptic gaze of the metropole on issues of gender inequality, hegemonic masculinity and domestic violence proliferate in the supposed crime-free idyll – as rural society often is held in the imaginations of the wider public.

The essay-style structure of the individual chapters provides authors the space to think critically and creatively about these issues and challenges. Whilst contributors draw upon contemporary and classical arguments – and from a richness of traditions from theories of modernity, feminism, left realism and globalisation to name just a few – the ensemble of authors also attend to matters around technological change, the Anthropocene and with pointers to the future.

This book centres on rural transformations, and explicates the many ways that rural societies experience change: whether that be social change wrought by new economic ordering of the globe centring on technology; or institutional change resulting in the way in which the state and market penetrate civil society in rural areas. These changes themselves pose conceptual and empirical challenges to criminology, to capture the rural experience of crime, victimisation and harm.

It is always going to be a tough challenge to encapsulate a complete diversity of geographically located contributors in a single volume – and we are conscious that we have not been able to secure representation from around the world here – but are confident that we have assembled an ensemble of early-, mid- and established 'wise owls' to spark discussion and debate.

We hope you enjoy the book – and those that follow in the series – and that you yourself might be motivated to 'take up the cudgels' and contribute to the ongoing development and growth of the rural criminology sub-discipline.

1

Reimagining Rural Criminology in a Time of Change

Matt Bowden and Alistair Harkness

Introduction

In August 2021, the Intergovernmental Panel on Climate Change (IPCC) published its Sixth Assessment Report on the physical science of change (IPCC, 2021). It restates, quite unequivocally, that it is human influence that has led to the warming of the atmosphere, the cryosphere, the ocean and the biosphere – largely owing to the release of greenhouse gases since the start of the Industrial Revolution, but most particularly in recent years.

Since the 1980s, there has seen unprecedented warming of the planet – again attributed to human influence through greenhouse gas emissions. Somewhat depressingly, the IPCC reports on glacial decline in the Arctic Sea and notes that if the growth pattern continues in human-induced climate change, global sea levels will rise to an unprecedented degree, making coastal habitation impossible (IPCC, 2021). The report, in many ways, reiterates and updates what we already know, but offers a timely reminder of the nature and scale of transformation that is in train as we enter the third decade of the twenty-first century.

These changes – without doubt – will be felt in cities and towns across the planet. The working poor, in particular, will feel the brunt, as economies will by necessity need to transform and so many will be left behind.

But, crucially, these human-induced environmental changes will also lead to social, economic and cultural transformations in rural – and especially coastal – areas. Already, many industries located in rural areas are declining – whether it is the harvesting of peat for fuel or composting, or the highly intensive mining and fossil fuel operations that are scaling back and being replaced with more sustainable energy sources. That these will impact and

1

transform rural economies and societies is in no doubt. Let us not forget as well of the largely agrarian-based economies and communities in the South Pacific and elsewhere – countries such as Tuvalu, indeed – where a few centimetres of ocean rise will devastate entire populations (Ainge Roy, 2019).

There is a common myth internationally that rural areas are characterised by change that is either slow or static. The idea here is that the rural is somehow connected to the premodern notion of *gemeinschaft*, which as many of the chapters in this volume will attest is unsustainable. Rural spaces are restructured, reordered and respatialised by modernity and intersect with global processes such as migration, enhanced transportation and digital infrastructures, and penetration by state institutions. Rural areas are exposed to the risk society (Beck, 1992) and rural people have adopted strategies to protect themselves from crimes and various harms (Pytlarz and Bowden, 2019; Bowden and Pytlarz, 2020) as the solid institutions of modernity retreat, and further illustrated by these same authors in this book.

This book centres on rural transformations, and explicates the many ways that rural societies experience change: whether that be social change wrought by new economic ordering of the globe centring on technology; or institutional change resulting in the way in which the state and market penetrate civil society in rural areas. These changes themselves pose conceptual and empirical challenges to criminology, to capture the rural experience of crime, victimisation and harm.

Rural areas are subject to flows of capital, labour, migrants and data: they are the subject of political (mis)adventures, power struggles, land grabs for suburbanisation, state withdrawal and neglect. When these structuring forces change, rural communities, too, experience those changes and they provide the contextual backdrop, or the physical, social and symbolic spaces in which rural crime and responses to it take place. Moreover, these forces also align to shape the institutional and legal frameworks that structure rural life, together with the power of populist ideologies that wish to deny the scientific consensus on climate change.

The unprecedented burning of the Amazon forests by the Brazilian regime during the presidency of Jair Bolsonaro, for example, has done irreversible damage to the local and global ecosystems on an unprecedented scale; and the political populism of former US president Donald Trump and his fellow-traveller de-globalists throughout the world have promised rural peoples much, but delivered so very little. Brexit, the UK's withdrawal from the European Union, for example, resulted from a struggle within the British cultural elite to sever itself from what it believes to be the entrapments of European Union membership – one branch being strongly committed to multiculturalism, but a powerful other faction being imperially racist has capitalised upon the anti-establishment nationalism of the disenfranchised (Flemmen and Savage, 2017). This misadventure has resulted in political insecurity in Ireland, and destabilising the confidence of civil society in the predominately rural border communities in Ireland that depend on the retention of an open border for trade and everyday life to remain normal (see Hayward, 2021).

Reflecting more broadly on the themes that are encompassed in this book, we see that the shape of rural communities depends greatly on what is practised every day by rural people. In addition to everyday life, rural areas are structured by the actions of states, by the economy and technology – and so we must regard the rural as a distinct socio-spatiality. Moreover, the rural is connected to and shaped by local and global forces that organise both in and beyond its boundaries. The rural therefore intersects with economy, environment and politics at the macro level, but also with gender, class and ethnicity and with struggles for power, resources and identity that shapes its cohesion and (in)security.

This chapter serves as an introduction to *Rural Transformations and Rural Crime*, and is structured in three parts. First, it reflects upon the rural as a socio-spatial nexus that is composed of rural practices and shaped by the external world society and the state. Here, the chapter reflects further on the shared space between rural and green criminology with reference to the Anthropocene. Second, it considers some of the – often contradictory – ways in which the rural and rural people are represented in popular discourse. It contemplates some of these themes through the lens of rural criminology as a newly emerging subdiscipline, drawing primarily from the work of Donnermeyer and DeKeseredy (2014). Third, the chapter provides an overview of the various contributions in this book.

The rural: badlands or promised land?

Bruce Springsteen's album *Darkness at the Edge of Town* speaks, as do so many in Springsteen's oeuvre, of hard times, of the edge and of the space beyond the city limits. It captures the idea of the rural as an unknown place of 'badlands' or the feral zones beyond the tamed civilised spaces of the city.

It calls to mind the German adage *Stadtluft macht frei* (city air makes one free) standing for the period in early European history where cities were said to reflect a civilised existence beyond the supposed wildness of rural life. This idea also contributed to the urbanism of the Chicago School who imagined the city as a place where individuals migrating from the old, primarily agricultural world, could find a superior life in a more advanced division of labour offered by the city (Park, 1925) and thus would be free from the entrapments of tradition.

But 'the rural' must be understood in a number of ways as having distinct spatial and social characteristics that distinguish it from 'the urban'. Social theories of space have merit here, for they help us to understand that the rural consists of a physicality, an imagery and rural practices in everyday life (Halfacree, 2006; see also Chapters 8 and 9 of this volume).

While not specifically writing of the rural, we can draw from the work of French philosopher and spatial theorist Henri Lefebvre (1991) who distinguished between abstract space and social space. Abstract space relates to how space is ordered into systems of production, political organisation and control. Lefebvre viewed this ordering as a form of violence on space, and the task of a sociology of space was to unmask and reveal these contradictions. Similarly, as space is incorporated into production, social space becomes part of the spatial process in train and therefore socially constructs the meaning systems that attach to space, in how it is imagined and represented. When we think of space therefore with need to comprehend a twofold dynamic between a physical 'thing' and a social 'process' (Harvey, 1997).

In this way, we can see the rural as a physical geography that first exists in a natural state and then, as a result of a process of territorialisation, it is ordered in the formation of a state and reordered and rescaled to fit with transformations: globalisation, for example (Brenner, 1999). This imposes political and administrative boundaries on the rural, integrates it into a division of labour, and converts it into a means of production and, in the current era, into the global scale of capitalist production. Understanding the rural as part of a spatial ordering, we ought to look also at the way in which it is shaped by the state and its role in the governance of the rural. Changes in how public institutions do business has a territorial impact on the way space is governed and, in turn, affects everyday practice and everyday lives.

Brenner et al (2003) offer a useful threefold model of how the state orders space. 'State-space' can be considered in 'narrow', 'integral' and 'representational' terms. In the 'narrow' sense, state-space refers to the organisation of state territoriality and the evolving role of boundaries and borders within which an array of juridical and political institutions are involved in territorialising political power.

State-space in the 'integral' sense involves the way in which state institutions are deployed and mobilised strategically to the task of regulating and reorganising socio-economic relations. Hence, state-spatial strategies should be viewed as 'historically specific practices through which state institutions attempt to adjust to the constantly changing geo-economic and geo-political conditions in which they operate' (Brenner et al, 2003: 10). Many of the chapters in this volume pick up on these themes in the way in which rural institutions have become more fluid (Bowden and Pytlarz in Chapter 4), the way in which prisons are located in rural areas (Hale, Harkness and Mulrooney in Chapter 10), and the way in which the organisation is reshaped and respatialised (by Wooff in Chapter 8 and by Stenbacka in Chapter 9).

Finally, state-space in the 'representational' sense refers to the way in which the spatial practices of states shape the 'subjectivities and horizons in everyday life' and the way in which both scale-specific and space-specific strategies underpin particular interests with established and new state-spaces. Critical here is the way in which the state penetrates rural civil society and, in the current era, this takes the place through governance and regulation through formal institutions and networks.

These new configurations of rural space bring new issues, challenges and possibilities. These have been acute in societies in transition, such as in Eastern Europe and in the former states of the Soviet Union where state institutions have reconfigured the rural economy and introduced new forms of governance to affect that reshaping. In addition, climate change is a critical driver of new questions for humanity, forging responses from states to reconfigure spatial questions, and previously regarded as minor environmental crimes, become more prominent.

We live in a new era where geological time and human time have collided in the Anthropocene – where the condition of the planet is caused by humans and not the reverse. This epoch replaces the Holocene, where human societies could be constructed because of the temperate nature of the biosphere (Shearing, 2015). At the level of epistemology, humans are now determining and shaping the forces of nature, social science is potentially upended as we had previously regarded nature as an objective force, which caused effects to humans. Indeed, the Anthropocene poses a new paradox as to how humanity can protect itself from the worst excesses of itself (Hamilton, 2017), a topic discussed further by Rob White in Chapter 7 of this book.

For criminologists pondering these questions, environmental and climactic change in the Anthropocene is not just a standard security threat – but shows that humans now have an entangled fragility along with all living systems, requiring new ways of being, doing and organising:

> Central to these developments has been a pervasive (though not universal) sensibility – a way of being – which has understood nature (and nonhumans) as separate from and unaffected by humans and their actions. Within this way of being, humans and nature are understood as two entirely separate realms and survival by any means is the ultimate axiom. (Harrington and Shearing, 2017: 142–3)

Thinking about security has been framed within the context of the Holocene and therefore bounded within sovereign territoriality, or that security threats within a space can be merely controlled by a group. The security threats of climate change have outgrown these boundaries and are now no longer determined by the dualism of friend/enemy nor adhere to spatial lines. The security of our planet – and the resources we require to live and thrive – relies upon the introduction of an ethic of 'care' which requires us to go back to the original meaning of *securitas*: a state of being 'without a care'. Citing feminist authors, Harrington and Shearing (2017) argue that the adoption of caring virtues is required in national and international governance by humans as custodians of the environment – so as that we generate secure societies based on a shift in ethic from careless to careful.

An example in the criminological literature of these abstract spatial issues and environmental themes is the issue of water, highlighted by the work of Eman and Meško (2021) and their study of water regulation and governance in Slovenia. There has been growing concern, as we become more conscious of climate change, of the importance of water as a life-giving source and a public good that must be distributed fairly and equally. Yet, water has been to a large extent commodified and there have been attempts to reconfigure its governance through privatisation in various states, and by meta-governing bodies such as the European Union in its attempt to legitimise water privatisation.

Water crimes vary from concrete interference of aquifers, syphoning and pilfering from reserves to more abstract harms such as attacks on water utility companies as 'critical infrastructure' by cybercriminals. Eman and Meško's (2021) work underlines that these environmental crimes are also rural crimes: they take place in spatial contexts that are remote from the centres of governance and regulation, and thus out of sight and out of mind (see also White, Chapter 7). They call for a convergence of rural and environmental criminology on this issue and highlight the emergence of a socio-spatial politics of water, together with the emergence of water rights and regulation as a form of spatial (in)justice. A study by Eichholz et al (2013) on the cultural and economic capital redistribution of land in post-Soviet rural Uzbekistan reveal that farmers doing well after some privatisation were able to purchase pumps to ensure their water supply when irrigation stocks of publicly available water were lower, giving them an unequal advantage over other categories of agricultural producer.

Rural crime: imagery and myths

In their foundational work on rural criminology, Donnermeyer and DeKeseredy (2014) dispel four myths about the rural that are central in the discussions in this volume. The first of these is the assumption that there is a rural–urban dichotomy premised upon the idea of urban-normativity (Thomas et al, 2011). However, when put to scrutiny, rural areas are diverse spatially, socially and culturally – and hence they are likely to generate distinct types of crimes and transgressions. Scholars writing on aspects of socio-spatiality have shown that the dichotomous model is inadequate. Space might best be conceptualised as a continuum of urban and rural and divided into subcategories such as peri-urban, rural–urban or 'edge cities', 'urban fringe' and 'exurban' depending on how the particular contexts relate to one another (see Lerner and Eakin, 2011).

The second myth is that there is a higher level of collective efficacy which keeps rural crime rates low: however, as Donnermeyer and DeKeseredy (2014) summarise the literature on violence against women in rural areas, there is a type of collective efficacy that promotes this crime based upon the 'old boys' club', the male-support networks that share misogynistic values that maintain patriarchy.

The third myth is that rural crime rates have been historically low and are now increasing: this particularly relates again to the absence of 'street crime', but rates of victimisation for rural separated and divorced women in the US exceeds that for urban women. In addition, what matters here is which crimes are in the frame and which are left out: theft of livestock and farm equipment are specific forms of crime not typically found in urban areas by definition, but are endemic in rural parts of the US and Australia.

The final myth is that the conflicting imagery of rural as either idyllic or horrid: the rural is supposedly peaceful, green and unspoilt but this sits alongside mass media and internet 'horrifications' and 'pornification' of the rural in slasher movies and internet porn. This reflects an ongoing ideology of urbanism as a free and civilised existence, as against the darkness and mystique that surrounds the rural. Donnermeyer and DeKeseredy (2014: 24) point out that this imagery 'lower[s] rural people's status, regardless of their sex and age, and pathologize[s] their culture'.

In cultural representations, the rural is both the 'promised land' and the 'badlands', the font of virtue and nature, and the cauldron of evil and destruction. It is regarded as a playground for the urban. It is a place of retreat that we wish to have preserved in a particular image of purity, simplicity and civility. In one of the most cited articles in the scholarly journal *Sociologica Ruralis*, Bessière wrote:

> As a reaction to the complexity of the modern world in which social links either are falling apart or weakening, rural areas are chosen as holiday destinations seem to offer the possibility for socializing or for finding a community identity. Therefore, people dream of friendly relationships, true and genuine values, roots. (Bessière, 1998: 22)

It is therefore expected that those who are custodians of the countryside will behave in a particular way so as it can be utilised for its leisure and alimentary function. This image of the rural is in a perpetual dialectic with those depicted by the rural 'horror show'. There is no greater image of that purity than the rural as a supply of food, for we also look to the rural as a preserved environment for what we eat, or indeed the water we drink.

The marketing of rural tourism and the products of farming rest heavily upon the image of purity, serenity and 'natural'. Yet the rural is also the site for environmental destruction through extractive industries mining for minerals and fossil fuels which, too, 'horrifies' the landscape. For McClanahan (2020) 'horror' and 'dread' are two categories essential in rural, green and cultural criminological analysis: they are not an error imposed by contemporary cultural representations as such as Donnermeyer and DeKeseredy (2014) and others imply, but are real subjective experiences. The horror movie draws us from the perspective of the gaze of the sympathetic (metropolitan) 'terrified outsider'. McClanahan argues:

> While horror ... exists first and foremost in the mind – it is a problem of subjectivity without much to found it in the objective material world – it must be imagined in a material landscape, and those landscapes are frequently rural. What better setting, after all, for a genre that requires the dialectic of desire and dread than a landscape whose mean requires the dialectic between desire (the idyll) and dread (the anti-idyll)? (McClanahan, 2020: 639)

It is against this backdrop of social, technological and environmental change that we have assembled the contributions in this book to speak to the ongoing and the new themes for rural criminology in the twenty-first century.

The framework of this book

This book is the first in the Bristol University Press 'Research in Rural Crime' series. It began its life with an initial meeting of minds at the American Society of Criminology conference at New Orleans in 2016 and later at the 2019 meeting in San Francisco. The series aims to capture – in mid-length monographs and edited collections – the recent boom in activity in the rural criminological space. As a first volume, the challenge has been to coalesce leading authors in the field to spell out the major achievements and gaps in theory and empirical research in rural criminology. The aim, therefore, has been to produce a series of essays that are conceptual and theoretical in nature, that benchmark the state of the art in the field, and that provide an agenda for rural criminology in the coming years. It is also the intention to address some of the global themes outlined in this introductory chapter thus far and for them to be explored through a thematic lens.

We assume that rural and urban are homologous – that one is the opposite of the other; the rural in this sense is defined by its unique socio-spatial and topographical characteristics; and by extension, the absence of these features, would define, its contrary opposite. Taking the approach that there is a rural–urban continuum, Vania Ceccato suggests in Chapter 2 that there exist no sharp breaking points between these ideal–typical constructs, but that the rural exists as a 'flow' of people and materials rather than necessarily fixed entities. While the rural has been defined in popular and academic discourses as idyllic and crime-free, Ceccato postulates 15 different reasons why we should care about rural crime and safety. Among these reasons, she points out, is that low crime rates are not synonymous with the absence of harmful acts, and that distance may complicate official crime reporting. Rural areas are heterogenous and are changing – and in this context rural society faces the challenges of crime, violence and security just as much as the urban.

Identifying a list of 22 theoretical and empirical gaps, Joseph F. Donnermeyer sets out in Chapter 3 to develop a guide for research on crime and criminal justice in the context of rural space. Donnermeyer draws from Merton's theories of the middle range with reference to two paradigms – place-based theory and the left realist square of crime. Theories can be, and often are, underdeveloped, understated or name-dropped but never anchored, explained or justified: grand theorising or explanation sometimes lack specificity. Mid-range theory has the value of orienting researchers to the data and Donnermeyer provides insightful examples from middle-range theories including 'primary socialisation theory', 'civic community theory' and 'male-peer support' theory. Chapter 3 is a clarion call from Donnermeyer to 'get our hands dirty' with theory-generating and theory-building work in rural criminology.

Taking up the issue of rural safety and security from the lens of 'late modern governance' in Chapter 4, Matt Bowden and Artur Pytlarz make a similar argument to Ceccato that the rural areas are a 'space of flow', as with the urban. This is particularly true, they argue, of countries that have undergone particular forms of globalisation and which are anchored into the informational capitalist economy, where the rural has also been integrated and transformed. Citing a range of approaches within 'theories of modernity', they draw heavily from Bauman's ideas on 'liquid modernity', where solid institutions of the modern have been undermined by the globalisation of finance and manufacturing and generate, by the nature of this transformation, fear and insecurity. They use these conceptual tools to show how people wish to create a security bubble for themselves and in their 'theoretical case' in rural areas: this can be seen in the way in which people use forms of information as a means to arm themselves against insecurity.

Critical criminological approaches are often marginalised from research grants because their recommendations challenge the more mainstream states of mind of both policymakers and administrative criminology. Feminist criminology, Walter S. DeKeseredy argues in Chapter 5, challenges the hegemony of the mainstream by bringing together theoretically rich, empirically well-grounded contributions from remote rural places to inform public and scholarly debate. Indeed, challenging the hegemony of male privilege, radical feminist theory and research has been instrumental in highlighting the plight of women and girls as victims of violence and abuse. Such abuse, DeKeseredy points out, originates in the privilege of patriarchy.

DeKeseredy presents a series of empirical contributions illuminating this point, and brings together feminism with a mid-range theoretical approach highlighting how males offer peer support to one another though a form of mutual male-to-male reinforcement that perpetuates violence against their female partners, particularly in the context of divorce or separation. There remain many gaps in our understanding of woman abuse in rural spaces and DeKeseredy highlights the need for both quantitative and qualitative research to be applied to distinct and specific categories of violence across a more diverse range of categories reflecting rural difference including women with disabilities, LGBTIQ+ communities, indigenous people and ethnic groups.

A major aim of this volume is to explore how local cases address more universal concerns or indeed, how we can learn from applying conceptual frameworks to understanding and addressing problems associated with rural crime. In Chapter 6, James Windle brings together the conceptual framework of left realism and draws lessons from the case of agricultural theft in Ireland. Deploying the call of left realism to 'take crime seriously', Windle argues that this means listening to the fears of rural communities and farmers in particular, and incorporating their perspectives and understandings in our empirical work.

The chapter provides an intense overview of left realism, highlighting the approach as one that researches the actual experiences of crime, through victim surveys for example. Central to the left realist approach is the 'square of crime', an open system for assessing how the state and the criminal justice system, the public, the victim and the offender interact with one another to construct crime and respond to it. The chapter sets out a number of key strategies in a left realist agenda applied to agricultural theft in particular stressing the need to overcome the reluctance of farmers to reveal their victim experiences; finding more approachable ways to survey farm households; tailoring research instruments based upon some local knowledge of farm life; specifically researching the gendered differences of victimisation; and taking all points of the square of crime into consideration, researching the motivations of farm crime offenders.

The remoteness of rural areas makes charting and monitoring environmental harms more complicated. Therefore, much of the destruction of the natural environment, the biosphere we rely upon to sustain human existence, takes place outside of media and governmental gazes. This is a 'light touch' regulatory environment in which the harmful and destructive extraction of natural resources and pollution takes place out of sight, and thus out of mind. Rob White in Chapter 7 charts the impact of climate change including trends on global warming and greenhouse gas emissions and food (in)security. Critically, the chapter challenges us to think as criminologists within the paradigm of the Anthropocene – a geological epoch replacing the temperate Holocene which enabled humans to thrive – and to the concept of 'ecocide': the criminal acts that destroy ecosystems of both humans, other species and natural forces.

Recasting a rights perspective, therefore, requires that we go beyond a human rights framework to recognise those of non-humans. This requires a situation where both states and corporations are held accountable for the destruction of the worlds of other species. While these harmful acts can take place in one location, they are not geographically fixed in their impact. Consider water, for example – destruction in one location can have downstream effects on fish, other animals and on humans. On a world scale these threats lead to conflict and to the destruction of civilisation as we know it.

Having an understanding of the rural itself at a theoretical level is critical for engaging in relationships with rural people. Policing in rural communities perceived this way is a relational act carried on and through the everyday lives of rural people. Andrew Wooff sets out a conceptual model on the totality of rural space in Chapter 8. This involves the materiality of space, representational space and the sociality of space in everyday practice in the social lives of rural people. Policing, Wooff argues, has become more distant and abstract, which seems to run counter to claims to be policing in and with the community. He offers two linked case studies of policing in Scotland, which shifted from local police forces to a centralised model. This has removed police at the centre from the value of local knowledge in responding to safety and security issues in rural locales. Organisational changes in policing impacts on the everyday lives of rural people in by removing police from the rural context.

Taking a similar relational approach and also using the triangulation of physical space, representations and everyday practices, Susanne Stenbacka in Chapter 9 focuses on rural power relations, stressing the salience of space and human interactions in space. Stenbacka draws from the case of police reform in Sweden, which reduced its number of police authorities and closed many regional command centres by 2018. Critical in this chapter are core–periphery relations and how organisational and administrative units are related and ranked relative to one another and, critically, how resources are allocated to policing. Rationalising police organisation (which is represented formally as a betterment) can bring about a perception of police withdrawal, or that rural spaces are policed less. Stenbacka shows that in the middle, professionals adapt new processes alongside formal regulations, such as how they respond to stretched areas of responsibility. The withdrawal of police is more about how people perceive their value in the spatial context of the rural than on the risk of being caught breaking the rules on drink driving.

In Chapter 10, Rachel Hale, Alistair Harkness and Kyle Mulrooney consider the politics of punishment and the realities of prisons in rural areas in terms of popular punitiveness and the political decisions surrounding locations of prisons. The chapter brings us on to the terrain of the confluence between more conservative attitudes in rural areas that supports more punitive responses to crime, and a neoliberal governance that is looking for more cost-effective carceral solutions. This chapter proposes that while it is convenient for many critical commentators to pour scorn on rural communities for welcoming prisons, this does little to impact on the economic realities of rural decline. While the prisons and other carceral institutions sited in rural area can be regarded as an 'economics of misery', it is understandable if it is a welcome development, albeit not a desirable venture.

In Chapter 11, the final chapter, Alistair Harkness, Matt Bowden and Joseph F. Donnermeyer reflect on where rural criminology has come from, and where it might be heading to. They first recall their own journeys towards each other's orbits and how each of us are accidental rural criminologists. They have come into this space through distinct personal trajectories and have a chance to shape it, now that they have arrived. This crossing of borders is a key theme here, and the authors note the globalising nature of rural crime which grew as technological frontiers enabled spatial borders to be crossed, linking many parts of the world together, from the railways of the eighteenth and nineteenth centuries to Zoom in the twenty-first. Borders by their nature are peripheral, representing the edges of territories and across which streams a range of contraband driving local shadow economies. Borders are also metaphors for our own divisions that we impose in the academy. The authors muse on how rural criminology as a subdiscipline in its own right is an effective crossing of our own boundaries, and in the process can create an inclusive and dynamic space for research, scholarship and practice.

References

Ainge Roy, E. (2019) ' "One day we'll disappear": Tuvalu's sinking islands', *The Guardian*, 16 May. Available from: https://www.theguardian.com/glo bal-development/2019/may/16/one-day-disappear-tuvalu-sinking-isla nds-rising-seas-climate-change [Accessed 14 September 2021].

Beck, U. (1992) *Risk Society: Towards a New Modernity*, trans M. Ritter, London: Sage.

Bessière, J. (1998) 'Local development and heritage: traditional food and cuisine as tourist attractions in rural areas', *Sociologia Ruralis*, 38(1): 21–34.

Bowden, M. and Pytlarz, A. (2020) 'The development of rational models of crime prevention: a critique of situationist common sense in rural contexts', in A. Harkness (ed) *Rural Crime Prevention: Theory, Tactics and Techniques*, Abingdon: Routledge, pp 30–42.

Brenner, N. (1999) 'Beyond state-centrism? Space, territoriality, and geographical scale in globalization studies', *Theory and Society*, 28(1): 39–78.

Brenner, N., Jessop, B., Jones, M. and MacLeod, G. (2003) 'Introduction: state space in question', in N. Brenner, B. Jessop, M. Jones and G. MacLeod (eds) *State/Space: A Reader*, Maldon, MA: Blackwell, pp 1–26.

Donnermeyer, J.F. and DeKeseredy, W.S. (2014) *Rural Criminology*, Abingdon: Routledge.

Eichholz, M., Van Assche, K., Oberkircher, L. and Hornidge, A.-K. (2013) 'Trading capitals? Bourdieu, land and water in rural Uzbekistan', *Journal of Environmental Planning and Management*, 56(6): 868–92.

Eman, K. and Meško, G. (2021) 'Water crimes and governance: the Slovenian perspective', *International Criminology*, 1(3): 208–19.

Flemmen, M. and Savage, M. (2017) 'The politics of nationalism and white racism in the UK', *British Journal of Sociology*, 68(S1): S233–S264.

Halfacree, K. (2006) 'Rural space: constructing a three-fold architecture', in P. Cloke, T. Marsden and P. Mooney (eds), *The Handbook of Rural Studies*, Thousand Oaks, CA: SAGE, pp 44–62.

Hamilton, S. (2017) 'Securing ourselves *from* ourselves? The paradox of "entanglement" in the Anthropocene', *Crime, Law and Social Change*, 68(5): 579–95.

Harrington, C. and Shearing, C. (2017) *Security in the Anthropocene: Reflections on Safety and Care*, Bielefeld: Transcript.

Harvey, D. (1997) 'Between space and time: reflections on the geographical imagination', in T. Barnes and D. Gregory (eds) *Reading Human Geography*, London: Arnold, pp 19–27.

Hayward, K. (2021) *What Do We Know and What Should We Do About the Irish Border?* Thousand Oaks, CA: Sage.

IPCC (Intergovernmental Panel on Climate Change) (2021) *Climate Change 2021: The Physical Science Basis*, Geneva: Intergovernmental Panel on Climate Change. Available from: https://www.ipcc.ch/report/ar6/wg1/downloads/report/IPCC_AR6_WGI_Full_Report.pdf [Accessed 14 September 2021].

Lefebvre, H. (1991) *The Production of Space*, Hoboken, NJ: Wiley-Blackwell.

Lerner, A.M. and Eakin, H. (2011) 'An obsolete dichotomy? Rethinking the rural–urban interface in terms of food security and production in the global south', *Geographical Journal*, 177(4): 311–20.

McClanahan, B. (2020) 'Earth-world-planet: rural ecologies of horror and dark green criminology', *Theoretical Criminology*, 24(4): 633–50.

Park, R.E. (1925) 'The city: suggestions for investigation of human behavior in the urban environment', in R.E. Park and E.W. Burgess (eds) *The City*, Chicago: University of Chicago Press, pp 1–46.

Pytlarz, A. and Bowden, M. (2019) '"Crime-talk", security and fear in the countryside: a preliminary study of a rural Irish town and its hinterland', *International Journal of Rural Criminology*, 4(2): 138–72.

Shearing, C. (2015) 'Criminology and the Anthropocene', *Criminology and Criminal Justice*, 15(3): 255–69.

Thomas, A.R., Lowe, B.M., Fulkerson, G.M. and Smith, P.J. (2011) *Critical Rural Theory: Structure, Space, Culture*, Lanham, MD: Lexington Books.

2

Fifteen Reasons to Care About Rural Crime and Safety

Vania Ceccato

Introduction

Many works of fiction and science have highlighted the distinctiveness of criminogenic conditions of the countryside. From fiction, one of the most known quotes written by Sir Arthur Conan Doyle in the late nineteenth century comes from *The Adventure of Copper Beeches*. Dr Watson and Sherlock Holmes are aboard a train to the country when, as they pass Aldershot, Watson glances out the window at the passing houses:

> 'Are they not fresh and beautiful?', Watson cried with all the enthusiasm of a man fresh from the fogs of Baker Street.

Then Holmes replies:

> 'You look at these scattered houses, and you are impressed by their beauty. I look at them, and the only thought which comes to me is a feeling of their isolation and of the impunity with which crime may be committed there'. (Doyle, 1892: 9)

Watson is not alone. Far too often 'the rural' has been taken for granted as a place free of problems; the rural idyll (Bell, 2006). Fast-forward more than a century later and, despite there being an increase in scholarship in criminology, most aspects of rural crime and safety perceptions in rural contexts have received scant attention or been overlooked completely. This chapter challenges the notion of the rural idyll and other assumptions of crime and safety in rural environments by highlighting 15 reasons why scholars, decision-makers and society as a whole should care about victimisation and safety perceptions of people living in the rural–urban continuum.

Building on previous research (in particular Ceccato, 2015, 2016), this chapter focuses on issues of crime and safety in a variety of environments, ranging from remote areas to those belonging to the urban fringe. The concept of the rural–urban continuum is used here to stress the idea that 'there are no sharp breaking points to be found in the degree or quantity of rural–urban differences' (Planning Tank, 2017), but rather a flow of people and goods in which crime takes place. Finally, the importance of problems with crime and safety across countries, including examples of those of the Global South, are addressed. While 'crime' indicates levels of victimisation, the concept of 'safety' is used here as a general term that indicates safety perceptions or perceived safety in rural areas. Thus, perceived safety can be high (when an individual feels safe) or low (when an individual is in fear and feels unsafe) regardless of the levels of crime or victimisation. The chapter concludes by drawing attention to the contemporary dynamics of rural areas and calls for new societal and academic action to make crime and safety in the countryside a subject worth examining in its own right.

Why care about crime and safety in rural areas?

What follows is a consideration of 15 reasons why crime and safety are relevant issues in a rural context.

Crime is not simply an urban phenomenon

People's perceptions of rural areas as being free of crime are important in defining rurality, both in fiction (as in the earlier example given by Dr Watson) and in everyday life. This assumption of the rural as the perfect place stems from the notion of a 'rural idyll'. The rural idyll (for example Short, 1991; Bell, 1997) is considered to be the socially constructed and commonly shared idealised image, or stereotype, of life in villages, often depicted as quiet places and as harmonious, cohesive and homogeneous communities surrounded by a hinterland of farmers and ranchers with little or no conflict (Squire, 1993; Lockie and Bourke, 2001; Wangüemert, 2001): a place where the world is still and unaffected by global changes (Short, 1991; Bell, 1997, 2006; Short, 2006).

Although the idea stems from imperial England at the turn of the nineteenth century, the myth of the rural idyll is very much alive and can be found anywhere on the globe, from England to Argentina, from Sweden to Australia. Indeed, as suggested by Donnermeyer et al (2013), the rural idyll myth works to exaggerate rural 'strangeness' and, in so doing, works to broaden the assumed gap that separates rural and urban life. Crime affects the nature of rural areas. While the rural idyll creates rural space as an object of desire because it is not urban, rural space may also be represented as an object of dread because it is not urban (Bell, 1997; Scott and Biron, 2010).

Low crime rates do not mean 'no problems'

Far too often we take for granted that 'because there is less crime in the countryside, crime is not a problem for people living there' (Yarwood, 2001: 206). In rural areas, lower crime rates alone do not measure the impact crime has on those living in the countryside. A homicide (or any serious crime) in a rural area may have a stronger and more long-term impact on those living there than it would have had in a metropolitan area. Even if such impacts could be measured with a metric, crime rates alone might be poor indicators of the problems encountered in rural areas. This is because they may be low as a result of low reporting rates, triggered by a number of factors (Ceccato and Dolmen, 2011). Reporting rates in rural areas may be affected by long distances, a lack of trust in the police or the normalisation of certain types of crime. It is no surprise that rural crime consistently ranks among the least studied social problems in criminology (Donnermeyer, 2012; DeKeseredy, 2015).

Rates of crime reporting may be low in rural areas

In Australia, Barclay et al (2004) showed that the reporting rate is lower because farmers have a high tolerance for several criminal behaviours. Distance from police stations is behind differences in the willingness to report a crime to the police (Stassen and Ceccato, 2021). Women are less likely to report violence for numerous reasons (DeKeseredy et al, 2007). Some illegal acts have become normalised and part of 'doing business' (Stassen and Ceccato, 2021). In Sweden, farmers avoid reporting an offence if it is not serious (LRF, 2018). Fear can be revealed by silence in rural areas. One example is the lack of trust in authorities and criminal justice, as victims and witnesses refrain from witnessing and revealing local criminal groups in fear of retaliation (Ceccato and Ceccato, 2017) or in fear of ostracism if violence on the part of perpetrators becomes public (DeKeseredy et al, 2012).

Low rates of reported violence against women can be associated with a code of silence imposed by patriarchal community values. Websdale (1998) shows how some women were afraid to call the police because they knew that their abuser was socially networked with police personnel and that little or no action would be taken in their defence. In other cases, local women do not help because they themselves are experiencing similar problems and their own struggles prevent them from helping others (DeKeseredy and Schwartz, 2008: 112). In addition, the literature suggests that social and geographical isolation in rural areas can be particularly problematic for ethnic minority groups when seeking advice and reporting racial discrimination and abuse (Garland and Chakraborti, 2006, 2012; Chakraborti and Garland, 2011; Robinson and Gardner, 2012; Greenfields, 2014).

The 'rural' is a heterogeneous and complex space

In Europe in 2018, 39 per cent of the population lived in cities, 32 per cent in towns and suburbs and 29 per cent in rural areas (Eurostat, 2020) Despite this, the idea of the 'rural' composed of homogeneous environments is commonly fed by mediated images of what rural and urban are expected to be (Halfacree, 1993; Wells and Weisheit, 2004). Jansson (2013) argues that the problem is not to recognise that urban and rural are different but rather to identify 'forgotten places' that may fall in the rural–urban continuum. These places are suburbs, small towns and other in-between spaces. With information communication technology (ICT) in a globalised world, some areas are the real 'other places' and yet may be rural in some aspects and urban in others.

Rural areas are under constant transformation

It is increasingly recognised that rural areas are global, hybrid spaces that are shaped by forces far beyond their local reality (Woods, 2011; Shortall and Warner, 2012). In some cases, the restructuring process has forced rural communities to move away from traditional economies towards more diversified local employment bases (Krannich et al, 2011). Crime is part of the transformation occurring at different paces and on various scales around the rural world (Ceccato, 2013), in and beyond rural communities. Globalised networks of crime are having a profound impact on rural places and people. More recently, examples include people trafficking, slavery, drugs, hate crime against animal production, violence against women and minorities, international theft, 'county drug lines' and environmental crimes (Yarwood, 2022), each demanding new ways to tackle crime and ensure people's safety. These transformations are not specific to the Global North (Tapiador, 2008; Woods, 2011; Siwale, 2014).

Crime is influenced by the very nature of rural areas

Certain crime opportunities may only be present in rural areas. Low population density affects crime opportunities and detection. It is no surprise that hotspots of diesel theft from tractors are concentrated in farm-based municipalities; similarly harassment and attacks against ranchers (for example, of mink or cattle) are found only in farms that specialise in animal production

(Ceccato et al, forthcoming). If people are not present in a place, a crime may go undetected for some time, such as with the dumping of rubbish in forests (Ceccato, 2013).

Other conditions that may promote crime in rural areas are the high tolerance for certain types of behaviour and crime itself among individuals of the local community (Barclay et al, 2004; Barclay et al, 2007). Hotspots of crime may be found in particular 'towns marketed as centres for mass tourism and youth tourism' and 'those where poverty combines with tourism' (Mawby, 2007: 21). In addition, crimes in the rural include cases in which farmers are the offenders, a perspective which has been greatly ignored by mainstream criminology (Collins, 2016). Other examples include illegal criminal enterprises, such as in the meat trade (Smith and McElwee, 2013), environmental wildlife crimes (Caniglia et al, 2010; Fyfe and Reeves, 2011; Wellsmith, 2011; Maingi et al, 2012; Loeffler, 2013) and the illegal killing of predators or 'pests' (Enticott, 2011; Gargiulo et al, 2016).

Safety perceptions in rural areas are complex and unequal

People living in rural areas often declare feeling safer overall than people living in urban areas. However, safety perceptions reflect unbalanced levels of victimisation, such that the poor are over-represented among crime victims (Nilsson and Estrada, 2006; Tseloni et al, 2010; BRÅ, 2014). Some of these feelings relate to a lack of an individual's sense of order and continuity in regard to one's experiences in life (Giddens, 1991). Research also shows that safety perceptions reflect people's sense of place, where 'place' refers to the immediate settings and conditions of their daily life, but also their sense of their place in a larger societal context (Hope and Sparks, 2000). International literature confirms that this process goes along with long-term social and economic exclusion and discrimination that manifest differently by gender, ethnicity, and residents versus newcomers (Chakraborti and Garland, 2011; Babacan, 2012; Jensen, 2012; Scott et al, 2012; Ceccato, 2018).

Other processes relate to macro changes in communities, such as rapid population inflow and crime. For instance, in Sweden half of respondents to the national victims' survey who live in larger municipalities (that had a population increase) stated they worried more frequently about crime than those living in more rural municipalities (Ceccato, 2016). Nowadays, with access to the internet and social media, overall anxieties are said to be generated by a lack of individuals' embedded biography with a plurality of social worlds, beliefs and diversification of lifestyles. Victimisation becomes less dependent on location or proximity, and with that the fear of being a victim of crime may be fed by boundary-less 'glocal' forces. An individual living on Manhattan in New York may run the same risk of being targeted by computer fraud or any other cybercrime as someone living in the remote rural areas of Sweden (Ceccato, 2013).

Violence occurs in global rural contexts

There is no doubt that those living in rural areas of the Global South are not immune to acts of violence. This is particularly true in South and Central America, Africa and most of Asia, where violence encompasses fights between spouses and neighbours, armed robbery, organised cargo theft, child labour, prostitution, slavery, human trafficking, smuggling, 'honour' homicides, killings in land reform and environmental conflicts, and police-related violence (Ceccato and Ceccato, 2017). Topics of research interest include rural patterns of violence (Steeves et al, 2015; Ceccato and Ceccato, 2017), the effects of lighting on homicide (Arvate et al, 2018), the case of Somalian pirates (Collins, 2016), violence in Turkish rural regions (Çaya, 2014), estimations of homicide rates in Cambodia (Broadhurst, 2002) and violent farm crime in Zimbabwe (Rutherford, 2004). Research also calls for more evidence on the relationship between poverty and violence in rural areas (Melde, 2006; Lee and Slack, 2008). In addition, there is a need for new theoretical frameworks capable of understanding differences in dynamics of crime across the world, especially in countries in the southern hemisphere (Carrington et al, 2016).

Commodification of security is emerging

Commodification of rural areas is taking different shapes and affecting levels of crime and safety. Commodities turn into goods when value is associated with the price of observing a landscape, petting animals or living in a safe rural gated community. The commodification of the rural is perhaps more often associated with rural tourism and the inflow of temporary population. Countries in the Global South show examples where gated communities are increasingly part of the countryside (Spocter, 2013).

Private security is part of the same process of commodification of the rural as it has taken over several responsibilities that used to be associated with the public sector, in other words, law enforcement. Privatisation of security (as a public good) potentially has a negative impact on the provision, distribution and quality of security services, in particular on those who are not seen as obvious consumers (Goold et al, 2010).

Drug production, use and dealing threaten rural areas

Owing to their isolation, rural areas have been associated with drug production (Weisheit et al, 1994). More recently, though, the countryside is also associated with the distribution and consumption of illicit substances. In the UK, for example, there has been observed an increase of 'county lines' drug dealing (Harding, 2020), namely 'the practice of urban gangs recruiting vulnerable young people in rural and coastal settlements to distribute drugs' (Yarwood, 2022). Enabled by new technologies and social media, dealers can exert control over widening areas and so enrol young people into remote illicit networks.

In Sweden, Stenbacka (2021) assessed the presence of drugs in rural places and the way that impacts rural people and places. In rural America, there have also been several studies reporting on marijuana cultivation and methamphetamine production (Garriott, 2016; Weisheit and Brownstein, 2016) as well as organised drug production and related violence (van Dun, 2014). In the Global South, Anderson (2018) reports on opium poppy cultivators among the Karen people in Thailand, providing the perspective of how the restrictions of rights of ethnic minorities can lead to drug production being a last means of survival. A commonality in these studies is the realisation that rural areas are not sufficiently prepared to combat drug-related crime. This is owing to a combination of a transformation of access and distribution of drugs (via the internet or county lines) and the limited supply of police resources in combination with large geographical areas of responsibility.

Policing and crime prevention are urban-centric

Most crime prevention models are imported from urban areas to rural ones as examples of good practice, with little concern about potential differences in contexts (Ceccato, 2013). In Sweden, neighbourhood watch schemes and safety audits have been important examples of community safety practices in rural areas. The lack of attention at the national level to crime in rural areas and its prevention is a general problem.

In recent decades, a wide diversity of agencies and agents, including the volunteer sector, have attempted to deliver policing and security in pluralistic or autonomous ways (Loader, 2000). In addition, in most countries, rural policing is often under-resourced, exclusionary and too parochial to deal with increasingly globalised, multi-scalar threats (Yarwood, 2015).

Rural crime prevention is adopting technological measures

Although still in its infancy, technology in situational crime prevention in rural areas is attracting more attention. Aransiola and Ceccato (2020) reviewed the literature searching for applications of modern technologies in situational crime prevention, finding that traditional crime prevention (locking doors, use of guard dogs, raising fences and so on) are still the most common in rural areas, while modern measures (CCTV, security lights, alarms and drones) are generally more supplemental. CCTV and alarms have been shown to have little to no effect in preventing crime, especially on farms, though are better at detecting and monitoring wildlife crime (Liedka et al, 2019; Aransiola and Ceccato, 2020). Different technologies have been used to prevent farm theft (Harkness and Larkins, 2020) and housebreaking (Hamid and Yusof, 2013) and to reduce violent crime (Arvate et al, 2018).

The combat of crime using new technologies should be considered in further research and as part of rural policing strategy. In particular, there is a need to investigate whether and how ICT and digitalisation in general are affecting the ways in which people interact with the police (Stassen and Ceccato, 2021), as it is unclear how to best adapt current methods of policing under conditions of changing technologies.

The theoretical legacy is urban-centric and dominated by the Global North

Most of the current theories in criminology used by criminologists and the like are urban-centric with little or no reference to contexts outside the big cities. Empirically, they are based on 'urban neighbourhoods' as a model, often limited to the city borders. These theories also tend to be 'stuck in time', as they do very little to offer an understanding of the current complexity of crimes that happen in globalised rural areas. They fail to recognise differences in dynamics of crime across the world, especially in countries from the Global South (Carrington et al, 2016).

More recently, criminologists have begun to contest the theoretical urban-centric legacy. Donnermeyer et al (2013), for instance, contest the assumption that places with low crime must manifest high levels of social organisation, while areas with low social organisation must inevitably display more crime. They suggest that there are multiple forms of social organisation in the rural, allowing individuals to simultaneously participate in multiple networks, some of which may be criminal: 'it is quite possible that many rural communities have a social or moral order which keeps some crimes such as violence in the "dark"' (Donnermeyer et al, 2013: 71).

The intersectional perspective on safety is critical

Traditionally, studies in domestic violence in rural areas have adopted a gender approach, providing a more nuanced perspective to studies that historically had treated women as having universal safety needs, usually patterned after White male individuals (DeKeseredy and Joseph, 2006; DeKeseredy and Schwartz, 2008; DeKeseredy et al, 2012). Yet, much remains to be done on the intersectionality of safety (Crenshaw, 1989) in rural contexts – both in research and practice. It has to be sensitive to how, when and why gender intersects with age, class and ethnic belonging, which together may result in multiple dimensions of disadvantage, victimisation and/or poor safety perceptions.

Crime and safety are intertwined with sustainable rural development

The United Nations' 2030 Agenda for Sustainable Development identifies crime and fear of crime as major threats to sustainability (United Nations, 2015). An unsustainable environment is commonly characterised by 'images of poverty, physical deterioration, increasing levels of crime, and fear of crime' (Cozens, 2002: 131). Mihai and Iatu (2020) remind us that in many countries of the Global South, populations living in the rural–urban continuum are more prone to chronic poverty, famine, social exclusion and environmental injustice, particularly in developing countries in Africa, Asia and Latin America.

A sustainable future demands holistic approaches in which daily basic needs of populations can be covered by reliable public services combined with technical, socio-economic and environmental conditions that support regional rural–urban linkages (Mihai and Iatu, 2020). In particular, dealing with the problems of crime and poor safety perceptions requires, among other things, a clearer definition of the roles of public and private actors in providing security services as well as a better understanding of the safety of those living in the rural–urban continuum in a hybrid and globalised world.

Conclusion

Criminology has until recently neglected the nature of crimes that happen outside the urban realm. This is no surprise given that crime tends to be concentrated in urban areas and the rural has been regarded as a retreat from urban problems. This chapter has attempted to untangle this simplistic view by discussing a number of issues that show facets of the countryside as both safe and criminogenic and, more importantly, a hybrid place worth examination in its own right.

A crucial consideration is why low crime rates in rural areas are mistakenly taken as a sign that crime is not a problem for those living there. Avoiding the myths of the rural idyll is a necessary step towards more nuanced perspectives on safety in the country. Both research (for example in criminology) and practice (such as policing) could benefit from implementing the notion of the rural–urban continuum, giving researchers and practitioners the opportunity to account for the dynamics of rural areas and the complexity of the lives of those who live there. Argued here is that crime is not simply an urban phenomenon but embodies the same characteristics of the environment in which it is embedded; in certain cases, crime commission is only possible at situational rural contexts. In addition, crime in rural areas is in constant transformation given local and global influences, imposing challenges for policing and, not least, for the long-term sustainability of rural areas.

There is, thus, an emergent call for theoretical frameworks that can provide a better understanding of crime and safety in rural conditions, which recognises the hybrid globalised nature of these spaces, their contextual differences and the safety needs of people living in them.

References

Anderson, B. (2018) 'Zomia's vestiges: illegible peoples and legible crimes in Omkoi, northwest Thailand', *South East Asia Research*, 26(1): 38–57.

Aransiola, T.J. and Ceccato, V. (2020) 'The role of modern technology in rural situational crime prevention: a review of the literature', in A. Harkness (ed) *Rural Crime Prevention: Theory, Tactics and Techniques*, Abingdon: Routledge, pp 58–72.

Arvate, P., Falsete, F.O., Ribeiro, F.G. and Souza, A.P. (2018) 'Lighting and homicides: evaluating the effect of an electrification policy in rural Brazil on violent crime reduction', *Journal of Quantitative Criminology*, 34(4): 1047–78.

Babacan, H. (2012) 'Racism denial in Australia: the power of silence', *Australian Mosaic*, 32: 1–3.

Barclay, E., Donnermeyer, J.F. and Jobes, P.C. (2004) 'The dark side of gemeinschaft: criminality within rural communities', *Crime Prevention and Community Safety*, 6(3): 7–22.

Barclay, E., Donnermeyer, J.F., Scott, J. and Hogg, R. (eds) (2007) *Crime in Rural Australia*, Sydney: Federation Press.

Bell, D. (1997) 'Anti-idyll: rural horror', in P. Cloke and J. Litte (eds), *Contested Countryside Cultures: Otherness, Marginalisation and Rurality*, London: Routledge, pp 94–108.

Bell, D. (2006) 'Variation on the rural idyll', in P. Cloke, T. Marsden and P. Mooney (eds), *Handbook of Rural Studies*, Thousand Oaks, CA: Sage, pp 149–60.

BRÅ (2014) *Nationella trygghetsundersökningen 2006–2013: regionala resultat*, Stockholm: BRÅ. Available from: https://www.bra.se/download/18.35c6 81d4143337cb6b21074/1390229096985/2014_3_NTU_Regionala_resul tat.pdf [Accessed 12 August 2021].

Broadhurst, R. (2002) 'Lethal violence, crime and state formation in Cambodia', *Australian and New Zealand Journal of Criminology*, 35(1): 1–26.

Caniglia, R., Fabbri, E., Greco, C., Galaverni, M. and Randi, E. (2010) 'Forensic DNA against wildlife poaching: identification of a serial wolf killing in Italy', *Forensic Science International: Genetics*, 4(5): 334–8.

Carrington, K., Hogg, R. and Sozzo, M. (2016) 'Southern criminology', *British Journal of Criminology*, 56(1): 1–20.

Çaya, S. (2014) 'Violence in rural regions: the case of modern Turkey', *Procedia: Social and Behavioral Sciences*, 114: 721–6.

Ceccato, V. (2013) 'Integrating geographical information into urban safety research and planning', *Proceedings of the Institution of Civil Engineers: Urban Design and Planning*, 166(1): 15–23.

Ceccato, V. (2015) 'Rural crime and community safety', *Journal of Rural Studies*, 39: 157–9.

Ceccato, V. (2016) *Rural Crime and Community Safety*, Abingdon: Routledge.

Ceccato, V. (2018) 'Fear of crime and overall anxieties in rural areas: the case of Sweden', in M. Lee and G. Mythen (eds), *The Routledge International Handbook on Fear of Crime*, Abingdon: Routledge, pp 354–67.

Ceccato, V. and Dolmen, L. (2011) 'Crime in rural Sweden', *Applied Geography*, 31(1): 119–35.

Ceccato, V. and Ceccato, H. (2017) 'Violence in the rural global south: trends, patterns, and tales from the Brazilian countryside', *Criminal Justice Review*, 42(3): 270–90.

Ceccato, V. and Yarwood, R. (2021) 'The geographies of crime and policing in the global countryside', *Professional Geographer*, ahead of print, https://doi.org/10.1080/00330124.2021.1990090 [Accessed 28 February 2022].

Ceccato, V., Lundqvist, P., Abraham, J., Göransson, E. and Svennefelt, C.A. (forthcoming) 'Crimes against animal production in Sweden: an assessment of 2009–2019s media archives', *International Criminal Justice Review*.

Chakraborti, N. and Garland, J. (eds) (2011) *Rural Racism*, Abingdon: Routledge.

Collins, V.E. (2016) 'The nomadic pastoralist, the fisherman and the pirate: a historical overview of the rural dimensions of piracy in Somalia', in J.F. Donnermeyer (ed) *The Routledge International Handbook of Rural Criminology*, Abingdon: Routledge, pp 93–100.

Cozens, P.M. (2002) 'Sustainable urban development and crime prevention through environmental design for the British city: towards an effective urban environmentalism for the 21st century', *Cities*, 19(2): 129–37.

Crenshaw, K. (1989) 'Demarginalizing the intersection of race and sex: a black feminist critique of antidiscrimination doctrine, feminist theory and antiracist politics', *University of Chicago Legal Forum*, 1989: 139–67.

DeKeseredy, W.S. (2015) 'New directions in feminist understandings of rural crime and social control', *Journal of Rural Studies*, 39: 180–7.

DeKeseredy, W.S. and Joseph, C. (2006) 'Separation and/or divorce sexual assault in rural Ohio: preliminary results of an exploratory study', *Violence Against Women*, 12(3): 301–11.

DeKeseredy, W.S. and Schwartz, M.D. (2008) 'Separation/divorce sexual assault in rural Ohio: survivors' perceptions', *Journal of Prevention and Intervention in the Community*, 36(1/2): 105–19.

DeKeseredy, W.S., Donnermeyer, J.F., Schwartz, M.D., Tunnell, K. and Hall, M. (2007) 'Thinking critically about rural gender relations: toward a rural masculinity crisis / male peer support model of separation/divorce sexual assault', *Critical Criminology*, 15(4): 295–311.

DeKeseredy, W.S., Dragiewicz, M. and Rennisson, C.M. (2012) 'Racial/ethnic variations in violence against women: urban, suburban, and rural differences', *International Journal of Rural Criminology*, 1(2): 184–202.

Donnermeyer, J.F. (2012) 'Rural crime and critical criminology', in W.S. DeKeseredy and M. Dragiewicz (eds) *Routledge Handbook of Critical Criminology*, Abingdon: Routledge, pp 289–301.

Donnermeyer, J.F., Scott, J. and Barclay, E. (2013) 'How rural criminology informs critical thinking in criminology', *International Journal for Crime, Justice and Social Democracy*, 2(3): 69–91.

Doyle, A.C. (1892) *The Adventure of Copper Beeches*, London: George Newnes.

Enticott, G. (2011) 'Techniques of neutralising wildlife crime in rural England and Wales', *Journal of Rural Studies*, 27(2): 200–8.

Eurostat (2020) 'Urban and rural living in the EU', *Europa-news*, 7 February. Available from: https://ec.europa.eu/eurostat/web/products-eurostat-news/-/edn-20200207-1 [Accessed 12 August 2021].

Fyfe, N.R. and Reeves, A.D. (2011) 'The thin green line? Police perceptions of challenges of policing wildlife crime in Scotland', in R.I. Mawby and R. Yarwood (eds) *Rural Policing and Policing the Rural: A Constable Countryside?*, Farnham: Ashgate, pp 169–82.

Gargiulo, F., Angelino, C.V., Cicala, L., Persechino, G. and Lega, M. (2016) 'Remote sensing in the fight against environmental crimes: the case study of the cattle-breeding facilities in southern Italy', *International Journal of Sustainable Development and Planning*, 11(5): 663–71.

Garland, J. and Chakraborti, N. (2006) ' "Race", space and place: examining identity and cultures of exclusion in rural England', *Ethnicities*, 6(2): 159–77.

Garland, J. and Chakraborti, N. (2012) 'Another country? Community, belonging and exclusion in rural England', in N. Chakraborti and J. Garland (eds) *Rural Racism*, Abingdon: Routledge, pp 122–40.

Garriott, W. (2016) 'Methamphetamine and the changing rhetoric of drugs in the United States', in J.F. Donnermeyer (ed) *The Routledge International Handbook of Rural Criminology*, Abingdon: Routledge, pp 275–82.

Giddens, A. (1991) *Modernity and Self-Identity: Self and Society in the Late Modern Age*, Cambridge: Polity Press.

Goold, B., Loader, I. and Thumala, A. (2010) 'Consuming security? Tools for a sociology of security consumption', *Theoretical Criminology*, 14(1): 3–30.

Greenfields, M. (2014) 'Gypsies and Travellers in modern rural England', in G. Bosworth and P. Somerville (eds) *Interpreting Rurality: Multidisciplinary Approaches*, Abingdon: Routledge, pp 219–34.

Halfacree, K. (1993) 'Locality and social representation: space, discourse and alternative definitions of the rural', *Journal of Rural Studies*, 9(1): 23–37.

Hamid, L.A. and Yusof, W.Z.M. (2013) 'Experiential approach as a design innovation solution to prevent house breaking crime', *Procedia: Social and Behavioral Sciences*, 107: 145–52.

Harding, S. (2020) *County Lines: Exploitation and Drug Dealing Among Urban Street Gangs*, Bristol: Policy Press.

Harkness, A. and Larkins, J. (2020) 'Technological approaches to preventing property theft from farms', in A. Harkness (ed), *Rural Crime Prevention: Theory, Tactics and Techniques*, Abingdon: Routledge, pp 226–44.

Hope, T. and Sparks, R. (2000) *Crime, Risk, and Insecurity: Law and Order in Everyday Life and Political Discourse*, Abingdon: Routledge.

Jansson, A. (2013) 'The hegemony of the urban/rural divide: cultural transformations and mediatized moral geographies in Sweden', *Space and Culture*, 16(1): 88–103.

Jensen, M. (2012) 'Rasism, missnöje och "Fertile Grounds" Östergötland Sverige jämförs med Birkaland Finland: Sverigedemokraterna vs Sannfinländarna', bachelor thesis, Linköping University, Linköping. Available from: http://www.diva-portal.org/smash/record.jsf?pid=diva2:479299 [Accessed 28 February 2022].

Krannich, R.S., Luloff, E. and Field, D.R. (2011) *People, Places and Landscapes: Social Change in High Amenity Rural Areas*, New York: Springer.

Lee, M.R. and Slack, T. (2008) 'Labor market conditions and violent crime across the metro–nonmetro divide', *Social Science Research*, 37(3): 753–68.

Liedka, R.V., Meehan, A.J. and Lauer, T.W. (2019) 'CCTV and campus crime: challenging a technological "fix"', *Criminal Justice Policy Review*, 30(2): 316–38.

Loader, I. (2000) 'Plural policing and democratic governance', *Social and Legal Studies*, 9(3): 323–45.

Lockie, S. and Bourke, L. (2001) *Rurality Bites: The Social and Environmental Transformation of Rural Australia*, Annandale, NSW: Pluto.

Loeffler, K. (2013) 'Breeding wildlife to extinction in China', *Journal of Applied Animal Welfare Science*, 16(4): 387.

LRF (2018) *Grön entreprenör: Affärsmöjligheter i hela landet* [Green entrepreneur: business opportunities throughout the country], Lantbrukarnas Riksförbund. Available from: https://www.lrf.se/imageva ult/publishedmedia/q29e0k2et35yvn1wzgba/Gr-n_entrepren-r_3_upp lagan_sept_2018.pdf [Accessed 12 August 2021].

Maingi, J.K., Mukeka, J.M., Kyale, D.M. and Muasya, R.M. (2012) 'Spatiotemporal patterns of elephant poaching in south-eastern Kenya', *Wildlife Research*, 39(3): 234–49.

Mawby, R.I. (2007) 'Crime, place and explaining rural hotspots' *International Journal of Rural Crime*, 1: 21–43.

Melde, C. (2006) 'Social disorganization and violent crime in rural Appalachia', *Journal of Crime and Justice*, 29(2): 117–40.

Mihai, F.-C. and Iatu, C. (2020) 'Sustainable rural development under Agenda 2030', in M.J. Bastante-Ceca, J.L. Fuentes-Bargues, L. Hufnagel, F.-C. Mihai and C. Iatu (eds) *Sustainability Assessment at the 21st Century*, IntechOpen. Available from https://www.intechopen.com/chapters/69950 [Accessed 12 August 2021].

Nilsson, A. and Estrada, F. (2006) 'The inequality of victimization: trends in exposure to crime among rich and poor', *European Journal of Criminology*, 3(4): 387–412.

Planning Tank (2017) 'Rural-urban continuum and causes of rural-urban continuum', Planning Tank, 5 January. Available from: https://planningt ank.com/settlement-geography/rural-urban-continuum [Accessed 12 August 2021]

Robinson, V. and Gardner, G. (2012) 'Unravelling a stereotype: the lived experience of black and minority ethnic in rural Wales', in N. Chakraborti and J. Garland (eds) *Rural Racism*, Abingdon: Routledge, pp 85–107.

Rutherford, B. (2004) 'Desired publics, domestic government, and entangled fears: on the anthropology of civil society, farm workers, and white farmers in Zimbabwe', *Cultural Anthropology*, 19(1): 122–53.

Scott, J. and Biron, D. (2010) '*Wolf Creek*, rurality and the Australian gothic', *Continuum*, 24(2): 307–22.

Scott, J., Carrington, K. and McIntosh, A. (2012) 'Established-outsider relations and fear of crime in mining towns', *Sociologia Ruralis*, 52(2): 147–69.

Short, B. (2006) 'Idyllic ruralities', in P. Cloke, T. Marsden and P. Mooney (eds), *Handbook of Rural Studies*, Thousand Oaks, CA: Sage, pp 133–48.

Short, J.R. (1991) *Imagined Country: Environment, Culture and Society*, London: Routledge.

Shortall, S. and Warner, M. (2012) 'Rural transformations: conceptual and policy issues', in M. Shucksmith, D.L. Brown, S. Shortall, J. Vergunst and M.E. Warner (eds) *Rural Transformations and Rural Policies in the US and UK*, New York: Routledge, pp 3–18.

Siwale, J. (2014) 'Challenging Western perceptions: a case study of rural Zambia', in G. Bosworth and P. Somerville (eds) *Interpreting Rurality: Multidisciplinary Approaches*, Abingdon: Routledge, pp 15–30.

Smith, R. and McElwee, G. (2013) 'Confronting social constructions of rural criminality: a case story on "illegal pluriactivity" in the farming community', *Sociologia Ruralis*, 53(1): 112–34.

Spocter M. (2022) 'A comparison of security in city and small-town gated developments in the Western Cape province, South Africa', *Journal of Asian and African Studies*, 57(2):165–81.

Squire, S.J. (1993) 'Valuing countryside: reflections on Beatrix Potter tourism', *Area*, 25(1): 5–10.

Stassen, R. and Ceccato, V. (2021) 'Police accessibility in Sweden: an analysis of the spatial arrangement of police services', *Policing: A Journal of Policy and Practice*, 15(2): 896–911.

Steeves, G.M., Petterini, F.C. and Moura, G.V. (2015) 'The interiorization of Brazilian violence, policing, and economic growth', *Economia*, 16(3): 359–75.

Stenbacka, S. (2021) 'Local policing in a global countryside: combating drugs in rural areas', *Professional Geographer*, ahead of print. Available from: https://doi.org/10.1080/00330124.2021.1990089 [Accessed 24 February 2022].

Tapiador, F.J. (2008) *Rural Analysis and Management: An Earth Science Approach to Rural Science*, Berlin: Springer.

Tseloni, A., Mailley, J., Farrell, G. and Tilley, N. (2010) 'Exploring the international decline in crime rates', *European Journal of Criminology*, 7(5): 375–94.

United Nations (2015) 'Transforming our world: the 2030 agenda for sustainable development', *United Nations Department of Economic and Social Affairs*. Available from: https://sdgs.un.org/2030agenda [Accessed 4 April 2022].

van Dun, M. (2014) 'Exploring narco-sovereignty/violence: analyzing illegal networks, crime, violence, and legitimation in a Peruvian cocaine enclave (2003–2007)', *Journal of Contemporary Ethnography*, 43(4): 395–418.

Wangüemert, M.M. (2001) 'La Pampa: Historia de una pasión argentina'[The pampas: an Argentinian passion], in B.T. Ramírez (ed) *Propiedad de la tierra, latinfundios y movimientos campesinos: Actas de las VIII Jornadas de Andalucía y América*, Huelva: Universidad de Santa María de la Rábida, pp 357–69.

Websdale, N. (1998) *Rural Woman Battering and the Justice System: An Ethnography*, Thousand Oaks, CA: Sage.

Weisheit, R.A. and Brownstein, H. (2016) 'Drug production in the rural context', in J.F. Donnermeyer (ed) *The Routledge International Handbook of Rural Criminology*, Abingdon: Routledge, pp 235–44.

Weisheit, R.A., Wells, L.E. and Falcone, D.N. (1994) 'Community policing in small town and rural America', *Crime and Delinquency*, 40(4): 549–67.

Wells, L.E. and Weisheit, R.A. (2004) 'Patterns of rural and urban crime: a county-level comparison', *Criminal Justice Review*, 29(1): 1–22.

Wellsmith, M. (2011) 'Wildlife crime: the problems of enforcement', *European Journal on Criminal Policy and Research*, 17(2): 125–48.

Woods, M. (2011) *Rural*, Abingdon: Routledge.

Yarwood, R. (2001) 'Crime and policing in the British countryside: some agendas for contemporary geographical research', *Sociologia Ruralis*, 41(2): 201–19.

Yarwood, R. (2015) 'Lost and hound: the more-than-human networks of rural policing', *Journal of Rural Studies*, 39: 278–86.

Yarwood, R. (2022) 'Policing the global countryside: toward a research agenda', *The Professional Geographer*, 74(2): 343–9.

3

Theoretical and Empirical Gaps in Rural Criminology

Joseph F. Donnermeyer

Introduction

As the title of this chapter states, it is about both theoretical and empirical gaps in rural criminology. For the purposes of this chapter, a gap will be defined as: first, a failure to develop rural-based theory and/or to actively conduct research on particular rural criminological topics; second, a failure to apply theory to help define research or, reciprocally, apply research to help revise and upgrade theory; and third, a failure to apply both theory and research to the development of crime prevention and criminal justice strategies for the benefit of rural police and other criminal justice professionals, citizens and citizen groups concerned about the security of rural communities around the world.

This chapter serves as a clarion call to scholars, young and old, to help fill these gaps, address these failures and pay attention to those things previously neglected. The good news is that rural criminology has matured to the point that it can no longer be described as newly emerging, but as having grown fast enough that some topics are insufficiently developed to the point that they can now be considered left behind. Those are the gaps!

The division between theoretical and empirical gaps is itself both artificial and arbitrary because in a perfect world, theory and research are not completely different forms of scholarship, even though they form distinctive intellectual activities for what the complete scholar should attempt to do when addressing a particular criminological or criminal justice topic. One-dimensional scholars[1] are those who spend all or nearly all of their intellectual energies on theory without ever 'getting their hands dirty' by collecting their own data or, conversely, devote themselves to either qualitative or quantitative data collection and data analysis without thinking much about the theoretical implications of their research. There are plenty of one-dimensional scholars across the broad spectrum of subfields within criminology, including rural criminology.

Theoretical flaws

In their well-respected and widely read book *Criminological Theory: Context and Consequences*, Lilly et al (2015) do not actually provide a clear-cut definition of theory. Yet, in the discussion that forms the introduction to their book, they make several good points about theorising. For example, 'crime is a complex phenomenon, and it is a demanding, if intriguing, challenge to explain its many sides' (Lilly et al, 2015: 1). They emphasise that explaining crime (hence, theory that is tested) is more than common sense.

Theory may be defined in a thousand different ways, but the keyword 'explanation' always seems to appear in these definitional attempts to understand phenomena, from the expansion and contraction of the universe to the ups and downs of crime rates. Theories provide meaning and clarify relationships between various aspects of what scholars are trying to explain. It is hoped that the clarity provides ways to test these relationships by collecting data, and that all of these scholarly activities can be put to the test of peer review by others trained in the same science or discipline. In this sense, therefore, theory and research are not as different as the head and the tail of a coin, but nonetheless, they do require all criminologists as scientists to become competent in different skills.

Theory-building may be more of a mental process of thinking abstractly about relationships, and of revising explanations as one thinks more and more about a theory, while research is a more concrete, specific set of activities associated with management of the steps in the research process and what skill sets are required to collect data, analyse data and interpret the results. And let us not forget that clear, straightforward writing is necessary to describe what one is thinking about in terms of criminological explanations and how one is engaged in research to test a theory that is to be shared with colleagues.

Three of the biggest flaws exhibited by scholars in all sciences, and they show up frequently through presentations at criminological conferences, are as follows. First, there is the 'name-dropper' who claims to be guided by 'strain theory', or 'routine activities theory' or some other theory about crime, but never explains why. The token mentioning of theory becomes an attempt to invoke a patina of scientism to the presentation. Nowadays, it is likely that the name-dropper relied on a quick read of a Wikipedia entry to create a theoretical illusion.

Second, and perhaps the more frequently occurring, is the person who proudly claims that their analysis explained 5 (or 10, or 20) per cent of the variance, which provides proof of the theory they selected while ignoring the vast percentage not explained, never questioning the theory itself, and failing to think about ways to improve its explanatory powers. It must be the methodology that is at fault, not the theory itself or the fact that the presenter also engaged in the first flaw by using theory as a type of window dressing.

Third, there are those who purposively obfuscate the theory they seek to apply to a criminological phenomenon through obtuse language, hoping that multisyllabic words strung together in a single sentence will convince the audience of their theoretical cleverness. Those same individuals may also double-up by employing overly complex data analytic procedures of both the quantitative and qualitative kind, or explain their analysis in an overly complex manner in order to impress their audience and deflect possible criticism of their scholarship through a form of linguistic intimidation.

Hopefully, as rural criminology continues to expand its theoretical and research horizons, it will avoid these decades-long flaws that seem to be so much a part of the cultural tapestry that decorates so many get-togethers of criminologists. This wish forms the ultimate objective of this chapter.

The value of middle-range theory

Partial or middle-range theories are a way to build up a field of study, and that certainly pertains to rural criminology. Why? Because it allows scholars with rural crime interests to create rural contextualised theories, rather than merely borrowing, wholesale, mainstream criminological theories without first considering the extent to which those theories may lack external validity for rural contexts. At the same time, a middle-range approach allows rural scholars to avoid simplistic negativisms about criminological theories as inappropriate for rural settings. Why not borrow, even wholesale, from a theory when it seems a good idea for helping to create and frame a research question, how the data will be collected, how the collected data will be analysed, and how the analysed data will be interpreted. However, always keep in mind that a good theory is not to be dogmatically worshipped as an immutable statement of truths. Criminological theories are not religious icons, even if some scholars seem to treat them that way and use them to lord their faux intellectualism over others. Theories should be treated as 'living documents' to be revised, repaired, revamped and rewritten.

The creation of the phrase 'middle-range theory' is attributed to the sociologist Robert King Merton (1910–2003), whose book *Social Theory and Social Structure* (1957), remains influential today. In it, he saw middle-range theory as solving both the problems of grand theories that lack specificity to guide research, and research that often fails to integrate findings into broader generalisations. To quote from two portions of his book (one only need substitute criminological for sociological):

[O]ne must admit that a large part of what is now called sociological theory consists of general orientations toward data ... we have many concepts but few confirmed theories ... many 'approaches', but few arrivals. (Merton, 1957: 9)

It seems probable that if special inquiries trace out the theoretical connections between ... forms of behavior, they will develop one of those theories of the middle range which consolidate otherwise segregated hypotheses and empirical uniformities. (Merton, 1957: 280)

Hence, middle-range theory in rural criminology ought to straddle a realm that can be found between grand approaches or views about crime and criminal justice issues and specific data-driven research about crime and criminal justice issues. Theory frames research, but reciprocally, research aids theory development.

There are, at the time of this writing, three middle-range theories with strong rural roots. They are briefly discussed in the chronological order of their development.[2] The first is called Primary Socialisation Theory and emerged from work by social scientists at the Tri-Ethnic Center for Prevention Research at Colorado State University during the 1990s. Its focus was on explaining variations in rates of substance use by adolescents, and a substantial amount of their focus was on rural youth, although their intent was not solely on adolescents living in rural communities (Oetting et al, 1998). It is a multilevel model focused on individual characteristics (such as risk-taking); three primary sources of socialisation (schools, close friends, family) likely to influence adolescent behaviour; and the mediating effects of community characteristics.

A second middle-range rural-based theory is represented in the scholarship of Matthew Lee (2008). It is called civic community theory and works from the ecological model of a community by Kasarda and Janowitz (1974), who viewed places as composed of networks of friendship/kinship and membership in community-located organisations. Lee (2008) asks the research question: to what extent are crime rates correlated with various measures of the civic engagement of a community's members? Indicators of civic engagement may include rates of church membership and voting in state and local elections, homeownership, plus the number of locally owned business establishments, among others.

The third middle-range theory with strong rural roots is male-peer support by DeKeseredy (DeKeseredy and Schwartz, 2009; DeKeseredy, 2021; see also DeKeseredy in Chapter 5 of this volume). It is more reliant on qualitative research than the other two rural-based middle-range theories. Simply, it is not possible to establish valid rates of violence against women, especially cases of domestic violence, in rural settings (or urban settings) based on police data because so much of it is not reported. This theory explores the highly patriarchal nature of many rural communities, especially in the Appalachian region of the US, and its connection to violence by males against their female partners, focusing specifically on the dangerous times for these women during separation and/or divorce. Male-peer support theory links the ways masculinity as a cultural trait reinforces networks of males (that is, peers) that provide support through rationalisations for normalising their abusive behaviour against women.

All three middle-range theories borrow from traditional criminological theories, such as social learning theory and subcultural models for explaining criminal behaviours (Lilly et al, 2015). Yet, they represent innovative theorising to fit both a rural-orientation and a middle-range theory approach. The real problem for rural criminology is not innovative, theoretical thinking, but that there are only three such theories accounting for rural context, so far! Many theoretical gaps are left.

Theoretical gaps

Here are 16 examples, with a caveat that the citations to specific authors in these paragraphs about shortcomings are not intended as criticisms of their scholarship. Simply, the goal is to call attention to the theoretical gaps in rural criminology. Plus, there is a second caveat. The order of presentation of each gap is not to be viewed as any kind of prioritisation. It is merely a list, like a shopping list, for future theorising within rural criminology.

Rural policing

First, there is little or no theoretical dialogue about rural policing, regardless of the country that forms the focus for policing studies. There is research on the general trend towards the consolidation or centralisation of police services, mostly to the neglect of rural peoples and communities, but no perspective about how shifts in policing resources impact rural localities (Mouhanna, 2016; Ruddell and Lithopoulos, 2016; Yarwood and Wooff, 2016). Further, there is a modest body of scholarship related to the policing of indigenous people in rural communities (Cunneen and Tauri, 2016; Jones et al, 2016). Often, the literature bemoans the vast differences in arrest rates of indigenous populations to the general population of a country, which is attributed to aspects of discriminatory policing practices, inequality and poverty, yet there is no real theory to encapsulate, conceptually, what these patterns mean. However, from these already rich literatures about rural policing, it is now possible to develop middle-range theories.

Indigenous communities

Second, there is limited scholarship regarding the differences and commonalities across regions of the world of Indigenous communities in relation to crime and criminal justice issues, beyond discriminatory policing. It is often observed that some Indigenous communities exhibit very high rates of substance misuse and violence (Cunneen and Tauri, 2016; Jones et al, 2016), but there are no perspectives attempting to explain variations in criminal behaviours across various rural places where Indigenous populations are concentrated. If this were done, the high criminality label associated with indigenous communities is likely to be challenged as just another rural stereotype. Indigenous communities, like rural communities more generally, vary in their expressions of alcoholism, substance abuse, violence and other crimes, but it will take good middle-range theorising and related research to make this happen.

Fear of crime and perceptions of safety and security

Third, there is a large volume of empirically derived rural-based literature on fear of crime, and other dimensions related to perceptions of rural peoples about security (Donnermeyer, 2019a; Meško, 2020), but little of it provides a theoretical framework for understanding these issues in ways that the disparate studies can be synthesised into an improved comparative framework. Models of fear generally emphasise perceived vulnerability (Lee, 2001). It could be argued that perceived vulnerability is the same across various kinds of communities, and is more likely based on age, sex or some other individual-level characteristic. Hence, community size is not very relevant. But, the trick then is to begin to build a rural-based middle-range theory that considers rural context and confronts this assumption for its relative degree of veracity. Some populations, for example, are especially vulnerable because of their physical and social isolation, such as found in the work of DeKeseredy and Schwartz (2009) on violence against rural women. As well, other vulnerable populations and their perceptions can only be understood within the context of their rural locations.

LGBTIQA+

Fourth, rural communities around the world have far more diversity than what the criminological world has ever imagined. This diversity is certainly associated with aspects of crime and criminal justice, and this is nowhere more apparent than the very limited research, and practically zero theorising, about crime in relation to LGBTIQA+ people who live in rural localities. To assume that these folks only live urban lifestyles and that issues associated with hate crimes against LGBTIQA+ people is solely within city environs, is incorrect. Does a rural landscape for issues LGBTIQA+ people and crime issues help redefine how scholars see rural communities?

Hate, anti-government, militias, nationalists, separatists and other groups

Fifth, a firmer middle-range rural-based framework is needed on hate groups, anti-government groups and militias and, for that matter, nationalist and separatist groups anywhere in the world in relation crime and criminal justice issues. There is certainly much journalistic commentary on this subject, some of which is rigorous enough to inform a scholarly frame, but there is much work to do because the rural criminological literature has mostly ignored the topic. Most theoretical work on these groups adopt a social movement perspective, such as resource mobilisation theory (Blee and Creasap, 2010). The question is, to what extent does rural context inform and revise these frameworks?

Interethnic violence, interracial violence and genocide

Sixth, closely related to the fifth theoretical gap is the need for a stronger rural criminological focus through the development of rural-based middle-range theories on interethnic and interracial violence and of genocide in countries around the world (Karstedt et al, 2021). Since the Second World War, there have been nothing but roiling times for many regions, especially former colonial countries of Africa, Asia and South America. It is not simply a matter of presuming that social change, weak governments and countries whose resources are now exploited by capitalistic interests from wealthier countries create this kind of violence. So much of it seems to occur in rural localities, yet there is little consideration for rural context in the current literature. How might understanding the way rural places mediate violence of this type add value and possibly revise current scholarship on this topic?

Interpersonal violence

Seventh, the middle-range theory of male-peer support has already received backing for generalisability beyond the US to other countries (DeKeseredy, 2021). However, many other forms of interpersonal violence as expressed in a rural context have not been examined. To what extent do both social structural conditions, as statistically explored by Lee (2008) and associates through civic community theory and of rural cultural contexts allow scholars to formulate new middle-range theories of violent crime? Previous criminological scholarship often approached the subject from a subcultural point of view, such as the idea from the US that there is a subculture of violence in the southern and more rural regions of the country (Hayes and Lee, 2005). The thesis does not stand up to the evidence, and can be considered as a prime example of the conceptual fallacies of functionalist-thinking, but has more merit when reframed in terms of larger social structural considerations, including the ravages of capitalism on rural people and communities around the world. In a US context, the example would be its Appalachian region with the long-term decline of coal mining and deindustrialisation.

Violence, harassment and other crimes against women

One might think that this eighth gap was already covered in the discussion of the work of DeKeseredy and Schwartz (2009) and others who have considered violence against rural women. However, there is much more about which to think. Consider, for example, the work of Saunders (2015) who examined sexual harassment in rural workplaces of Australia and its relationship to aspects of male dominance and patriarchy. In this case, the theoretical gap is in the construction of middle-range theories that expand on what is meant by patriarchy and its expressions within the kinds of workplaces found more frequently in rural regions, from mining to farming. There is substantial evidence that some of the highest rates of harassment and both verbal and physical violence are against female farmworkers, with the evidence emerging from documentary forms of journalism and reports by non-government organisations (Barrick, 2016; Ramchandani, 2018; DeKeseredy, 2021). It is now time for rural criminological scholars to create the kinds of middle-range theories that will promote a worldwide understanding of the issue, and of effective responses.

Cybercrime

Ninth, there is much made by scholars of the rural–urban digital divide and whether or not the divide is disappearing with time. Regardless, the image that cybercrime for people living in rural communities is not much of a problem persists. Cybercrime exhibits a great variety of types, from scams and frauds to cyberbullying and other forms of coercive control often directed towards rural women and girls (Harris, 2020). It is now time to develop one or more middle-range theories that can contextualise cybercrime as experienced by people living in rural communities and how the impacts of cybercrime may be differentially experienced with rural and urban localities. Harris' work (2020), and the scholarship of others as well, lays the basis for filling in this theoretical gap in rural criminology.

The trafficking of everything

The tenth gap is perhaps the most daunting to fill because it is identified as the 'trafficking of everything'. Humans, food, flora, fauna, drugs, archaeological artefacts and so on and so on: all are subject to illegal movements both within and across countries. For each type of commodity, including humans, there are already cadres of scholars who attempt to understand the issue (Mackenzie and Green, 2009; Sollund, 2019), but little attempt to consider the commonalities of trafficking across various types of commodities. One commonality is that almost all commodities that are trafficked have a significant rural dimension, whether transnational or not. Yet, the rural dimension is often overlooked because the focus is on amelioration (a good thing!), and on commodity-specific thinking. The fact that these various commodities often have rural origins and urban destinations is acknowledged, but not fully examined. How do the conditions at the point of origin point to aspects of social structure that influence the probability of trafficking? How would a network approach help us to understand the relationship between the rural origins of trafficking and their connections to various destinations, which are more likely to be urban? Further, in the case of drug trafficking in particular, but possibly other commodities as well, trafficking may be in the opposite direction, that is, from urban to rural.

Drug production, trafficking, use and abuse

Despite the virtues of primary socialisation theory, it falls short of understanding the full context of the production, trafficking and abuse/consumption of illegal substances. The evidence for the lack of depth within primary socialisation theory can be seen in the reading of only two books. The first is a monograph by Garriott (2011) from his ethnographic study about the impact of methamphetamines in a two-county area in the state of West Virginia in the US. Garriott (2011) details how meth use came to be the norm and a part of small-town living there. Similarly, Stallwitz (2012) detailed in her ethnographic study the normalisation of heroin use in the Shetland Islands, UK, developing the theme of community-mindedness, which itself can be considered as a fourth example of middle-range theory. By community-mindedness, she meant the acceptance of heroin use by the general population in this rural region, so long as the users were not disruptive of everyday community life. Here again, middle-range theories that are focused on community context and less so on individual characteristics, would represent a real advance in rural criminological theorising.

Farm victimisation

Studies of farm victimisation, as a body of research, were among the first historically in the development of rural criminology (Barclay, 2016). Yet, this research represents the twelfth theory gap. Heretofore, farm crime research has adopted routine activities theory and situation crime prevention (Clack, 2015), but farm victimisation is ripe for much deeper theorising.

Recognising that farms are, for the most part, capitalist enterprises, they are automatically part of the social class systems of the societies where they are located (Donnermeyer, 2018). Farmers own land, and they rent land. They raise crops and livestock, and they sell them. They are capitalist enterprises, but still owned and managed mostly by families as a way to control labour in a business that is dependent on the seasonality of various activities. How do all of the social structural and economic dynamics of particular farming regions contextualise a wider, and perhaps more critical perspective, for an understanding of farm victimisation? Given large differences in farming systems around the world and of the place of farmers within the social class structures of these societies, can there be a middle-range theory with a global reach?

Farmers as offenders

The thirteenth gap in the literature is also about farmers, but this time as offenders (Donnermeyer, 2014; Smith and McElwee, 2016). It is not only victimisation that should be considered when thinking about crime on the farm. Farmers can be involved in human trafficking (Byrne and Smith, 2016) and of the abuse of farmworkers. Farmers may be stealing equipment, livestock and farm supplies from their neighbours. They may be involved in the clandestine production of drugs or loaning property on their agricultural operations for illegal activities by others. Male farmers may be abusive to their partners and their children. In other words, because farms are largely family-based businesses, the kinds of offences that can be committed by farmers are quite wide (Bunei et al, 2016).

Natural resource extraction, energy boomtowns and crime

Number 14 on the list of theoretical gaps is a topic frequently addressed in the empirical literature by rural criminologists, but without a great deal of theorising (Ruddell, 2017). It would seem that there is no better topic on which to apply the principles of social disorganisation theory than to the rapid changes – such as population increase, transitory workers and crime – that occur in rural localities where natural resources and energy extraction activities begin. Nothing could be further from the truth. In fact, these very invasive forms of economic activities do create very transformational change, although often short term and temporary, but are nonetheless better understood as a type of reorganisation.

Middle-range theorising about how rural communities are influenced by change of this magnitude is very much analogous to the need for middle-range theory of rural-focused studies about the impact of drug use by Garriott (2011) and Stallwitz (2012), who both documented changes that occurred over several years, perhaps a decade, but not much more. What rural criminologists need to understand is that rural communities are not unchanging entities, which, when subjected to outside social and economic forces, are suddenly disorganised and disrupted. To think otherwise is to practise another variation on what is known as the rural idyll, that is, of idealising rural localities as places of stability and little crime until something from the outside disturbs the tranquillity (Shucksmith, 2018).

Environmental crimes and harms

The 15th theoretical gap is environmental crime. Perhaps the biggest contribution to rural criminology by the field known as green criminology is the distinction between crime and harm (Lynch, 2019). Yet, green criminology often seems stuck on the rhetoric of describing environmental harms as 'bad' rather than the development of middle-range theories. That may be a tough and unfair judgement, but is meant to serve as a call for the development of middle-range theories about a variety of important criminological topics related to the environment, from poaching and wildlife trafficking to violations of environmental regulations by individuals, corporations and governments alike, and much more.

In particular, environmental crimes often have a strong rural dimension, and it is within the identification of the rural dimensions of environmental crimes and harms that a cadre of middle-range theories can be developed. Often, these will involve aspects of exploitation of rural environments by corporations or the state. Further, environmental crimes and harms affect Indigenous peoples and communities, and rural regions with ethnic minorities and disenfranchised people. State and corporate crime, in fact, forms the 16th and final theoretical gap to be identified for this chapter.

State and corporate crime

It is recognised that the development of middle-range theories on state and corporate crime for the advance of rural criminology is not a single theoretical gap. It would actually require a very large, thick monograph to address state and corporate crime in terms of their rural dimensions and it would require a fully developed monograph that would probably contain a dozen or more middle-range theories. Regardless, along with other theoretical gaps – such as Indigenous communities, LGBTIQA+, farmers as offenders, natural resource extraction/boomtowns, and environmental crimes and harms – a focus on middle-range theories about the role of the state and corporations would add a much-needed critical criminological approach to the criminological subfield of rural criminology. It is impossible to develop middle-range theories on state and corporate crime without considering issues associated with political economy, economic and political inequalities, and economic exploitation (Stretesky et al, 2014).

Empirical gaps

The reader should immediately notice that this section on empirical gaps is a much shorter section than the one on theoretical gaps. There is a simple reason for this lopsidedness. Each of the 16 identified theoretical gaps is also an empirical gap! Once developed, all theory needs continuous research. So, what is left for a section on empirical gaps? Here is a short, but important list.

First, how is rural to be defined? Official government definitions are useful when secondary data is plumbed to examine crime rates and make rural–urban comparisons, but they are indeed arbitrary indicators that mostly cannot account for rural diversity (Dubois et al, 2019). Further, the task of finding a universal definition of rural – that is, one that can be applied to anywhere in the world – is like trying to search successfully for mermaids, unicorns and honest politicians. One implication of a claim that the search for a universal rural is entirely fruitless is the need to discard any kind of dichotomous thinking, be it the old, stale *gemeinschaft-gesellschaft* concepts (Tönnies, 1955 [1887]) or the newest theoretically useless dichotomy of a southern versus a northern criminology and its rhetorical use of such bloated words as the 'metropole' (Moosavi, 2019) to refer to the dominance of the city and subordinate or dependent status of the hinterland.

The solution? First, researchers need to be very, very clear about their own operational definition of rural when reporting their results. Simply, the need is to inform other rural criminological scholars through the specificity of their measures. Second, it may be time to collect and collate the plethora of operational definitions so that scholars can discern and appreciate the diversity without running down the 'rabbit hole' assumption of seeking to find universal sociological traits. Other than the fact that rural places have smaller populations and are not adjacent to cities or suburbs, all else is variable.

Second, images of rural areas and rural peoples should be collected and analysed, from various descriptions of a rural idyll (Shucksmith, 2018) to the ways that rurality is depicted in movies and other media outlets (DeKeseredy et al, 2014). Some work is completed in this regard, such as a series published through Lexington Press titled Studies in Urban–Rural Dynamics, edited by Fulkerson and Thomas, such as their 2016 publication *Reimagining Rural: Urbanormative Portrayals of Rural Life*. What is needed now is an analysis about how these images could potentially inform theoretical frameworks to advance a rural criminology, or be dismissed as mental rubbish.

Third, despite the extensive rural criminological work on violence against women, there is remarkably little rural scholarship on child abuse and elder abuse. However, some scholarship may be found in various social work and social services journals. For example, in the journal *Trauma, Violence, & Abuse*, a 'scoping literature review' on rural child mistreatment can be found (Maguire-Jack et al, 2021). A keyword search of the journal also indicates a number of articles from other countries with a focus on abuse among rural populations. What this illustrates is that some empirical gaps are not the absence of research, but of the lack of synthesis of the literature, especially because many rural criminological topics can be researched by scholars from a wide variety of scientific disciplines who have little or no connection to mainstream criminology.

Fourth, perhaps the biggest underdeveloped issue, empirically (and theoretically), is one with too many dimensions to count. It is access to justice by rural peoples around the world. This issue is indeed related to the consolidation of police services to urban centres and fewer resources devoted to rural communities. Another dimension of access is the relationship of the police to Indigenous people, of LGBTIQA+ people, and of various racial, ethnic and other minority groups and special subcultures who live in rural areas and who may be unequally served by both law enforcement and criminal justice agencies. As victims, their reporting to the police may not be received with the same seriousness or credibility as people from the so-called mainstream, but experience a much swifter response should they be identified as suspects. In essence, unequal access to justice among rural people and rural communities is a largely unexplored form of marginalisation, an expression of inequality and an indicator of a segmented (not disorganised) social structure.

The fifth empirical gap is not really about research per se, but about the application of rural criminological research to prevention and practice. Two exemplars that are exceptions to this generalisation are Wendt's (2009) *Domestic Violence in Rural Australia*, and the book edited by Harkness (2020) titled *Rural Crime Prevention: Theory, Tactics and Techniques*. Through qualitative interviews, Wendt's book is about the life experiences of victims and service providers to tell a story about male patriarchy in rural settings. Harkness's edited work combines summaries of important rural criminological topics alongside chapters by 'practitioners' (the police, planners, a forest service ranger and others) on the same topic. Both illustrate that the so-called empirical gap is not about a particular topic per se, but about the application of research to the development of crime prevention strategies within rural contexts.

The sixth and final empirical gap may be the most important of all. That gap is the synthesis of rural criminological literature. Rural criminology is growing sufficiently fast that it has left behind a large scattering of scholarship that is not well integrated: that is, packaged as a coherent body of work. It is certainly both a form of empirical scholarship and a type of theoretical scholarship to synthesise and bring coherence to the extant rural criminological literature.

Paradigms for building middle-range theories and closing empirical gaps

Words like 'theory' and 'paradigm' often are used rather loosely to refer to the same thing, but in fact, they are distinctive in their functions. While theory is an explanation, as mentioned at the beginning of this chapter, a paradigm is a model or guide. A successful paradigm ought to lead to good theorising and closing theoretical gaps. In turn, good theorising ought to lead to a sharper research focus, thereby closing empirical gaps.

There are two paradigms identified which can guide the future development of middle-range theories for rural-focused scholarship. The first emphasises theories based on the diversity of rural communities around the world. It is not a paradigm that has anything to do with crime and criminal justice issues per se. Developed by Ruth Liepins (2000), it shows the interplay of spaces/structures with both meanings (such as culture) and practices (such as behaviours), resulting in six kinds of relationships.

It is these relationships that can guide the development of middle-range theories and related hypotheses for empirical testing with both quantitative and qualitative data. Even though all 16 theoretical gaps could be filled with a paradigm of place, a place-based paradigm is especially pertinent to understanding fear of crime (#3), LGBTIQA+ populations (#4), interpersonal violence (#7), violence and harassment (#8), cybercrime (#9), drug production, trafficking and use (#11), farm victimisation (#11), natural resource extraction/boomtowns (#15) and environmental crimes and harms (#16).

The second paradigm is more explicitly critical in its orientation. It is the square of crime (Young, 1992; see also Windle's Chapter 6 in this volume), which is a set of four broad categories that take greater account of the state's role in understanding crime and criminal justice issues. It includes the police and other state-sponsored agencies, the public, the offender and the victim. The interplay of the police and the public determines the efficacy of the police and other forms of social control agencies within a society, while the interplay of offenders and victims determines the impact of crime. Meanwhile, the relationship of the police and other agencies determines which offenders become part of the criminal justice system. Like the first paradigm, it is applicable to all 16 theoretical gaps, but seems more pertinent to policing (#1), Indigenous communities (#2), hate groups, militias and so on (#5), interethnic and interracial violence and genocide

(#6), the trafficking of everything (#10), farmers as offenders (#13) and food crime (#14).

Conclusion

It would not be difficult to identify many more theoretical and empirical gaps in the rural criminological literature. For example, why was food crime (Gray and Hinch, 2018) not included? The reason is that the literature there is more consumer-oriented, hence, as much urban if not more, than it is rural in focus. Nor would it be onerous to claim that some of the gaps identified for this chapter do not really exist.

The goal of this chapter was to demonstrate that theory-building and research are like good mates, perhaps even partners, making new insights and expanding the rural criminological family. It is hoped that by filling the gaps with good scholarship, rural criminology will continue to be like a cohesive kinship system well into the twenty-first century.

Notes

[1] The phrase 'one-dimensional scholar' borrows from Herbert Marcuse's (1964) critical analysis of the industrial and post-industrial age in a book titled *One-Dimensional Man: Studies in the Ideology of Advanced Industrial Society.*
[2] For a fuller discussion of each, refer to Donnermeyer (2019b).

References

Barclay, E. (2016) 'Farm victimisation: the quintessential rural crime', in J.F. Donnermeyer (ed) *Routledge International Handbook of Rural Criminology,* Abingdon: Routledge, pp 107–16.

Barrick, K. (2016) 'Human trafficking, labor exploitation and exposure to environmental hazards: the abuse of farmworkers in the US', in J.F. Donnermeyer (ed) *Routledge International Handbook of Rural Criminology,* Abingdon: Routledge, pp 147–56.

Blee, K.M. and Creasap, K.A. (2010) 'Conservative and right-wing movements', *Annual Review of Sociology,* 36: 269–86.

Bunei, E., McElwee, G. and Smith, R. (2016) 'From bush to butchery: cattle rustling as an entrepreneurial process in Kenya', *Society and Business Review,* 11(1): 46–61.

Byrne, R. and Smith, K. (2016) 'Modern slavery and agriculture', in J.F. Donnermeyer (ed) *Routledge International Handbook of Rural Criminology,* Abingdon: Routledge, pp 157–66.

Clack, W.J. (2015) 'Criminological theories: an analysis of livestock theft cases', *Acta Criminologica: South African Journal of Criminology,* 25(2): 92–106.

Cunneen, C. and Tauri, J. (2016) *Indigenous Criminology,* Bristol: Policy Press.

DeKeseredy, W.S. (2021) *Woman Abuse in Rural Places,* Abingdon: Routledge.

DeKeseredy, W.S. and Schwartz, M.D. (2009) *Dangerous Exits: Escaping Abusive Relationships in Rural America*, New Brunswick, NJ: Rutgers University Press.

DeKeseredy, W.S., Muzzatti, S.L. and Donnermeyer, J.F. (2014) 'Mad men in bib overalls: media's horrification and pornification of rural culture', *Critical Criminology*, 22(2): 179–97.

Donnermeyer, J.F. (2014) 'On expanding the concept of green collar crime', *The Critical Criminologist*, 22(2): 2–5.

Donnermeyer, J.F. (2018) 'The impact of crime on farms: an international synthesis', *Acta Criminologica: South African Journal of Criminology*, 31(4): 1–22.

Donnermeyer, J.F. (2019a) 'The importance of place: safety and security of rural peoples and communities in an urbanizing world' [Pomen kraja: varnost ruralnega prebivalstva in ruralnih okupnosti v urbaniziranem svetu], *Revija za kriminalistiko in kriminologijo*, 70(5): 399–408 [in English].

Donnermeyer, J.F. (2019b) 'The international emergence of rural criminology: implications for development revision of criminological theory for rural contexts', *International Journal of Rural Criminology*, 5(1): 1–18.

Dubois, K.O., Rennison, C.M. and DeKeseredy, W.S. (2019) 'Intimate partner violence in small towns, dispersed rural areas, and other locations: estimates using a reconception of settlement type', *Rural Sociology*, 84(4): 826–52.

Fulkerson, G.M. and Thomas, A.R. (eds) (2016) *Reimagining Rural: Urbanormative Portrayals of Rural Life*, Lanham, MA: Lexington Books.

Garriott, W. (2011) *Policing Methamphetamine: Narcopolitics in Rural America*, New York: New York University Press.

Gray, A. and Hinch, R. (2018) *A Handbook of Food Crime: Immoral and Illegal Practices in the Food Industry and What to Do About Them*, Bristol: Policy Press.

Harkness, A. (ed) (2020) *Rural Crime Prevention: Theory, Tactics and Techniques*, Abingdon: Routledge.

Harris, B.A. (2020) 'Technology and violence against women', in S. Walklate, K. Fitz-Gibbon, J. Maher and J. McCulloch, J. (eds) *The Emerald Handbook of Feminism, Criminology and Social Change*, Bingley: Emerald, pp 317–36.

Hayes, T.C. and Lee, M.R. (2005) 'The southern culture of honor and violent attitudes', *Sociological Spectrum*, 25(5): 593–617.

Jones, N.A., Lithopoulos, S. and Ruddell, R. (2016) 'Policing rural Indigenous communities: an examination of practices in Australia, Canada, New Zealand and the United States', in J.F. Donnermeyer (ed) *Routledge International Handbook of Rural Criminology*, Abingdon: Routledge, pp 355–64.

Karstedt, S., Brehm, H.N. and Laura, C.F. (2021) 'Genocide, mass atrocity, and theories of crime: unlocking criminology's potential', *Annual Review of Criminology*, 4: 75–97.

Kasarda, J.D. and Janowitz, M. (1974) 'Community attachment in mass society', *American Sociological Review*, 39(3): 328–39.

Lee, M. (2001) 'The genesis of "fear of crime"', *Theoretical Criminology*, 5(4): 467–85.

Lee, M.R. (2008) 'Civic community in the hinterland: toward a theory of rural social structure and violence', *Criminology*, 46(2): 447–78.

Liepins, R. (2000) 'New energies for an old idea: reworking approaches to "community" in contemporary rural studies', *Journal of Rural Studies*, 16: 23–35.

Lilly, R.J., Cullen, F.T. and Ball, R.A. (2015) *Criminological Theory: Context and Consequences* (6th edn), Thousand Oaks, CA: Sage.

Lynch, M.J. (2019) 'Green criminology and environmental crime: criminology that matters in the age of global ecological collapse', *Journal of White Collar and Corporate Crime*, 1(1): 50–61.

Mackenzie, S. and Green, P. (2009) *Criminology and Archaeology: Studies in Looted Antiquities*, London: Hart.

Maguire-Jack, K., Jespersen, B., Korbin, J.E. and Spilsbury, J.C. (2021) 'Rural child maltreatment: a scoping literature review', *Trauma, Violence, & Abuse*, 22(5): 1316–25.

Marcuse, H. (1964) *One-Dimensional Man: Studies in the Ideology of Advanced Industrial Society*, Boston, MA: Beacon Press.

Merton, R.K. (1957) *Social Theory and Social Structure* (revised edn), London: Collier-Macmillan.

Meško, G. (2020) 'Rural criminology: a challenge for the future', *European Journal of Crime, Criminal Law and Criminal Justice*, 28(1): 3–13.

Moosavi, L. (2019) 'A friendly critique of "Asian criminology" and "Southern criminology"', *British Journal of Criminology*, 59(2): 257–75.

Mouhanna, C. (2016) 'From myth to myth: rural criminology in France', in J.F. Donnermeyer (ed) *Routledge International Handbook of Rural Criminology*, Abingdon: Routledge, pp 65–74.

Oetting, E.R., Donnermeyer, J.F. and Deffenbacher, J.L. (1998) 'Primary socialization theory: the influence of community on drug use and deviance', *Substance Use and Misuse*, 33(8): 1629–65.

Ramchandani, A. (2018) 'There's a sexual-harassment epidemic on America's farms', *The Atlantic*, 29 January. Available from: https://www.theatlantic.com/business/archive/2018/01/agriculture-sexual-harassment/550109/ [Accessed 28 April 2021].

Ruddell, R. (2017) *Oil, Gas, and Crime: The Dark Side of the Boomtown*, New York: Palgrave Macmillan.

Ruddell, R. and Lithopoulos, S. (2016) 'Policing rural Canada', in J.F. Donnermeyer (ed) *Routledge International Handbook of Rural Criminology*, Abingdon: Routledge, pp 399–408.

Saunders, S. (2015) *Whispers from the Bush: The Workplace Sexual Harassment of Australian Rural Women*, Sydney: Federation Press.

Shucksmith, M. (2018) 'Re-imagining the rural: from rural idyll to Good Countryside', *Journal of Rural Studies*, 59: 163–72.

Smith, R. and McElwee, G. (2016) 'Criminal farmers and organised crime groups: a UK case study', in J.F. Donnermeyer (ed) *Routledge International Handbook of Rural Criminology*, Abingdon: Routledge, pp 127–36.

Sollund, R.A. (2019) *The Crimes of Wildlife Trafficking: Issues of Justice, Legality and Morality*, Abingdon: Routledge.

Stallwitz, A. (2012) *The Role of Community-Mindedness in the Self-Regulation of Drug Cultures: A Case Study from the Shetland Islands*, Dordrecht: Springer.

Stretesky, P., Long, M. and Lynch, M. (2014) *The Treadmill of Crime: Political Economy and Green Criminology*, Abingdon: Routledge.

Tönnies, F. (1955) [1887] *Community and Society*, London: Routledge and Kegan Paul.

Wendt, S. (2009) *Domestic Violence in Rural Australia*, Sydney: Federation Press.

Yarwood, R. and Wooff, A. (2016) 'Policing the countryside in a devolving United Kingdom', in J.F. Donnermeyer (ed) *Routledge International Handbook of Rural Criminology*, Abingdon: Routledge, pp 375–86.

Young, J. (1992) 'Ten points of realism', in J. Young and R. Matthews (eds) *Rethinking Criminology: The Realist Debate*, Thousand Oak, CA: Sage, pp 24–68.

4

Late Modernity and the Governance of Rural Security: From Solid to Liquid

Matt Bowden and Artur Pytlarz

Introduction

Criminology – like many of the social sciences; sociology in particular – emerged from attempts at understanding and responding to the transformations taking place in urban society during the twentieth century. A working assumption in this chapter is that rural areas are not static, but rather are permeable to social and technological changes as are urban spaces. Such transformations are evident especially in Ireland, which has been regarded for the last 20 years or more as one of the most globalised societies on earth as measured by the Swiss-based KOF Globalisation Index (Gygli et al, 2019; KOF, 2020). Until the 1960s, Ireland was regarded as a primarily agricultural society with a prominent farm-based economy that was involved in producing for export to the UK, its former colonial power. Farm employment reduced dramatically from the 1970s, from 45 per cent of the labour force in 1973 to 7 per cent by 2003 – and further still in the first two decades of the twenty-first century to around 4.5 per cent on average (Central Statistics Office, 2003–20).

Ireland's economic growth has been fuelled by high-tech manufacture and more recently Ireland has become a leading European base for global technology corporations. Intel, which directly employs 4,500 people manufacturing a high proportion of the world's computer chips, was constructed in a field outside a rural village in County Kildare, 20 kilometres (12 miles) from Dublin. The campus on which it sits covers 145 hectares (360 acres), built on what was once a stud farm, and the company has invested

US$15 billion in it since 1989 (IDA, 2014; Intel, 2019). Such high-tech growth has not only changed the physical make-up of the geographic space, but has radically introduced new patterns of settlement, social mobility and culture that have been repeated over and again in rural areas – hence transforming space and patterns of life on a local scale. Changing technologies offer new opportunities and produce new risks and in this chapter we aim to capture these transformations drawing from sociological and criminological narratives that capture these changes in the late twentieth and early twenty-first centuries.

Sociologists writing on theories of modernity have been widely influential within criminology and have sought to capture the nature of security and insecurity associated with these social, spatial and technological transformations. Security is a condition of trust, confidence and stability: it connotes an absence of fear, yet social transformations precipitate insecurity and uncertainty as patterns of life begin to change. Giddens (1984) first began to map the idea of new modernity based upon individual reflexivity as a response to risk and uncertainty of modern life, as societies began to live though significant market-focused economic reform (such as through the early days of Thatcherism in the UK, Reaganist economic reforms in the US and those of Hawke and Keating in Australia in the 1980s): the neoliberal economy and governance began to rapidly disembed societies from tradition.

Later, Giddens (1991) would liken modernity to a juggernaut, a huge and overwhelming force, transforming everything in its path: bringing humanity to new places, potentially, but also involving new risks, uncertainties and insecurities. The challenge, he implied, was to find new ways to steer this fast-moving social transformation by having greater individual and collective reflexivity. Individuals, therefore, had to be more flexible and should adapt by embracing change in their individual life-projects (Giddens, 1991).

Late modernity, according to its proponents, generates fear and insecurity and, as a consequence, stimulates the new security industry or 'security field' (Bowden, 2021). This chapter attends to six key matters, each accounting for the range of complementary and competing theories of modernity that have greatly informed criminological thinking in respect of security and its governance. The chapter:

1. outlines ideas about how modernisation disembeds traditional practices and locales;
2. uses Bauman (2000) to say something about change and insecurity;
3. emphasises the concept of 'flows' as a way of thinking about our late-modern times as a flow process;
4. considers the issue of risk, drawing upon Ulrich Beck's (1992) ideas about risk society;

5. uses Young's (2007) dystopian framing of the dizziness of late-modern times to consider the idea of the security bubbles we live in; and
6. turns to the ideas of David Garland (2001) to think about how communities and individuals are asked to assume their own agency in taking responsibility for security.

Importantly, the chapter highlights some of the ways in which this new modernity can impact on rural transformation (Thomas et al, 2011), providing a theoretical case drawing from current research in Ireland looking at how previous ethnographic research has captured the social change in rural communities. Finally, the chapter takes a closer look at the way in which local people in rural areas are asked to take more responsibility for their own security, and highlights some of the ways in which they have adapted.

Modernity and late modernity in the rural locale

Disembedding social life

One might regard rural life as a series of regular practices that give rise to particular patterns of living, where individuals have to take stock of their social circumstances and alter practices to enable the reproduction of the social patterns in which they live. Modernity changes people and their communities by disembedding them from traditional practices.

In his book *The Constitution of Society*, Giddens (1984) wrote that such repetitive activities located on time and space are not intended by the actor, but what arises is a structured way of living. Giddens highlights that the conditions that change or help structures to continue reproduce those systems. This is the basis of his 'structuration theory': individuals are not passive but are active agents in the making and remaking of structures and social systems. Hence, the modern agent practises reflexively through constant monitoring of the self, revisiting previous actions and behaviours in order to modify current social practices.

Later, in his book *The Consequences of Modernity*, Giddens (1991) refers to the conditions of a new 'high' or 'late' modernity in which actors need to take account of what is communicated by expert knowledge for individuals to act reflexively. Trust in abstract systems is necessary to reap the promise of this stage of development and without it, individuals cannot participate in modern life. An example Giddens provides is that of the credit card, which enables the actor to transact in a global context on a global scale. It is not money in the physical paper sense that is tied to the national, but abstract money – a system in which the agent has to trust in order to engage. Modernity enables participation on this wider scale and therefore has a disembedding effect.

For Giddens, modernity is a momentous force that he likens to a juggernaut: it has immense transformative power that we, through collective effort, can try to steer to counter the disembedding effects by re-embedding globally constructed abstracts and adapting them in the local context of place. Hence, he argues for 'reflexive modernity' in which individuals, institutions and the state need to reimagine the local by embedding expert knowledge and abstract systems – we take the science on board, so to speak, and we transform both ourselves and our civil society.

Rural patterns of living are being disembedded in this image of change, but adopting expert knowledge and new technologies, reimagines and reconfigures communities. The rural is a 'local' that is transformed by modernisation and thus changes space, social relations, systems of governance and outcomes. Take health, for example: it has been argued that we need to see health as not isolated or particular in the locale but integrated with more complex, abstract systems where rural people can be enabled to access better health (Bourke et al, 2012), and therefore improve their well-being.

'The unholy trinity': late-modern insecurity

'Rural', in the common perception, is a place of little or at least a very slow pace of change. A peaceful rural life built around family, community and traditions helps to maintain the image of the 'rural idyll' (Donnermeyer and DeKeseredy, 2014). Yet, for Bauman (2000), the family or the community represent the old *solid institutions* of modernity. As he argues in his book *Liquid Modernity* (Bauman, 2000), the progress and impact of globalisation has led to the disconnection of capital from labour. With the capital becoming an international or even extraterritorial enterprise, it is constantly on the move and labour still grounded to the fixed location unable to catch up with capital unless it goes through the constant process of adaptation. One of the main characteristics of early modern times was that it was fixed to place, anchored by social mechanisms that rendered it 'heavy' or 'solid': institutions such as class, work, community or family. These institutions act as a 'safe harbour', offering stability and a frame of reference for all members of society. Yet, nowadays with the progress of globalisation and the fluidity of capital, they have become subject to change and therefore 'weightless' and 'liquid'. These liquidising powers have moved the social mode of operation from the 'system' to 'society', from 'politics to life-policies', and from 'territorialism' and 'settlement' to 'nomadism' and 'extraterritorial elite'.

Importantly, fast-going social and political change, together with the impact of globalisation, has even more impact on individuals: it becomes impossible to slow down the velocity of change and to predict future directions and outcomes. Therefore, individuals tend to choose to focus on the problems they can or believe they can control and focus on problems that are within the reach of their own action. Furthermore, as the 'old solids' crumble, this becomes a very self-centred enterprise:

> [W]e seek *substitute* targets on which we unload the surplus existential fear that has been barred from its natural outlets. … Those of us who can afford it fortify ourselves against all visible and invisible … dangers through locking ourselves behind walls, stuffing the approaches to our living quarters with TV cameras, … driving armoured vehicles (like the notorious SUVs). (Bauman, 2007: 11)

Furthermore, for Bauman, globalisation and the accompanying changes have a much deeper and structural impact on the postmodern society: the 'liquidating' power touches not only the family or work but also the nation state as the 'solid' form of governance. Bauman argues that in the new reality of a fast-globalised world, politics is losing the majority of its former power (note, for example, the demise of social democracy and the rise of populism, neoliberalism and neoconservatism in many jurisdictions) (Bauman, 2017). Hence, the government as an institution is unable and/or not willing to offer much security or certainty, ceding this task to individuals.

With such powerless political institutions focused more on finding new sources of fear than providing solutions, the reality of living in 'liquid modernity' is that we all face what Bauman called an 'unholy trinity': uncertainty, insecurity and unsafety which 'results in the perpetual thirst for more safety, a thirst which no practical measures can quell' (Bauman, 2000: 181). This precipitates a multiplicity of effects – the demise of trust, the rise of fear; adjustments and accommodations once thought unnecessary or unworkable become manifest (for a case example, see Leonard, 2014). For Bauman, we have transformed from a solid modernisation to a liquid modernity: this underlines the need to understand how space is being transformed by fluid processes, and where 'flows' are critical to capturing our contemporary globalised times.

Informational capitalism and the spatial logics of flows of flows

While writing primarily on cities over much of his career, Manuel Castells (2000) provides a critical set of insights that helps connect questions of space with the advancement of the current mode of capitalist economy based upon information. The Information Age is based upon new systems or milieux of innovation that Castells understands as relationships of production and management that are oriented towards new knowledge, products and processes. In this context, physical and social space is integrated into the new logics created by 'informationalism' centred on flows: of information, people, capital, data, images and symbols. Critically, this spatial logic becomes dominant as it is driven by the interests of the elites whom it serves: it has material effects on space but is driven by key social actors. The 'space of flows' is thus physical and social space captured by the informational capitalist elite and it dominates the interests of society which are rooted in the dominated 'space of place'. For Castells, the space of flows is the organisation of time-shared social practices working through flows rather than place. In particular, this has a networked form where the elites are connected both globally and locally, move in flow space and places are reconfigured for their needs, resulting in greater securitisation to shore up exclusion (Castells, 2000: 446).

The point here is to draw attention to the implications of informational capitalism for the reconfiguration of space. One strategy to connect productive zones together is through greater telecommunications infrastructure – utilising rural spaces for production but also for data centres, energy supply, mobile telephony and so on. Flow space requires increased physical infrastructure to enable greater connectivity for flows. The car system then requires new networks of roads to link productive regions and cities and to enable commuting, shopping and leisure, usurping and repurposing space previously regarded as rural, for retail parks, shopping malls, theme parks and tourist attractions (see Featherstone, 2004). Flows upset the previous spatial logic because they work in and alongside territorial sovereignty in which the global is mingled or 'glocalised' creating 'neo-worlds'; and hence flows render institutions in nation states 'a fetter on the emerging glocal modes of production' (Luke, 1995: 101). Flows bring new connecting infrastructures including roads, highways and motorways that dissect rural spaces, create new routes of access and egress and expose the rural to new risks. Flows also change the images we have of the rural.

For Thomas et al (2011), there are three principal images of rural space. First is the 'rural as wild', with the urban as 'civilised'. Here the rural is regarded, under the cultural hegemony of the urban, as being ripe for exploitation. Second is 'rural as simple', as a relic of the past to which we look for a sense of authenticity. Third is the 'rural as an escape', as a retreat from the urban, which implies that it must be preserved in a state that is consumable for visitors. The transformation of society based on technological advancements in the twentieth and early twenty-first centuries in building a type of 'accelerated modernity' where growth is required to stay still (Rosa, 2013), and in rural areas sets off a new politics over flows in a variety of domains including energy, tourism, sustainability and security.

Rural security as the redistribution of risk

Ulrich Beck (1992) offers another view on socio-political changes shaping late modernity. His main idea revolves around the concept of 'risk', which he described as a systematic way of dealing with hazards and insecurities induced by modernisation in the post-industrial society. This, he argues, became the dominant tendency in the postmodern social world and became evidence of social transformation towards the 'risk society' – one organised and focused mainly on real and potential risks and the ways of dealing with them, and this becomes a dominant mindset of contemporary society. For Beck, risk is associated with anticipation, of destruction that has not yet happened but is threatening in the future.

Risk, therefore, represents the shift of focus from the past to the future, and in the risk society the place of history is taken by the future. So arises a new practice at the subjective level whereby individuals have to craft the future by anticipating its destructive potential. From a crime prevention perspective (especially in the form of private activities such as alarms, CCTV systems or other situational measures) crime prevention can be viewed as an activity undertaken at present, as an answer or countermeasure to threats that potentially occur. Each individual and collective, therefore, has to accommodate this probability. Risk upsets the scale in which people act at the subjective level in how, for example, rural youth might calculate their mobility options in their rural locale, and regarding these chances as not getting very far (Looker and Naylor, 2009).

For Beck (1992), in the risk society the scientist's monopoly of rationality seems to be broken: science cannot objectively investigate risks, because all statements concerning risk are based on speculative assumptions or probability statements that cannot be proved without the actual incident. Therefore, the risks are subject to interpretation and, often, a negotiation between various agents of modernity and affected groups. In that reality, the position of science is just one of many voices in the public sphere. Thus, it is possible that crime prevention strategies or state intervention rely more on the wide discourse, including media, politicians, potential victims and the police force, competing alongside the recommendations from the experts. Their views have to compete in a discursive field which is emotionally charged (Pytlarz and Bowden, 2019).

Furthermore, Beck notes that with the increased focus on risks and hazards, democracy itself faces new challenges: as the risk society becomes a social organisation, it precipitates a tendency towards a shift in the form of governance where there is a totalising and legitimised emphasis on hazard prevention. As Beck (1992) asserts, the political price of preventing potential dangers threatens the democratic political system. The system is often caught in a dilemma: acting on the potential risks by suspending fundamental democratic principles and turning towards an authoritarian state; or governing to protect the individual freedoms yet at the same time exposing communities to potential dangers. Such a view moves the focus to the impact of increased security measures, such as CCTV or Text Alert Schemes now present in rural communities in Ireland, and on such institutions of civil society such as personal freedom and anonymity. Therefore, rural becomes a place of the constant contest between the right to privacy and personal freedoms versus the right to self-protection through increased surveillance.

The vertigo of late modernity and the safety bubble

For Young (2007), at the core of the social transformation into the late modern is an exclusive dystopia, manifest in a model of a social organisation built around division and exclusion running through the nation state. This vision contrasts to modernity which was focused on welfare, rehabilitation and integration. In this new model, the excluded are the underclass who are regarded by the powerful as living in idleness and crime. As Young averred, the main function of this group is to play the role of a scapegoat for the troubles of wider society as the winners can blame the losers for any social and political maladies. As such, the excluded reinforce the 'winner's' sense of ontological security. Tyler (2020: 29) has captured this as the exercise of 'stigma power' – the 'socio-political machining of stigma in service of extractive forms of capitalism'.

In late modernity, there is a rise of administrative criminology which is concerned with managing crime rather than reforming offenders or battling the causes of crime. It does not pretend to eliminate crime, but rather to minimise risk and harm. It seeks merely to separate the criminals from the 'decent' citizens, the troublemaker from the peaceful shopper. At its foundation lies the belief that eliminating criminal behaviour is impossible, and it eschews the dispositional origins of crime in the deviant or their milieux, favouring situational crime prevention (see Bowden and Pytlarz, 2020). Thus, in the context of rural crime, the answer to the problems perhaps does lies not in the operation of the criminal justice system but in recognising that individuals should ensure they reduce their exposure to harm and should minimise or eliminate their contact with potentially harmful individuals.

Furthermore, for Young (2007), an answer to this risk is reinforce the *Umwelt*: an attitude of constant awareness and calculation of how to minimise the exposure to crime and potential damage. In this context, *Umwelt* is a bubble everybody has around them and that bubble is the area where one feels safe and secure. At the same time, the area outside *Umwelt* is an arena of apprehension, fear and danger. Importantly, that secure area expands and shrinks whether one is at home or on the street. It has also a strong gender, age, class and ethnic component. Therefore, *Umwelt* is a dynamic structure shaped by social context and the world around it. Fear can be generated by far events such as a distant weather event, or more closely the *Umwelt* can be shaped by fear in the community as it is exposed to the risks brought by a new motorway. A new way of defending oneself, therefore, is to take responsibility; to harden oneself to risks.

The crime complex and the redistribution of responsibility

Sociological and criminological theorists have grasped late modernity as a way of capturing social transformation that manifests itself in a new defensiveness against crime. This is what Garland (2000) referred to as the 'crime complex', a cultural turn in late modernity where crime is designed out and people are forced to retreat to protected, privatised spaces. The cultural turn is based upon the belief that criminal justice systems are ineffective and hence self-protection and surveillance come to be accepted as normal. This, for Garland (2000), captures the late-modern dystopia – a private member society where people buy in safety based upon fear of victimisation which takes place against an emotionally charged discourse about crime that impacts on daily routines. We choose cars over walking; chaperone children and retreat behind self-provided security infrastructure; spaces not so tamed are wild and ungoverned and accompanied by, to a considerable extent, the flight of the middle class from cities to suburbs and beyond to commuting from rural spaces.

There is, according to Garland (2001), a realisation that the state cannot prevent crime and provide security reflected in the persistence and normalisation of high crime rates, which had become taken for granted. There follows, for Garland, a series of adaptations including routinisation of justice agencies, policing and, in many cases, the privatisation and outsourcing of justice and policing functions. According to Garland, adaptation seeks to relocate and redistribute responsibility – and in this context set up community corrections, community diversion and community policing schemes. The second part of this adaptation was the 'responsibilisation strategy'. Thus, the growth of crime prevention partnerships involving criminal justice agencies and non-state sectors that are designed to persuade citizens to act appropriately. However, the responsibilisation strategy has been made more difficult by the prior monopoly enjoyed by the state, in that the state was always the exclusive authority in relation to crime control.

Responsibilisation effectively accompanies the 'new regulatory state' in criminal justice (Braithwaite, 2000) as the neoliberal state recoils to a miniature version of its previous incarnation. For Garland (2001), responsibilisation goes cheek-by-jowl with the 'new criminology of everyday life' and should be viewed as a routine risk to be calculated rather than a moral lapse or act of deviance. The new theory of situationalism thus defeated earlier attempts at reforming the offender through penal welfarism, and was replaced with new situationalism – the return to calculated, reasoned decision-making involving individual prudentialism. In turn, this gives rise to a practice of self-governing in terms of security and safety in late modernity that impacts all spaces, rural and urban (Bowden and Pytlarz, 2020).

This chapter, thus far, has taken a theoretical journey though the various accounts of these late-modern times. How do the themes and trends we identify manifest themselves in context? What follows is a discussion of the case of Ireland and its late-modern transformation and an exploration as to how these issues manifest themselves in rural communities.

The case of Ireland: rural security and insecurity in a highly globalised society

The development of criminology owes much to the urbanism of the Chicago School as it sought to capture the anomic conditions of a rapidly expanding city as immigrants flocked from the old world to the new in the late nineteenth and early twentieth centuries. Predating this, however, in the early period of cities in Europe, an ideology emerged that saw the urban as superior and the rural as deviant, dark and edgy, and so emerged the ideology of urban-normativity (Thomas et al, 2011). The city was a place of liberation, civility and rationality leading to the formation of capitalism, and captured from the outset in the phrase *Stadtluft macht frei* ('urban air makes one free') and by contrast the rural was associated with magic, darkness and danger (Holton, 1986). Engagements that we have had with theories of modernity thus far in the twenty-first century within criminology have tended to deal with crime, security and safety primarily based on urban cases (Hancock, 2001; Bourgois, 2003; Wacquant, 2008).

Hence, an ongoing study of crime, risk and resilience in the countryside (Pytlarz and Bowden, 2019) emerged to ascertain the extent to which the rural experience resonates with the theory and whether it reflects a similar politics to that of the urban. What follows is an outline of social change from rural ethnographies of Ireland, accompanied by a brief case vignette of issues from fieldwork.

Modernisation of Ireland

Until the signing of the Anglo-Irish Treaty in 1921, Ireland was governed under the colonial government of the UK, and after several hundred years of rebellion and insurrection achieved its independence. In the mid-1840s, the failure of the potato harvests (upon which most smallholders depended to feed their families) precipitated a famine that resulted in the deaths of one million people and mass emigration from rural Ireland of approximately 2.5 million people (O'Gráda, 2007).

The modernisation of Ireland accompanied its embracing in the 1960s of foreign direct investment as the basis of an industrial strategy, and thus as a late entrant ideally placed itself for a form of 'high tech growth' (Ó Riain, 2004). The subsequent emergence of the Celtic Tiger economy of the 1990s and 2000s was premised upon its interventionist 'flexible developmental state' (Ó Riain, 2000). Change in the countryside has been gradual. Ireland favoured a form of dispersed industrialisation (Whelan et al, 1992) whereby branch plants of foreign firms could be located in small regional towns or in rural areas with good road and rail infrastructure. The changing social relations in these areas of the country has been captured in a series of studies whereby the national interest came to dominate and insert itself as community interest (see Harris, 1983). Let us start to account for this period of rural change with reference to a series of ethnographies that have captured rural life in Ireland since the 1930s.

Excavating modernities in rural Ireland: three historic contributions

Between 1932 and 1934, two young American anthropologists visited Ireland and conducted a field study of a rural community in county Clare (Arensberg and Kimball, 2001 [1940]). They came seeking the image of the pre-industrial world as they believed rural Ireland at that time was still an example of such, from which using a structural functionalist analysis they could characterise social change in the developed industrial world (Byrne et al, 2015). What they observed was a place of order and tradition. The social structure was bonded and held together by tradition: small family farms based on a kinship system, amplified by communal mutual aid. At the time, agriculture was a predominant industry, the rural smallholders and their ways of living were lauded by the political elite, giving them a culturally dominant position nationally.

Industrialisation and outward migration from the island from the 1960s saw a shift away from the rural community to a more advanced urban-based economy and society. This is captured well by Hugh Brody (1973) in his book *Inishkillane: Change and Decline in the West of Ireland*, which recorded a completely different image of rural Ireland. The former cultural hegemony of rural Ireland was gone, together with the young generation who emigrated to the city looking for a better life. The traditional primogeniture (right of succession to the first born) model forced younger members of the family to look at the city as a viable option; a new generation therefore discovered urban life and the urban values. Brody (1973) accounted for the transformation of traditional small farm communities from integrated and working systems into demoralisation: where villages became characterised by an ageing population, loneliness and isolation became the common. In a sense, this sparks a first noticeable impact of modernisation, to use Bauman's (2000) logic, whereby the 'mobile' younger generation left behind the static and immobilised older population who were tied to the 'heavy' land.

Writing at the height of the Celtic Tiger economy and society, Inglis (2008) observed another phase of rural transformation in Ireland as the economic model accelerated into its informational and globalised form. In his account, the rural village of Ballivor is a place of colliding global trends: the local customs of the rural community he was observing seemed to adapt to new challenges through the process which we could call 'the re-embedding' (Giddens, 1991) or 'glocalisation' as the local co-mingled with the global. Inglis (2008) observed how local conversations were imbued with information gleaned from the internet which, he suggested, constituted evidence of inhabitants of Ballivor being part of the global flow of information and integrated into local practices. On the other hand, the community in Ballivor is stratified into two groups: the established villagers – people who were born in the village and spent the whole lives there; and the newcomers – people who bought a house in the growing village, but whose work and leisure time revolves around the city, as they commute on daily basis.

Ballivor is close enough to the global node of Dublin where one finds the new global flow industries of informational capitalism, and far enough away to remain rural – a hybrid space allowing for hybrid identities. Both groups occupy the same territory but have little need to interact which each other. For example, being fixed to place, the villagers do their shopping in the local post office (a solid) while the mobile newcomers occupy flow space (Castells, 2000) and hence prefer the petrol station, emphasising Bauman's (2000) distinction between the solid and the fluid.

Governance of rural crime: responsibilisation and the incorporation of rural civil society

In fieldwork conducted with rural communities, some of the transformations noted by these scholars are evident. However, they are often uneven and not clear-cut. For example, it can be argued that late modernity exposes rural people to new risks: what were previously remote places have become connected through the networks of motorways. In this sense, rural communities have become part of the flow of the labour, goods and tourists. In recent years, distinct regions of Ireland have been marketed as niche destinations, such as the Wild Atlantic Way and the Historic East. While this is often connected with the improvement of the local economy, it brings new risks as well, as rural areas are converted into distinct flow products.

Commuting and resettlement by ex-urban residents transforms the composition and culture of rural areas each with a distinct experience of crime and with different feelings of insecurity. Exploring how crime enters the local discourse through 'crime talk', Pytlarz and Bowden (2019) show that there were distinct categories of rural resident: newcomers retained the idea of the rural idyll having witnessed crime in the city; while for local residents, they saw the village as being in decline: the underlying tone of the conversations was the nostalgia of the past. The responsibilisation, although present, was never fully implemented and the response to the risks was more nuanced.

Taking the idea that insecurity is an effect of late modernity and that there is an expansion in different forms of production of security (Bowden, 2019), this work focuses on how rural crime prevention, as a public good, has been taking shape in rural communities in Ireland. Critically, it can be shown from fieldwork that the adoption of new technological fixes like more sophisticated alarms systems or high-definition CCTV cameras has taken place, but that change goes much deeper.

Part of the Irish police's crime prevention strategy is the roll out of an SMS text-based crime prevention scheme – the Text Alert Scheme. The majority of rural communities have adopted the crime prevention strategy by their participation in the scheme, based on an SMS technology network that connects rural communities with the police force and engages rural dwellers in a specific trade-off: safety for information; police receive information from the public; and the police can then provide alerts to a wider public through phone texts (Bowden and Pytlarz, 2020). What we see here should be understood as a process of production and maintenance of safety based on the exchange of information.

This has few implications for the understanding nature of safety in the Irish countryside, which one might regard as being composed of a mixture of hard and soft or indeed solid and fluid elements. While on the one hand the official police website encourages citizens to protect themselves with hard/ solid solutions – high fences, a good intruder alarm, better locks – there is an equal emphasis on having access to information. This appears in a variety of forms: the SMS text network, Facebook pages set up by local residents, cooperation and networking with other communities and CCTV systems (Bowden and Pytlarz, 2020). For many rural residents, to be safe means to be informed, or at least to be included in the flow of information – being outside of the information flow is enough to create insecurity. Here it is argued that information is a form of cultural capital and a critical part of late-modern security production in rural areas.

Communities engage in manifold forms of gathering information, which they use as capital in contacts with the police force or other players in the security field. Rural safety is going through the change itself (Bowden and Pytlarz, 2020). Frustrated at times with the lack of value for money, local residents move away from the monologic Text Alert Scheme (information is dispatched centrally by the police) and towards setting up their own Facebook and WhatsApp groups. In some ways, this reflects a shift from a form of rural security 1.0 to rural security 2.0 which allows local residents to be both consumers and producers of crime prevention information, with at times very little quality control checks. This is a new space in that it signals the emergence of what could be termed 'liquid security' based upon information flow and a dynamic based upon inclusion and exclusion. Therefore, security moves from a hard and solid to soft and fluid form as the rural community adapts by taking part in the production and consumption of security, as a means of constructing an *Umwelt*.

Conclusion

This chapter has sought to align fieldwork observations in rural communities in Ireland with broader narratives of late modernity that have been more typical in the contemporary literature on urban security (see for example Hughes, 2007; Edwards et al, 2013). To conclude, then, there exists a typical late-modern pattern in rural areas where the emphasis on adopting self-defensive security measures has taken hold through the use of situational crime prevention measures. This is now supplemented by more fluid forms of security and crime prevention based upon information. Rural communities are moving, therefore, into a period where abstract forms of security bring with them great promise and great risk: of creating safe and secure rural communities; and of potentially othering and marginalising – either through misuse of social media or by excluding some rural people from the flow of information.

However, a greater threat is stalking civil society in the form of cybersecurity threats and information-based scams that are now widely reported in the media. Additionally, as homes become smarter and turn to a wider range of internet-enabled devices, the WannaCry ransomware attack of 2017, for example, exposes the potential for greater informational insecurity in these fluid times where rural crime is becoming increasingly abstract and extraterritorial, and creating new challenges for research and theorising in relation to rural security. The 'capable guardian' (Cohen and Felson, 1979) in this context needs some revisiting for crimes take place regardless of the presence of people. While crime could easily have been tackled with a gate, a lock and a dog, it too has undergone liquefaction and shifted into its informational mode. The juggernaut of late modernity rolls on.

References

Arensberg, C.M. and Kimball, S.T. (2001) [1940] *Family and Community in Ireland* (3rd edn), Ennis, Ireland: Clasp Press.

Bauman, Z. (2000) *Liquid Modernity*, Cambridge: Polity Press.

Bauman, Z. (2007) *Liquid Times: Living in an Age of Uncertainty*, Cambridge: Polity Press.

Bauman, Z. (2017) *A Chronicle of Crisis: 2011 to 2016*, Online ebook. Berlin: Social Europe Editions. Available from: https://socialeurope.eu/book/chronicle-crisis-2011-2016 [Accessed 2 March 2022].

Beck, U. (1992) *Risk Society: Towards a New Modernity*, London: Sage.

Bourgois, P.I. (2003) *In Search of Respect: Selling Crack in El Barrio* (2nd edn), Cambridge: Cambridge University Press.

Bourke, L., Humphreys, J.S., Wakerman, J. and Taylor, J. (2012) 'Understanding rural and remote health: a framework for analysis in Australia', *Health and Place*, 18(3): 496–503.

Bowden, M. (2021) 'The security field: forming and expanding a Bourdieusian criminology', *Criminology & Criminal Justice*, 21(2): 169–86.

Bowden, M. and Pytlarz, A. (2020) 'The development of rational models of crime prevention: a critique of situationist common sense in rural contexts', in A. Harkness (ed) *Rural Crime Prevention: Theory, Tactics and Techniques*, Abingdon: Routledge, pp 30–42.

Braithwaite, J. (2000) 'The new regulatory state and the transformation of criminology', *British Journal of Criminology*, 40(2): 222–38.

Brody, H. (1973) *Inishkillane: Change and Decline in the West of Ireland*, London: Allen Lane.

Byrne, A., Edmondson, R. and Varley, T. (2015) 'Arensberg and Kimball and anthropological research in Ireland', *Irish Journal of Sociology*, 23(1): 22–61.

Castells, M. (2000) *The Rise of the Network Society* (2nd edn), Oxford: Blackwell.

Central Statistics Office (2003–20) *Statistical Yearbook of Ireland*, Cork: Central Statistics Office. Available from: https://www.cso.ie/en/statistics/statistic alyearbookofireland/ [Accessed 2 March 2022].

Cohen, L.E. and Felson, M. (1979) 'Social change and crime rate trends: a routine activity approach', *American Sociological Review*, 44(4): 588–608.

Donnermeyer, J.F. and DeKeseredy, W.S. (2014) *Rural Criminology*, New York: Routledge.

Edwards, A., Hughes, G. and Lord, N. (2013) 'Urban security in Europe: translating a concept in public criminology', *European Journal of Criminology*, 10(3): 260–83.

Featherstone, M. (2004) 'Automobilities: an introduction', *Theory, Culture & Society*, 21(4/5): 1–24.

Garland, D. (2000) 'The culture of high crime societies: some preconditions of recent "law and order" policies', *British Journal of Criminology*, 40(3): 347–75.

Garland, D. (2001) *The Culture of Control: Crime and Social Order in Contemporary Society*, Oxford: Oxford University Press.

Giddens, A. (1984) *The Constitution of Society: Outline of a Theory of Structuration*, Cambridge: Polity Press.

Giddens, A. (1991) *The Consequences of Modernity*, Cambridge: Polity Press.

Gygli, S., Haelg, F., Potrafke, N. and Sturm, J.-E. (2019) 'The KOF Globalisation Index – revisited', *Review of International Organizations*, 14(3): 543–74.

Hancock, L. (2001) *Community, Crime, and Disorder: Safety and Regeneration in Urban Neighbourhoods*, Basingstoke: Palgrave.

Harris, L. (1983) 'Industrialisation, women and working class politics in the west of Ireland', *Capital and Class*, 7(1): 100–17.

Holton, R.J. (1986) *Cities, Capitalism, and Civilization: Controversies in Sociology*, London: Allen & Unwin.

Hughes, G. (2007) *The Politics of Crime and Community*, Basingstoke: Palgrave Macmillan.

IDA (Industrial Development Authority) (2014) 'Intel – 25 years in Ireland', *IDA Ireland*. Available from: https://www.idaireland.com/how-we-help/resources/infographics/intel [Accessed 3 May 2021].

Inglis, T. (2008) *Global Ireland: Same Difference*, New York: Routledge.

Intel (2019) 'Intel celebrates 30 years in Ireland', *Intel Newsroom*, 22 November. Available from: https://newsroom.intel.ie/press-kits/intel-celebrates-30-years-in-ireland/#gs.2z1nfx [Accessed 10 June 2021].

KOF (Swiss Economic Institute) (2020) *KOF Globalisation Index*. Available from: https://kof.ethz.ch/en/forecasts-and-indicators/indicators/kof-globalisation-index.html [Accessed 10 June 2021].

Leonard, L. (2014) 'Cultural criminology, governmentality and the liquidity of the failing state: the view from Ireland', *Critical Criminology*, 22(2): 293–306.

Looker, D.E. and Naylor, T.D. (2009) '"At risk" of being rural? The experience of rural youth in a risk society', *Journal of Rural and Community Development*, 4(2): 39–64.

Luke, T.W. (1995) 'New world order or neo-world orders power: politics and ideology in informationalizing glocalities', in M. Featherstone, S. Lash and R. Robertson (eds) *Global Modernities*, London: Sage, pp 91–107.

Ó'Gráda, C. (2007) 'Making famine history', *Journal of Economic Literature*, 45(1): 5–38.

Ó Riain, S. (2000) 'The flexible developmental state: globalization, information technology and the "Celtic Tiger"', *Politics & Society*, 28(2): 157–93.

Ó Riain, S. (2004) 'Falling over the competitive edge', in M. Peillon and M.P. Corcoran (eds) *Place and Non-place: The Reconfiguration of Ireland*, Dublin: Institute of Public Administration, pp 19–29.

Pytlarz, A. and Bowden, M. (2019) '"Crime-talk", security and fear in the countryside: a preliminary study of a rural Irish town and its hinterland', *International Journal of Rural Criminology*, 4(2): 138–72.

Rosa, H. (2013) *Social Acceleration: A New Theory of Modernity*, trans J. Trejo-Mathys, New York: Columbia University Press.

Thomas, A.R., Lowe, B.M., Fulkerson, G.M. and Smith, P.J. (2011) *Critical Rural Theory: Structure, Space, Culture*, Lanham, MD: Lexicon Books.

Tyler, I. (2020) *Stigma: The Machinery of Inequality*, London: Zed Books.

Wacquant, L.J.D. (2008) *Urban Outcasts: A Comparative Sociology of Advanced Marginality*, Cambridge: Polity Press.

Whelan, C.T., Breen, R. and Whelan, B. (1992) 'Industrialisation, class formation and social mobility in Ireland', in J.H. Goldthorpe and C.T. Whelan (eds) *The Development of Industrial Society in Ireland*, Dublin: Gill and Macmillan, pp 105–28.

Young, J. (2007) *The Vertigo of Late Modernity*, London: Sage.

5

Feminist Perspectives on Woman Abuse in Rural and Remote Places: Pushing the Criminological Envelope

Walter S. DeKeseredy

Introduction

Like other rural critical criminologists, those who are feminists aggressively chip away at urban-normative, mainstream criminology and push criminology in general to be more imaginative. An 'imaginative criminology', in the words of Carlen (2017):

> eschews administrative criminology's quest for evidence of the already-known in favor of imagining the new, it is one manifestation of a broader critical criminology. Unlike administrative criminology, which involves a reflexive journey into an official past, imaginative criminology embarks on an uncharted voyage into an unofficial future. But, more than that, the promise of imaginative criminology is that it is well-designed to be a bridge between critical criminology and a critical politics of criminal justice policy. Imaginative criminology … does not pretend to exclude politics from critique. (Carlen, 2017: 19)

Sometimes referred to as 'right realism', administrative criminology – as demonstrated by most of the articles that now appear in *Criminology* and *Criminology and Public Policy* (the two official journals of the American Society of Criminology) – is very much alive and well today because university administrators (in a US context) pressure academic staff to seek grants from government agencies that have no interest whatsoever in implementing progressive policies recommended by critical criminologists (Carlen, 2017; DeKeseredy, 2022). These are some of administrative criminologists' main arguments:

- crime is not determined by social forces, but rather by forces within the individual;
- searching for the causes of crime is a 'distraction and a waste of valuable time' (Platt and Takagi, 1981: 45);
- individuals *choose* to commit crime, and fewer criminal choices will be made if the government creates more effective and appropriate punishments;
- improving social conditions will not reduce crime rates; and
- rehabilitation is an ineffective way of dealing with offenders (Wilson, 1985).

Feminist rural criminologists resist the hegemony of administrative criminology, and their imaginative empirical, theoretical and political work on woman abuse in rural and remote places makes important contributions to both critical criminology and criminology as a whole. The main objective of this chapter is to review the recent achievements of feminists who study woman abuse in rural locales and to articulate new research trajectories. This chapter begins by offering a definition of feminism and is followed by synopses of feminist empirical and theoretical contributions to the field. A number of recommendations for future research are made, starting with gathering reliable data on intimate femicide.

Definition of feminism

The word 'feminist' is frequently used in this chapter and scores of other publications, but there are at least 12 different feminist criminological ways of knowing (Renzetti, 2018).[1] There is no 'party line' and defining feminism is subject to much debate. Still, all feminist scholars, regardless of their disciplinary backgrounds, concur with the observation that 'feminism is not merely about adding women onto the agenda' (Currie and MacLean, 1993: 6). Daly and Chesney-Lind's (1988: 502) is one of the most widely used and cited conceptualisations of feminism in the criminological literature and thus it is offered here: 'a set of theories about women's oppression and a set of strategies for change'.

Two other things that most feminist criminologists have in common is examining how 'gender' and 'patriarchy' shape violations of social and legal norms and societal reactions to crime and deviance. Gender is 'the socially defined expectations, characteristics, attributes, roles, responsibilities, activities and practices that constitute masculinity, femininity, gender identity, and gender expressions' (Flavin and Artz, 2013: 11). Following Renzetti (2013: 8), patriarchy 'is a gender structure in which men dominate women, and what is considered masculine is more highly valued that that what is considered feminine'.

Feminist criminologists are well aware that there are varieties of patriarchy (Hunnicutt, 2009; Ozaki and Otis, 2016). They also recognise that not all men benefit equally in patriarchal societies and that some women have more privilege than others (Renzetti, 2018; DeKeseredy et al, 2021). Additionally, many contemporary feminists examine the intersection of race/ethnicity, social class, sexuality, immigration status and other types of inequality. Intersectionality has roots in 'Black feminist theory' and 'critical race theory' (Crenshaw, 1991; Potter, 2015; Collins and Bilge, 2016) and it is front and centre in almost all of the contemporary North American criminological literature on the violent experiences of inner-city African American girls and women. It has yet, however, to gain momentum in theoretical work on male to female violence in rural and remote locales. In fact, of all the feminist schools of thought, 'radical feminism' is the variant that is the most frequently applied to this topic. This is not surprising because radical feminism sparked the vast amount of empirical and theoretical work on woman abuse that we see today (Renzetti, 2018). Radical feminists argue that the most important set of social relations is found in patriarchy. All other social relations, such as class, are secondary and originate from male–female relations (Beirne and Messerschmidt, 2014).

While elements of radical feminism exist in all of the feminist theories of woman abuse in non-metropolitan areas, these offerings are integrative and blend elements of radical feminism with those of other perspectives (see DeKeseredy, 2021a). The scholars who crafted the theories to be briefly covered later in this chapter are highly cognisant of the fact that the offline and online abuse of women, regardless of where they live, is not only caused by patriarchy. Actually, in this current era, one would be hard pressed to find any feminist single-factor explanations of woman abuse (DeKeseredy, 2022).

All told, feminism offers alternative gendered ways of thinking about crime and societal reactions to it (Snipes et al, 2019). What is more, the study of gender and crime is among the most vibrant areas in criminology, and it has made important contributions to epistemology and practice. At the same time, there is still much more feminist empirical and theoretical work to be done, some of which is suggested in this chapter. The possibilities for future work in the field are exciting and stand to invigorate criminology as a whole.

Empirical contributions

One widely disseminated myth about feminist criminologists is that they categorically reject quantitative research.[2] It is also often said that feminist empirical, theoretical and policy objectives are incompatible with goals of mainstream science. Nothing can be further from the truth. Feminism is now 'less celebratory', much more 'self-critical' and more open to using traditional scientific methods than it is earlier days (McCormack, 1990; Smith, 1994; DeKeseredy, 2016).

Many feminists now acknowledge that their empirical concerns can be effectively addressed by adhering to the rules of orthodox science. For instance, though Molly Dragiewicz and Walter S. DeKeseredy are heavily influenced by radical feminist thought, they joined forces with Callie Rennison and examined US National Crime Victimization Survey (NCVS) data to determine whether rural women are more likely to experience intimate violence than their urban and suburban counterparts. DeKeseredy et al (2012) found that multiracial rural women had rates exceeding those of similar women in urban and suburban settings and Rennison et al (2013) found that a higher percentage of rural females are victims of intimate violence that are urban and suburban females. Furthermore, Rennison et al (2012) found that rural separated/divorced women report significantly higher rates of intimate rape / sexual assault than do urban and suburban separated/divorced women.

Historically, the NCVS was used mainly by orthodox criminologists, but the studies already described are salient examples of imaginative feminist quantitative work done in the US. Innovative quantitative research done by feminists in Australia also demonstrates geographic variations in woman abuse. The National Australian Longitudinal Study on Women's Health, for instance, found that rates of intimate partner violence against young women living in remote or very remote areas are the highest, and they are the lowest for those living in major cities (Dillon et al, 2016).

What are the key risk factors associated with non-lethal forms of woman abuse in non-metropolitan places? Imaginative feminist research also provides answers to this question, but they primarily come from qualitative investigations done by scholars based in the US and Australia. On top of pointing to the high rate of gun ownership, patriarchal male-peer support, male pornography consumption, separation/divorce, substance abuse, natural disasters and male hunting subcultures,[3] these researchers assert that there is a system of social practices that dominates and oppresses rural and urban females alike, but found that it operates differently in rural places. For example, the masculinisation of the rural, the dominance of man and mankind over women and nature, is represented as natural and unproblematic (Carrington et al, 2014).

While some types of men in urban vicinities, especially those who are Black and Indigenous, report adversarial relationships with police, men in rural communities who abuse women are more likely to be protected by an 'ol' boys network' that includes criminal justice officials (Websdale, 1998; DeKeseredy, 2021b). Referred to as 'mateship' in Australia (Wendt, 2009; Saunders, 2015), rural battered women know that local police officers may be friends with their abuser, and officers may refuse to arrest on the grounds of friendship (DeKeseredy, 2021a). Ponder what this rural Ohio survivor of separation/divorce told DeKeseredy and Schwartz (2009):

> 'Cops are number-one bad for unwanted sex, for forcing unwanted sex on their mates and violence. They've got to change the whole structure of the protective system with more women on the force. They're all men – how's a man gonna relate to what a woman just went through? It's a good ol' boys network. And it's terrible that our police have come to that. They're not protection.' (DeKeseredy and Schwartz, 2009: 93)

The influence of the rural good ol' boys network also exists in Tanzania (Jakobsen, 2016, 2018), Canada (Ruddell, 2017a), and Australia (Wendt, 2016). Rural criminal justice officials often 'know the man' (Websdale, 1998), and there are far fewer female police officers in rural areas than there are in more densely populated places. In the US, women constitute only 14 per cent of sworn law enforcement personnel in metropolitan places and only 8.1 per cent of these positions in small and rural agencies (Weisner et al, 2020). Several of DeKeseredy and Schwartz's (2009) rural Ohio interviewees knew this imbalance and this woman, like some others, sees hiring more female officers as an effective way to break up the ol' boys network:

> 'Put more women on the force because men have no compassion in these kinds of cases. ... And they really need to change the training for and teach these policemen what women are going through, how they are sexually abused by their husbands or anyone. But they don't know. They're all men. How's a man gonna relate to what a woman went through? The only way a person can relate to that is the same gender and that's why we need more women in the department.' (DeKeseredy and Schwartz, 2009: 107)

Australian feminists are beginning to uncover rich qualitative data on the co-occurrence of the offline and online victimisation of rural women. The latter type of abuse is what Harris and Vitis (2020: 330) define as 'spaceless violence' committed by 'unknown persons and those who "may" be known'. Major examples are technology-facilitated stalking and image-based sexual abuse that can target women anywhere they use electronic devices like smartphones or tablets. Common types of image-based sexual abuse are videos made by men with the consent of the women they were intimately involved with, but then distributed online without their consent following the women's termination of a relationship (Salter and Crofts, 2015; Henry et al, 2021).

The qualitative feminist work of Australian scholars George and Harris (2014), Harris (2018) and Harris and Woodlock (2019) is a much-needed addition to the body of knowledge on adult 'poly-victimisation', which is experiencing multiple abusive behaviours of various kinds (Mitchell et al, 2018). Except for a small number of studies of US college students (for example Marganski and Melander, 2018; DeKeseredy et al, 2019a, 2019b), almost all the extant literature on the overlap of cyber and in-person violence centres on adolescent bullying and thus new studies of rural adult women's experiences are warmly welcomed. The criminological community will probably soon discover that numerous rural women are targets of both face-to-face violence and technology-facilitated violence, especially since the digital gap between rural and non-rural residents is rapidly shrinking in advanced industrialised nations like the US (DeKeseredy, 2021b; Vogels, 2021).

Australian feminists, along with their US colleagues, also consistently show, using qualitative data, that widespread acceptance of violence against women and community norms prohibiting women from seeking social support, geographic and social isolation, and the absence of social support services and public transportation are related to various type of abuse outside what Hogg and Carrington (2016) refer to as 'the metropole'. What is more, Australian, US and Canadian research shows that rural mining is connected with woman abuse (Carrington and Pereira, 2011; Ruddell, 2017b): so is the emergence of resource-based booms in rural regions (Ruddell and Britto, 2020). The 'resource curse', of course, exists in other countries like Laos, Mozambique, Papua New Guinea, Peru and Sudan (Hogg and Carrington, 2016). Hopefully, more feminist scholars will follow in the footsteps of Miedema and Fulu (2018) and examine how the harmful effects of globalisation, such as mining companies 'scouring the world in search of new deposits' (Dansereau, 2006: 8), shape women's experiences with abusive men.

Like scores of other feminist scholars, this author devotes little attention to identifying the characteristics of the adult female targets of male violence for an important reason. Studying these people rather than the offenders can be interpreted as blaming women for their current or former partners' abusive conduct. Research that investigates how abused women differ from those who are not abused suggests that there is something 'wrong' with those who are victimised by men. The reality is that any woman is a possible object of physical violence, psychological abuse, sexual assault and other forms of male-to-female abuse (LaViolette and Barnett, 2014). What differs is not the woman but the man. If the man is a woman abuser, he will abuse any woman with whom he is or was intimate.

In addition to making the earlier contributions, feminist rural criminologists confirm that Kelly's (1987, 1988) continuum of sexual violence 'stands the test of time' (Kelly, 2012: xvii). The continuum ranges from non-physical acts like inappropriate sexual remarks in the workplace to physical ones like forced penetration. Though the idea of the continuum is generally used to portray moving from the least serious to most serious, to Kelly and the rural feminists who follow in her footsteps (Saunders, 2015; Harris, 2020; DeKeseredy, 2021a), all of these behaviours are equally serious. For these researchers, the acts they identify as existing on the continuum all pass or 'seep into' each other and they are all used to abuse and control women.

DeKeseredy's book *Woman Abuse in Rural Places* (DeKeseredy, 2021a) introduces the 'continuum of woman abuse'. It is similar, but still differs from that of Kelly in the sense that it includes non-physical and physical male abusive acts, as well as 'crimes of powerful'[4] not examined by her. Integrated in this continuum are: (1) what Collins (2016) refers to as direct forms of state-perpetrated violence against women; and (2) other violent crimes of capital against women. Prime examples of the former are US federal and state governments' assaults on women's reproductive rights (DeKeseredy, 2019) and 'the pervasive and enduring use of sexual violence by state militaries during both conflict and peacetime' (Collins, 2019: 179). It should be noted that Kelly's original continuum excludes many acts of corporate violence, but she later argued that wartime violence against women exists on it and that peacetime abuse is a 'shadow war' (see Kelly, 2000).

Violent crimes of capital are 'socially injurious acts that arise from the ownership or management of capital or from occupancy of positions of trust in institutions designed to facilitate the accumulation of capital' (Michalowski, 1985: 314). Millions of women not only face workplace sexual harassment, but also numerous additional health hazards in jobs often labelled 'pink ghettos'.

Also included DeKeseredy (2021a) are examples of 'state-corporate crimes' that are 'illegal or social injurious actions that occur when one or more institutions of political governance pursue a goal in direct cooperation with one or more institutions of economic production and distribution' (Kramer and Michalowski, 1990: 4). These crimes can be 'state-facilitated' or 'state-initiated' (Kramer and Michalowski, 2006). A widely discussed example of state–corporate crime is the Space Shuttle Challenger explosion on 28 January 1986 (Kramer, 1992). State officials and corporate executives (NASA [National Aeronautics and Space Administration] and Morton Thiokol, Inc.) teamed up to 'produce risky decision-making processes and unsafe actions' that cause the death of six astronauts (Rothe and Kauzlarich, 2016: 125).

Like definitions of crime that encompass such socially injurious behaviours as racism, poverty, unemployment, sexism, imperialism, inadequate social services (for example housing, childcare, education and medical care) and corporate and state wrongdoings (Schwendinger and Schwendinger, 1975; Elias, 1986), the continuum of woman abuse contributes to a broader-based analysis of woman abuse in rural places around the world. Numerous researchers have added to a rich social scientific understanding of harms that exist on Kelly's (1987, 1988) original continuum of sexual violence, but except for a small cadre of feminists (for example Collins, 2016), they have not paid enough attention to a wide range of crimes that are equally, if not more, harmful to women regardless of whether they live in rural, suburban or urban places.

Theoretical contributions

Feminist theories of woman abuse in non-metropolitan areas are refreshing departures from place-based explanations (for example, social disorganisation theory) that, until recently, were the dominant theoretical frameworks in rural criminology (Harris and Harkness, 2016).[5] In fact, feminist rural criminologists DeKeseredy and Schwartz (2009) were among the first group of scholars to show that 'collective efficacy' takes different shapes and forms. It can prevent property crimes (for example farm vandalism) while also contributing to woman abuse. Collective efficacy is generally defined as 'mutual trust among neighbors combined with the willingness to act on behalf of the common good, specifically to supervise children and maintain public order' (Sampson et al, 1998: 1). A salient variant of the 'common good' uncovered by DeKeseredy and Schwartz (2009) in rural Ohio was what Websdale (1998) defines as a 'rural patriarchy' that functioned to prevent women from leaving their abusive partners. This is an example offered by one of their interviewees:

> 'Another time, after I finally got away from him and I was having these problems. I was, I was on drugs real heavy um, and I was trying to get away from him. He was still calling me. This was just in the last nine months. Um, I called Victim Awareness in my town and um, told them that I had been abused by him. Oh, they kept telling me that they was going to do something about it, and they never did. The one other time I went to Victim Awareness, they told me that um, they were going to question the neighbors and stuff. And the neighbors said that um, you know, they said that the neighbors didn't, didn't see or hear anything. So, they – I didn't have enough ah proof, so. Basically, nothing was ever done. He's a corrections officer in the town that I lived in, and he's friends with the sheriff and whoever else.' (DeKeseredy and Schwartz, 2009: 10)

Another woman told DeKeseredy and Schwartz (2009: 10) that the police officers who responded to several of her 911 calls were more empathetic towards the man who abused her than they were to her: "They have this whole attitude that they never give up, so that when they respond to a woman, they're apologizing to him as they lead him away". Similarly, this respondent said, "Well, this is a rural area and all the cops know everybody and they're all family and they're very redneckish".

The concepts of patriarchy and 'male-peer support' are integral components of the theoretical literature on interpersonal forms of woman abuse in rural places. Two main examples are DeKeseredy et al's (2004) feminist / male-peer support model of separation/divorce sexual assault and DeKeseredy et al's (2007) rural masculinity crisis / male-peer support model of separation/divorce sexual assault. A unique feature of DeKeseredy et al's (2004) contribution is that it imbued rural-focused middle-range theory (Merton, 1949) with feminism.

The vast majority of men who abuse current or former female intimate partners are patriarchal (Pease, 2019). Even so, being patriarchal, alone, like all single factors, cannot on its own account for separation/divorce sexual assault in rural places. DeKeseredy and colleagues' central argument is that many patriarchal men who abuse women during and after separation/divorce have male friends with similar beliefs and values, and these peers reinforce the notion that women's exiting is a threat to men's masculinity. Moreover, patriarchal peer groups view beatings, rapes and other forms of male-to-female victimisation as legitimate and effective means of repairing 'damaged' patriarchal masculinity and reaffirming a man's 'right' to control his female partner (Messerschmidt, 1993; DeKeseredy et al, 2017).

Not only do these men verbally and publicly claim that sexual assault and other forms of abuse are legitimate means of maintaining patriarchal authority and domination, but they are also role models since many of them physically, sexually and psychologically harm their own intimate partners. Consider that 47 per cent of the 43 rural survivors of separation/divorce sexual interviewed by DeKeseredy and Schwartz (2009) said that their partners' friends physically or sexually abused women. As well, 67 per cent of the sample reported on a variety of ways in which their partners' male peers perpetuated and legitimated woman abuse.

Hall-Sanchez's (2014) study of rural separation/divorce sexual assault reveals that hunting trips are key contexts of male-peer support. This woman told her that:

'He would leave on Friday morning and return late Sunday. I would see him pack a few clothes but mostly beer, bullets, and porn. What a combination, right? I never understood how all that went together but he would tell me that they would drink, go scout the stuff and set up their spots in the woods, and come back to camp and drink, shoot targets, watch porn, guy talk, play cards, you know the usual guy stuff. They would tell dirty jokes and look at porn. So weird but I guess that is what made them "real" men. No women allowed and that is how they wanted it. That was a place where they could get away with demeaning women and get a pat on the back for "putting their women in their place". I'm sure all those guys did the same thing so it's no wonder. Sundays were always bad for me.' (Hall-Sanchez, 2014: 503)

Hall-Sanchez (2014), and DeKeseredy and Schwartz (2009) provide empirical support for the aforementioned two models. Their findings also verify a basic sociological assertion promoted by differential association and social learning theorists (for example Sutherland, 1947); that woman abuse is behaviour that is socially learned from interactions with others. As well, DeKeseredy and colleagues' (2004, 2007) offerings, and the data supporting them, challenge traditional social support theory, which emphasises only the beneficial features of social support (Heller and Swindle, 1983). The rural male-peer support data collected so far confirm Vaux's (1985: 102) claim that 'social support may facilitate the resolution of problems or the management of distress, but there are no guarantees that such a resolution is free of cost'.

It was previously stated that globalisation and natural resource extraction contribute to interpersonal variants of rural woman abuse. The extant literature, however, is under-theorised. This is not to say, though, that the research is not theoretically driven. DeKeseredy and Donnermeyer (2020) assert that this work, at first glance, appears resolutely critical in orientation, but it is also heavily guided by a thinly veiled version of social disorganisation theory and Durkheimian (1938, 1951) anomie theory, both of which ignore the influence of broader patriarchal forces. DeKeseredy and Donnermeyer (2020) offer a new empirically informed critical criminological theory that better explains the linkage between globalisation, natural resource extraction and woman abuse. DeKeseredy and Donnermeyer remind us that what is crucial in considering the links between globalisation, natural resource extraction and woman abuse is not to revisit the well-worn, erroneous path of social disorganisation theory.

There is not one theory specifically designed to explain corporate and state crimes against rural women. On the other hand, there are theories of corporate, state–corporate and state crime, some of which can be modified to explain the plight of rural women. One that immediately comes to mind is Collins's (2016) expansion of an integrated model of state crime that is rooted in the writings of Kramer and Michalowski (1990) and others who take a similar approach to theorising state and corporate crime.[6] Further, DeKeseredy (2021a) recently argued that instrumental and structural Marxist theories of the state, such as those constructed by Quinney (1975, 1980), should be revisited when trying to explain crimes of the powerful committed against rural women. Certainly, much more theoretical work, especially that informed by strands of feminist thought, is sorely needed.

Theoretical and empirical work in the field of crimes of the powerful is overwhelmingly gender-blind and that which is done is done primarily by White male scholars.

New trajectories

In the early 1980s, few, if any, violence against women scholars would have predicted the current amount of theoretical and empirical work on woman abuse in rural and remote places. We know much more about this issue than we did when Gagné (1992) published the results of her ethnographic study done in rural Appalachia. Furthermore, like other subfields of rural criminology, the study of woman abuse in non-metropolitan communities has become more internationalised. All the same, more work needs to be done, especially in non-English speaking countries (Donnermeyer, 2019).

Igniting a fresh wave of scholarship on woman abuse in rural areas involves taking a number of steps, one of which is gathering reliable data on intimate femicide. This is the killing of a female with whom a man currently has, has had or wants to have a sexual and/or emotional relationship (Ellis and DeKeseredy, 1997). Little is known about the extent and distribution of rural intimate femicide. In fact, there is scant research on any types of murder in rural communities (DeKeseredy, 2021a), and the word 'rural' is nowhere to be found in indexes included in scholarly monographs written and edited by some of the world's leading experts on male-to-female homicide (for example Dobash and Dobash, 2015; Walklate et al, 2020). Currently in its third edition, even Renzetti's widely read and cited *Sourcebook on Violence Against Women* (Renzetti et al, 2018) does not address rural intimate femicide, and the word 'rural' is only listed twice in the index.

Only a small amount of data gathered from male perpetrators of both lethal and non-lethal types of rural woman abuse of any sort are publicly available. Except for findings uncovered by few US studies[7] and the results of Yount et al's (2016) survey of 522 married men in Vietnam, all the data on the non-lethal harms covered in this chapter are derived from adult female survivors. This is not to say that these women do not provide valuable information. Indeed, they do, but male offender data provide a clearer understanding of: the number of men who abuse women; the number of assaults they commit; why they are abusive; and whether they commit multiple types of different kinds of abuse (Foubert et al, 2020; DeKeseredy, 2021b).

It is also time to stop going down the beaten path of focusing solely on rural, urban and suburban variations in woman abuse because, as Edwards (2015) correctly points out, this empirical approach: 'likely obscures a number of important contextual features, and future research would benefit from moving away from examining rurality or urbanicity as undifferentiated categories. More specifically, future work would benefit from the inclusion of explanatory variables to help contextualize differences ... detected across and within locales' (Edwards, 2015: 370).

Related to Edwards's call for including explanatory variables, it is also time to test hypotheses derived from the theories covered in this chapter using quantitative data. Actually, quantitative studies of any type of rural woman abuse done to date have not tested theories and have instead centred mainly on discerning geographic variations in women's victimisation (DeKeseredy, 2021b). As stated earlier, the bulk of data on determinants of rural woman abuse are derived from qualitative studies.

Another valuable contribution to the field would be prospective and longitudinal quantitative studies because most of the few surveys conducted so far[8] are cross-sectional, which makes it hard to find vulnerability and protective factors associated with offending and victimisation (Edwards, 2015). What should also be included in the wish list offered here is a longitudinal study of male offenders, including those who engage or have engaged in spaceless violence.

Numerous female adolescents and young adult women experience the harms covered in this chapter (Vagi et al, 2015; Maier and Bergen, 2019), but there is paucity of research on the victimisation of those living in non-metropolitan areas. There is also a dearth of published data on the prevalence, distribution, causes and consequences of the abuse of rural women with different abilities. Additionally, future studies should examine other marginalised rural women, such as lesbians, transwomen and women who are Indigenous and of colour. Intersectional feminist scholars constantly (and rightfully so) remind us that researchers should always be cognisant of who was not asked to participate in their studies and that they are not gathering data on their experiences (Gilfus et al, 1999).

Donnermeyer (2017: 129) remarked: 'There are simply too many rural issues to squeeze into a single journal article about a global criminology of the South and rural criminology'. Similarly, there are too many recommendations for future empirical and theoretical work to jam into one scholarly book chapter on feminist perspectives of the offline and online victimisation of women in rural and remote locales. This is all to the good. Having plenty of more research to do means that there is ample room for early and seasoned scholars alike to add to the literature reviewed here. The journey towards creating new feminist understandings of woman abuse outside the metropole is just beginning, and I encourage others to become fellow travellers.

Conclusion

While there may never be a unified criminology as called for by Agnew (2011) and there are still many (mainly White, heterosexual men) orthodox academics who resist feminist restructuring of criminological research

(Renzetti, 1993; DeKeseredy, 2021a), undeniably, feminists who examine woman abuse in rural and remote areas continue to push the criminological envelope. They are advancing rural criminology and all of criminology for reasons provided in this chapter. Owing, in large part, to the contributions covered here and to the efforts of other types of critical scholars, criminology is not 'essentially the same beast as it was in the early 1970s' (Winlow and Atkinson, 2013: 2). This does not mean that the work is done and feminist scholarship on woman abuse, like any type of criminology, is 'always in need of new direction' (Hayward, 2012: 142).

There are numerous pathways to be found on the journey towards developing fresh feminist research agendas and theoretical schools of thought. Consistent with Renzetti's (2013) cautionary note about her recommendations for new feminist criminological scholarship, this chapter, too, must recognise that suggestions for moving forward reflect a few personal priorities, some of which readers will agree with and some that they will reject. From a feminist standpoint, though, making concerns transparent is the right thing to do. In what is still one of the most widely read and cited sociological articles in the world, Howard Becker (1967) asks academics: 'Whose side are we on?' Although there are those who paint feminist researchers as 'idealogues' and depict themselves as objective scientists, in reality they are advancing a political agenda that support the goals of degendering the study of male-to-female violence and diminishing the severity of male-to-female abuse (Gondolf, 2012). Feminists scholars, on the other hand, put their politics up front for all to scrutinise and are committed to putting gender at the forefront of their research, theory construction and policy development (DeKeseredy and Dragiewicz, 2007). It is time for all criminologists to face up to the fact that 'all writing is political' (Sartre, 1964: 29).

Notes

[1] This section includes a revised version of work published previously by DeKeseredy (2020a, 2020b).

[2] This section includes modified portions of work published earlier by DeKeseredy (2021a, 2021b) and DeKeseredy et al (2016).

[3] See DeKeseredy (2021a) for an in-depth review of the extant literature on these risk factors.

[4] This is the title of Pearce's (1976) groundbreaking Marxist analysis of corporate and organised crime.

[5] This section includes modified parts of work published previously by DeKeseredy (2001), DeKeseredy et al (2007), DeKeseredy and Rennison (2020), DeKeseredy and Schwartz (2009), and Donnermeyer and DeKeseredy (2014).

[6] See DeKeseredy (2021a) for the roots of Collins' work.

[7] See Edwards (2015) for a review of the handful of US studies of perpetrators.

[8] One salient exception is Dillon et al's (2016) national, population-based study of Australian women.

References

Agnew, R. (2011) *Toward a Unified Criminology: Integrating Assumptions About Crime, People, and Society*, New York: New York University Press.

Becker, H. (1967) 'Whose side are we on?', *Social Problems*, 14(3): 239–47.

Beirne, P. and Messerschmidt, J.W. (2014) *Criminology: A Sociological Approach* (6th edn), New York: Oxford University Press.

Carlen, P. (2017) 'Doing imaginative criminology', in M.H. Jacobsen and S. Walklate (eds) *Liquid Criminology: Doing Imaginative Criminology*, Abingdon: Routledge, pp 17–30.

Carrington, K. and Pereira, M. (2011) 'Assessing the social impacts of the resources boom on rural communities', *Rural Society*, 21(1): 2–20.

Carrington, K., Donnermeyer, J.F. and DeKeseredy, W.S. (2014) 'Intersectionality, rural criminology, and re-imagining the boundaries of critical criminology', *Critical Criminology*, 22(4): 463–77.

Collins, P.H. and Bilge, S. (2016) *Intersectionality*, Cambridge: Polity Press.

Collins, V.E. (2016) *State Crime, Women and Gender*, Abingdon: Routledge.

Collins, V.E. (2019) 'Feminist perspectives on state crimes against women', in W.S. DeKeseredy, C.M. Rennison and A.K. Hall-Sanchez (eds) *The Routledge International Handbook of Violence Studies*, Abingdon: Routledge, pp 179–89.

Crenshaw, K.W. (1991) 'Mapping the margins: intersectionality, identity politics, and violence against women of color', *Stanford Law Review*, 43(6): 1241–99.

Currie, D.H. and MacLean, B.D. (1993) 'Preface', in D.H. Currie and B.D. MacLean (eds) *Social Inequality, Social Justice*, Vancouver, BC: Collective Press, pp 5–6.

Daly, K. and Chesney-Lind, M. (1988) 'Feminism and criminology', *Justice Quarterly*, 5(4): 497–538.

Dansereau, S. (2006) 'Globalization and mining labour: wages, skills and mobility', *Minerals and Energy – Raw Minerals Report*, 21(2): 8–22.

DeKeseredy, W.S. (2001) 'Patterns of family violence', in M. Baker (ed) *Families: Changing Trends in Canada*, Ryerson, ON: McGraw-Hill, pp 238–66.

DeKeseredy, W.S. (2016) 'Looking backward to move forward: revisiting some past feminist contributions to the study of violence against women', *Violence and Gender*, 3(4): 177–80.

DeKeseredy, W.S. (2019) 'Defenders of freedom or perpetrators and facilitators of crimes? Beyond progressive retreatism in the Trump era', *Victims & Offenders*, 14(8): 925–39.

DeKeseredy, W.S. (2020a) 'Enhancing feminist understandings of violence against women: looking to the future', in S. Walklate, K. Fitz-Gibbon, J. Maher and J. McCulloch (eds) *The Emerald Handbook of Feminism, Criminology and Social Change*, Bingley: Emerald, pp 337–55.

DeKeseredy, W.S. (2020b) 'Critical criminologies', in H.N. Pontell (ed) *Oxford Research Encyclopedia of Criminology and Criminal Justice*, New York: Oxford University Press. Available from: https://doi.org/10.1093/acrefore/9780190264079.013.549 [Accessed 3 March 2022].

DeKeseredy, W.S. (2021a) *Woman Abuse in Rural Places*, Abingdon: Routledge.

DeKeseredy, W.S. (2021b) 'Male-to-female sexual violence in rural communities: a sociological review', *Dignity: A Journal of Analysis of Exploitation and Violence*, 6(2): art 7. Available from: https://digitalcomm ons.uri.edu/dignity/vol6/iss2/7/ [Accessed 3 March 2022].

DeKeseredy, W.S. (2022) *Contemporary Critical Criminology* (2nd edn) Abingdon: Routledge.

DeKeseredy, W.S. and Dragiewicz, M. (2007) 'Understanding the complexities of feminist perspectives on woman abuse: a commentary on Donald G. Dutton's *Rethinking Domestic Violence*', *Violence Against Women*, 13(8): 874–84.

DeKeseredy, W.S. and Schwartz, M.D. (2009) *Dangerous Exits: Escaping Abusive Relationships in Rural America*, New Brunswick, NJ: Rutgers University Press.

DeKeseredy, W.S. and Donnermeyer, J.F. (2020) 'Globalization, natural resource extraction, and woman abuse in rural and remote areas', a work-in-progress paper presented at the annual meetings of the American Society of Criminology, Washington, DC, 19 November.

DeKeseredy, W.S. and Rennison, C.M. (2020) 'Thinking theoretically about male violence in rural places: a review of the extant sociological literature and suggestions for future theorizing', *International Journal of Rural Criminology*, 5(2): 162–80.

DeKeseredy, W.S., Rogness, M. and Schwartz, M.D. (2004) 'Separation/divorce sexual assault: the current state of social scientific knowledge', *Aggression and Violent Behavior*, 9(6): 675–91.

DeKeseredy, W.S. Donnermeyer, J.F., Schwartz, M.D., Tunnell, K.D. and Hall, M. (2007) 'Thinking critically about rural gender relations: toward a rural masculinity crisis / male peer support model of separation/divorce sexual assault', *Critical Criminology*, 15(4): 295–311.

DeKeseredy, W.S., Dragiewicz, M. and Rennison, C.M. (2012) 'Racial/ethnic variations in violence against women: urban, suburban, and rural differences', *International Journal of Rural Criminology*, 1(2): 184–202.

DeKeseredy, W.S., Hall-Sanchez, A., Dragiewicz, M. and Rennison, C.M. (2016) 'Intimate violence against women in rural communities', in J.F. Donnermeyer (ed) *The Routledge International Handbook of Rural Criminology*, London: Routledge, pp 171–9.

DeKeseredy, W.S., Dragiewicz, M. and Schwartz, M.D. (2017) *Abusive Endings: Separation and Divorce Violence Against Women*, Oakland, CA: University of California Press.

DeKeseredy, W.S., Schwartz, M.D., Nolan, J., Mastron, N. and Hall-Sanchez, A. (2019a) 'Polyvictimization and the continuum of sexual abuse at a college campus: does negative peer support increase the likelihood of multiple victimizations?', *British Journal of Criminology*, 59(2): 276–95.

DeKeseredy, W.S., Schwartz, M.D., Harris, B., Woodlock, D., Nolan, J. and Hall-Sanchez, A. (2019b) 'Technology-facilitated stalking and unwanted sexual messages/images in a college campus community: the role of negative peer support', *SAGE Open*, 9(1). Available from: https://doi.org/10.1177/2158244019828231 [Accessed 3 March 2022].

DeKeseredy, W.S., DeKeseredy, A. and DeKeseredy, P. (2021) 'Understanding *The Handmaid's Tale*: the contribution of radical feminism', in J.A. Grubb and C. Posick (eds) *Crime TV: Streaming Criminology in Popular Culture*, New York: New York University Press, pp 82–95.

Dillon, G., Hussain, R., Kibele, E., Rahman, S. and Loxton, D. (2016) 'Influence of intimate partner violence on domestic relocation in metropolitan and non-metropolitan young Australian women', *Violence Against Women*, 22(13): 1597–620.

Dobash, R.E. and Dobash, R.P. (2015) *When Men Murder Women*, New York: Oxford University Press.

Donnermeyer, J.F. (2017) 'The place of rural in a southern criminology', *International Journal for Crime, Justice and Social Democracy*, 6(1): 118–32.

Donnermeyer, J.F. (2019) 'The international emergence of rural criminology: implications for the development and revision of criminological theory for rural contexts', *International Journal of Rural Criminology*, 5(1): 1–18.

Donnermeyer, J.F. and DeKeseredy, W.S. (2014) *Rural Criminology*, Abingdon: Routledge.

Durkheim, E. (1938) *The Rules of Sociological Method* (8th edn), Chicago: University of Chicago Press.

Durkheim, E. (1951) *Suicide: A Study in Sociology*, trans J.A. Spaulding and G. Simpson, Glencoe, IL: Free Press.

Edwards, K.M. (2015) 'Intimate partner violence and the rural–urban–suburban divide: myth or reality? A critical review of the literature', *Trauma, Violence, & Abuse*, 16(3): 359–73.

Elias, R. (1986) *The Politics of Victimization: Victims, Victimology and Human Rights*, New York: Oxford University Press.

Ellis, D. and DeKeseredy, W.S. (1997) 'Rethinking estrangement, interventions, and intimate femicide', *Violence Against Women*, 3(6): 590–609.

Flavin, J. and Artz, L. (2013) 'Understanding women, gender, and crime: some historical and international developments', in C.M. Renzetti, S.L. Miller and A.R. Gover (eds) *Routledge International Handbook of Crime and Gender Studies*, Abingdon: Routledge, pp 9–35.

Foubert, J.D., Clark-Taylor, A. and Wall, A.F. (2020) 'Is campus rape primarily a serial or one-time problem? Evidence from a multicampus study', *Violence Against Women*, 26(3/4): 296–311.

Gagné, P. (1992) 'Appalachian women: violence and social control', *Journal of Contemporary Ethnography*, 20(4): 387–415.

George, A. and Harris, B. (2014) *Landscapes of Violence: Women Surviving Family Violence in Regional and Rural Victoria*, Geelong, Vic: Deakin University.

Gilfus, M.E., Fineran, S., Cohan, D.J., Jensen, S.A., Hartwick, L. and Spath, R. (1999) 'Research on violence against women: creating survivor-informed collaboration', *Violence Against Women*, 5(10): 1194–212.

Gondolf, E.W. (2012) *The Future of Batterer Programs: Reassessing Evidence-Based Practice*, New York: Northeastern University Press.

Hall-Sanchez, A.K. (2014) 'Male peer support, hunting, and separation/divorce sexual assault in rural Ohio', *Critical Criminology*, 22(4): 495–510.

Harris, B. (2018) 'Spacelessness, spatiality and intimate partner violence: technology-facilitated abuse, stalking and justice', in K. Fitz-Gibbon, S. Walklate, J. McCulloch and J. Maher (eds) *Intimate Partner Violence, Risk and Security: Securing Women's Lives in a Global World*, Abingdon: Routledge, pp 52–70.

Harris, B. (2020) 'Technology and violence against women', in S. Walklate, K. Fitz-Gibbon, J. Maher and J. McCulloch (eds) *The Emerald Handbook of Feminism, Criminology and Social Change*, Bingley: Emerald, pp 317–36.

Harris, B. and Harkness, A. (2016) 'Introduction: locating regional, rural and remote crime in theoretical and contemporary context', in A. Harkness, B. Harris and D. Baker (eds) *Locating Crime in Context and Place: Perspectives on Regional, Rural and Remote Australia*, Sydney: Federation Press, pp 1–12.

Harris, B. and Woodlock, D. (2019) 'Digital coercive control: insights from two landmark domestic violence studies', *British Journal of Criminology*, 59(3): 530–50.

Harris, B. and Vitis, L. (2020) 'Digital intrusions: technology, spatiality and violence against women', *Journal of Gender-Based Violence*, 4(3): 325–41.

Hayward, K.J. (2012) 'Using cultural geography to think differently about space and crime', in S. Hall and S. Winlow (eds) *New Directions in Criminological Theory*, Abingdon: Routledge, pp 123–44.

Heller, K. and Swindle, R.W. (1983) 'Social networks, perceived social support and coping with stress', in R.E. Reiner, L.A. Jason and J.N. Moritsugu (eds) *Preventive Psychology: Theory, Research and Practice*, New York: Pergamon, pp 87–103.

Henry, N., McGlynn, C., Flynn, A., Johnson, K., Powell, A. and Scott, A.J. (2021) *Image-Based Sexual Abuse: A Study of the Causes and Consequences of Non-consensual Nude or Sexual Imagery*, Abingdon: Routledge.

Hogg, R. and Carrington, K. (2016) 'Crime and violence outside the metropole: an Australian case study', in J.F. Donnermeyer (ed) *The Routledge International Handbook of Rural Criminology*, Abingdon: Routledge, pp 181–9.

Hunnicutt, G. (2009) 'Varieties of patriarchy and violence against women: resurrecting "patriarchy" as a theoretical tool', *Violence Against Women*, 15(5): 553–73.

Jakobsen, H. (2016) 'Community law enforcement in rural Tanzania', in J.F. Donnermeyer (ed) *The Routledge International Handbook of Rural Criminology*, Abingdon: Routledge, pp 409–17.

Jakobsen, H. (2018) 'How violence constitutes order: consent, coercion, and censure in Tanzania', *Violence Against Women*, 24(1): 45–65.

Kelly, L. (1987) 'The continuum of sexual violence', in J. Hanmer and M. Maynard (eds) *Women, Violence and Social Control*, Atlantic Highlands, NJ: Humanities Press International, pp 46–60.

Kelly, L. (1988) *Surviving Sexual Violence*, Minneapolis, MN: University of Minnesota Press.

Kelly, L. (2000) 'Wars against women: sexual violence, sexual violence and the militarized state', in S. Jacobs, R. Jacobson and J. Marchbank (eds) *States of Conflict: Gender, Violence and Resistance*, London: Zed Books, pp 45–65.

Kelly, L. (2012) 'Standing the test of time? Reflections on the continuum of sexual violence', in J.M. Brown and S.L. Walklate (eds) *Handbook on Sexual Violence*, Abingdon: Routledge, pp xvii–xxvi.

Kramer, R.C. (1992) 'The Space Shuttle Challenger explosion: a case-study of state-corporate crime', in K. Schlegel and D. Weisburd (eds) *White-Collar Crime Reconsidered*, Boston, MA: Northeastern University Press, pp 212–41.

Kramer, R.C. and Michalowski, R.J. (1990) 'Toward an integrated theory of state-corporate crime', paper presented at the annual meetings of the American Society of Criminology, Baltimore, MD, 9 November.

Kramer, R.C. and Michalowski, R.J. (2006) 'The original formulation', in R.J. Michalowski and R.C. Kramer (eds) *State-Corporate Crime: Wrongdoing at the Intersection of Business and Government*, New Brunswick, NJ: Rutgers University Press, pp 18–26.

LaViolette, A.D. and Barnett, O.W. (2014) *It Could Happen to Anyone: Why Battered Women Stay* (2nd edn), Los Angeles: Sage.

Maier, S.L. and Bergen, R.K. (2019) 'Male violence against women', in W.S. DeKeseredy, C.M. Rennison and A.K. Hall-Sanchez (eds) *The Routledge International Handbook of Violence Studies*, Abingdon: Routledge, pp 394–402.

Marganski, A. and Melander, L. (2018) 'Intimate partner violence victimization in the cyber and real world: examining the extent of cyber aggression experiences and its association with in-person dating violence', *Journal of Interpersonal Violence*, 33(7): 1071–95.

McCormack, T. (1990) 'Feminism and the new crisis in methodology', in W. Tomm (ed) *The Effects of Feminist Approaches on Research Methodologies*, Waterloo, ON: Wilfred Laurier University Press, pp 13–30.

Merton, R.K. (1949) *Social Theory and Social Structure* (enlarged edn), New York: Free Press of Glencoe.

Messerschmidt, J.W. (1993) *Masculinities and Crime: Critique and Reconceptualization*, Lanham, MD: Rowman and Littlefield.

Michalowski, R.J. (1985) *Order, Law and Crime: An Introduction to Criminology*, New York: Random House.

Miedema, S.S. and Fulu, E. (2018) 'Globalization and theorizing intimate partner violence from the Global South', in K. Carrington, R. Hogg, J. Scott and M. Sozzo (eds) *Palgrave Handbook of Criminology and the Global South*, New York: Palgrave Macmillan, pp 867–82.

Mitchell, K.J., Segura, A., Jones, L.M. and Turner, H.A. (2018) 'Poly-victimization and peer harassment involvement in a technological world', *Journal of Interpersonal Violence*, 33(5): 762–88.

Ozaki, R. and Otis, M.D. (2016) 'Gender equality, patriarchal cultural norms, and perpetration of intimate partner violence: comparison of male university students in Asian and European cultural contexts', *Violence Against Women*, 23(9): 1076–99.

Pearce, F. (1976) *Crimes of the Powerful: Marxism, Crime and Deviance*, London: Pluto Press.

Pease, B. (2019) *Facing Patriarchy: From a Violent Gender Order to a Culture of Peace*, London: Zed Books.

Platt, T. and Takagi, P. (1981) 'Intellectuals for law and order: critique of the new realists', in T. Platt and P. Takagi (eds) *Crime and Social Justice*, London: Macmillan, pp 30–58.

Potter, H. (2015) *Intersectionality and Criminology: Disrupting and Revolutionizing Studies of Crime*, Abingdon: Routledge.

Quinney, R. (1975) 'Crime control in capitalist society: a critical philosophy', in I. Taylor, P. Walton and J. Young (eds) *Critical Criminology*, London: Routledge and Kegan Paul, pp 181–202.

Quinney, R. (1980) *Class, State and Crime* (2nd edn), New York: Longman.

Rennison, C.M., DeKeseredy, W.S. and Dragiewicz, M. (2012) 'Urban, suburban, and rural variations in separation/divorce rape/sexual assault: results from the National Crime Victimization Survey', *Feminist Criminology*, 7(4): 282–97.

Rennison, C.M., DeKeseredy, W.S. and Dragiewicz, M. (2013) 'Intimate relationship status variations in violence against women: urban, suburban, and rural differences', *Violence Against Women*, 19(11): 1312–30.

Renzetti, C.M. (1993) 'On the margins of the malestream (or they *still* don't get it, do they?): feminist analyses in criminal justice education', *Journal of Criminal Justice Education*, 4(2): 219–34.

Renzetti, C.M. (2013) *Feminist Criminology*, Abingdon: Routledge.

Renzetti, C.M. (2018) 'Feminist perspectives', in W.S. DeKeseredy and M. Dragiewicz (eds) *Routledge Handbook of Critical Criminology* (2nd edn), Abingdon: Routledge, pp 74–82.

Renzetti, C.M., Edleson, J.L. and Bergen, R.K. (2018) *Sourcebook on Violence Against Women* (3rd edn), Thousand Oaks, CA: Sage.

Rothe, D.L. and Kauzlarich, D. (2016) *Crimes of the Powerful: An Introduction*, Abingdon: Routledge.

Ruddell, R. (2017a) *Policing Rural Canada*, Whitby, ON: de Sitter.

Ruddell, R. (2017b) *Oil, Gas, and Crime: The Dark Side of the Boomtown*, New York: Palgrave Macmillan.

Ruddell, R. and Britto, S. (2020) 'A perfect storm: violence toward women in the Bakken oil patch', *International Journal of Rural Criminology*, 5(2): 204–27.

Salter, M. and Crofts, T. (2015) 'Responding to revenge porn: challenges to online legal impunity', in L. Comella and S. Tarrant (eds) *New Views on Pornography: Sexuality, Politics, and the Law*, Santa Barbara, CA: Praeger, pp 233–53.

Sampson, R.J., Raudenbush, S.W. and Earls, F. (1998) *Neighborhood Collective Efficacy: Does It Help Reduce Violence?*, Washington, DC: US Department of Justice.

Sartre, J.P. (1964) *The Words*, London: Penguin.

Saunders, S. (2015) *Whispers from the Bush: The Workplace Sexual Harassment of Australian Rural Women*, Sydney: Federation Press.

Schwendinger, H. and Schwendinger, J. (1975) 'Defenders of order or guardians of human rights?', in I. Taylor, P. Walton and J. Young (eds) *Critical Criminology*, London: Kegan Paul, pp 113–38.

Smith, M.D. (1994) 'Enhancing the quality of survey data on violence against women: a feminist approach', *Gender & Society*, 8(1): 109–27.

Snipes, J.B., Bernard, T.J. and Gerould, A.L. (2019) *Vold's Theoretical Criminology* (8th edn), New York: Oxford University Press.

Sutherland, E.H. (1947) *Principles of Criminology* (4th edn), Philadelphia, PA: Lippincott.

Vagi, K.J., Olsen, E.O., Basile, K.C. and Vivolo-Kantor, A.M. (2015) 'Teen dating violence (physical and sexual) among US high school students: findings from the 2013 National Youth Risk Behavior Survey', *JAMA Pediatrics*, 169(5): 474–82.

Vaux, A. (1985) 'Variations in social support associated with gender, ethnicity, and age', *Journal of Social Issues*, 41(1): 89–110.

Vogels, E.A. (2021) 'Some digital divides persist between rural, urban and suburban America', *Pew Research Center*. Available from: https://www.pewresearch.org/fact-tank/2021/08/19/some-digital-divides-persist-betw een-rural-urban-and-suburban-america/ [Accessed 4 April 2022].

Walklate, S., Fitz-Gibbon, K., McCulloch, J. and Maher, J. (2020) *Towards a Global Femicide Index: Counting the Costs*, Abingdon: Routledge.

Websdale, N. (1998) *Rural Woman Battering and the Justice System: An Ethnography*, Thousand Oaks, CA: Sage.

Weisner, L., Otto, D.H. and Adams, S. (2020) 'Issues in policing rural areas: a review of the literature', ICJIA Research Hub. Available from: http://www.icjia.state.il.us/assets/articles/Rural2CoverPage-200320T21095517.pdf [Accessed 25 May 2021].

Wendt, S. (2009) 'Constructions of local culture and impacts on domestic violence in an Australian rural community', *Journal of Rural Studies*, 25(2): 175–84.

Wendt, S. (2016) 'Intimate violence and abuse in Australian rural contexts', in J.F. Donnermeyer (ed) *The Routledge International Handbook of Rural Criminology*, Abingdon: Routledge, pp 191–9.

Wilson, J.Q. (1985) *Thinking About Crime* (revised edn), New York: Vintage.

Winlow, S. and Atkinson, R. (2013) 'Introduction', in S. Winlow and R. Atkinson (eds) *New Directions in Crime and Deviancy*, Abingdon: Routledge, pp 1–18.

Yount, K.M., Higgins, E.M., VanderEnde, K.E., Krause, K.H., Minh, T.H., Schular, S.R. and Anh, H.T. (2016) 'Men's perpetration of intimate partner violence in Vietnam: gendered social learning and the challenges of masculinity', *Men and Masculinities*, 19(1): 64–84.

6

A Left Realist Approach to Rural Crime: The Case of Agricultural Theft in Ireland

James Windle

Introduction

Left realism originated as an applied theory to support communities to tackle crime in British working-class urban areas. While there are challenges to transferring theory from one context (British urban) to another (Irish rural), this chapter argues for the utility of a left realist approach to agricultural theft, using Ireland as a case study.

Globally, criminologists and crime scientists have paid scant attention to agricultural theft (Barclay and Donnermeyer, 2011; Windle, 2016). Some work has been conducted in Australia, the US and the UK, but there have been just two studies of farm crime in Ireland (Walsh and Walsh, 2017; Bowden and Pytlarz, 2020). While criminological research is relatively new in Ireland (Lynch et al, 2020), this lack of academic attention remains surprising: in 2016, around 10 per cent of the working population was employed in the agri-food sector and there were 137,500 farms in Ireland (Teagasc, 2020). Furthermore, the media – including specialist farming publications – commonly report that theft from farms is increasing and becoming more violent.

Agricultural theft should be taken seriously by researchers for three key reasons. First, it is expensive. Gallagher (2018a) reported in the *Irish Times* that in 2017, €1.4 million (US$1.7 million) worth of goods had been stolen in 1,100 incidents of farm theft reported to the Gardaí (the civil police force in Ireland):[1] the average value of stolen property was €300 (US$365) per incident. Theft increases insurance premiums for farmers who can afford to insure their property[2] while those without insurance cover can suffer significant economic costs. These costs are passed down to consumers which inflates the price of agricultural produce.

Second, fear of crime can affect farmers' quality of life: increasing stress levels; preventing families from taking holidays; and ultimately forcing some away from farming (Mears et al, 2007; K. Smith, 2020). Indeed, one Irish victim of theft reported sleeping with a shotgun next to his bed and that theft had reduced community cohesion: "Everyone is suspicious of people. You'd be nervous in your own bed at night" (Hamilton, 2019). Another elderly farmer, living alone in an isolated farm-house, reported suffering from depression after being the victim of repeat burglary and theft (Danaher, 2019; see Dáil Éireann, 2017). Third, agricultural theft can have significant environmental impacts. For example, livestock theft can result in illegal slaughter and distribution, which may contaminate the food chain (Jones, 2012), and stolen chemicals may be incorrectly used or disposed of.

Evidence-bases must be established before effective preventive policies and interventions can be formulated. This requires both empirical data and conceptual and theoretical frameworks. The objective of this chapter is, therefore, to take a small step towards rectifying the hidden nature of agricultural theft, and fear of theft, in Ireland by ironing out some conceptual and theoretical issues by applying a left realist perspective. The chapter begins by reviewing the results of Irish and international victimisation surveys. Left realism is then reviewed and its lessons are applied to agricultural theft. The final section draws lessons for Ireland from the international literature and proposes a left realist research agenda. While most chapters in this volume will have deliberately sought to avoid jurisdictional specificity, this would have run counter to left realism, which argues for local specificity as far as possible. The lessons from Ireland can, however, hopefully be of use to those in other regions.

Review of farm victimisations studies

The literature on farm crime remains relatively small. There have only been a small number of farm victimisation surveys. This section will review the results of these surveys, focusing on the level and scope of agricultural theft, and reported crime prevention measures.

An Australian study at the turn of the twenty-first century found that of 393 farmers surveyed, 87 per cent had been victimised in the previous two years. The theft of fuel, livestock, tools and equipment were the most frequently reported crimes (Barclay et al, 2001; Barclay and Donnermeyer, 2002). Another Australian study, in 2018, found that just over half (51.39 per cent) of 906 respondents indicated victimisation of farm theft, specifically, over the preceding three years (Harkness and Larkins, 2019; see also Harkness and Larkins, 2020). A 2020 survey of farmers in New South Wales, Australia, found that 81 per cent of farmers had been a victim of crime, with nine out of ten on two or more occasions and nearly two out of five more than seven times. The five types of victimisation experienced most by farmers were trespass, illegal shooting/hunting, theft of livestock, break and enter, and theft of equipment and tools (Mulrooney, 2021).

An American study surveyed 823 farmers in 2004 and 818 farmers in 2005: 62 per cent of farmers had been victimised in 2004 and 50 per cent in 2005. The theft of small tools were the most common offences; followed by chemical/fuel theft, breaking and entering, and large equipment theft. The theft of large plant was rare but had significant economic consequences. The offences that most concerned farmers were machinery theft, illegal dumping, burglary of farm buildings, and vandalism (Mears et al, 2007).

In a British study which surveyed 40 farms in the late 1990s, 82.5 per cent of farmers had been the victim of theft in the previous two years. While theft of, or from, vehicles was the most commonly reported crime, 42.5 per cent had their farm buildings or workshops broken into, often resulting in the theft of tools. The main residence was burgled in 17.5 per cent of cases but livestock theft was relatively rare, and there were seldom sizeable livestock losses (Sugden, 1999). These results are very different from Australian studies, which tend to indicate high levels of livestock theft (McCall and Homel, 2003) and such theft appears to have increased in Britain during the 2010s (Martin, 2020).

Of 1,022 Scottish farmers' surveyed by George Street Research (1999), 32 per cent had experienced a crime in the previous five years, most commonly vandalism, petty theft and illegal dumping, with a smaller number of farmers being victims of burglary. The greatest financial loss was reported to come from livestock theft. More recently, an online survey of 126 British farmers found that 62 per cent had been victimised: just under half had been victimised once, 23 per cent twice, 29 per cent three times or more (Smith and Byrne, 2017) and approximately 50 per cent of farmers who responded to a survey in Wales had been victimised, with farm machinery and livestock being the most commonly reported crimes (Morris et al, 2020).

There has been just one farm victimisation survey in Ireland, by Walsh and Walsh (2017: 4). The survey, administered in 2016, recruited 861 participants from 'across all sectors and counties'. It asked participants about their experiences between January 2014 and May 2016. While the report lacks critical analysis or theoretical underpinning, it does present some useful, if somewhat basic, data on national averages: 34 per cent of participants had experienced no crime, 25 per cent had experienced one agricultural crime and 41 per cent had experienced more than one incident. Of the 75 per cent who had been victimised, 43 per cent had been a victim of theft, 47 per cent of vandalism, criminal damage and/or trespass, 5 per cent of assault and

5 per cent of fraud. While just over half of participants experienced only one incident of theft, 28 per cent experienced two incidents and 16 per cent three or more incidents. Fuels and oil were the most commonly stolen items, experienced by 22 per cent of participants, followed by tools (21 per cent), machinery and equipment (17 per cent),[3] livestock (10 per cent), vehicles (9 per cent), building materials (7 per cent), crops (6 per cent), fodder (4 per cent), chemicals (2 per cent) and others (including weapons) (2 per cent). Robberies occurred in only 3 per cent of thefts with just eight reported incidents of threat of violence and six of actual violence.

Why are farms victimised?

Farms can make attractive targets. They are 'notoriously difficult to protect' (Sugden, 1998: 83), often consisting of large expanses of land spread across remote locations, and frequently shielded from would-be guardians by natural barriers. The goods found within farms are attractive to potential offenders. There are portable and profitable goods (such as fuel and power tools) and less portable but much more profitable goods (such as plant) (Donnermeyer and Barclay, 2005).

Barclay and colleagues (2001) investigated how the farm environment can influence victimisation. They found, in their sample of 393 farmers, that the further away a farm was from an urban area and the hillier the terrain the more likely it was to have experienced livestock theft. Farms and farm buildings visible from houses were associated with lower levels of breaking and entering, trespassing and theft. Farms surrounded by dense cover (such as trees, bushes) were more likely to report higher levels of stock theft and illegal trespassing (also Barclay and Donnermeyer, 2011). This is summarised by Barclay and Donnermeyer (2002: 58) as 'the ease of accessibility makes a farm a more suitable target, as does the lack of sufficient guardianship' and, in a later paper: as 'visibility decreased, crime increased' (Barclay and Donnermeyer, 2011: 14).

Several studies have found that farms situated near urban areas and main roads are most at risk of victimisation (George Street Research, 1999; McCall and Homel, 2003; Mears et al, 2007). Smith and Byrne (2017 found that farms with less than 250 hectares in size were significantly more likely to be a victim of crime and repeat victimisation was more likely to occur in isolated farms, although they found no evidence of a link between proximity to urban areas. Mears and colleagues (2007) similarly found that the utility of target-hardening efforts are largely dependent upon the physical environment and the existence of capable guardians. That is, locking and/ or hiding property reduced theft when there was light land cover; however, the likelihood of theft increased when cover was dense, regardless of target hardening. Furthermore, potential for theft increased when farmers left machinery in isolated fields for long periods (also Sugden, 1999).

These conclusions conform to findings about business crime more generally. Burrows et al (1999), for example, found that businesses where there was minimal customer contact (which would include farming) were at greater risk of victimisation, especially if capable guardians were absent for long periods and if premises were surrounded by yard areas with multiple entry points (as is the case on most farms).

Jobes and colleagues (2000) found that rural Australian communities that had greater 'residential instability' experienced higher rates of breaking and entering. That is, the less a farmer's social capital in an area the more susceptible they are to burglary and theft, a conclusion which also supports the guardianship findings of other surveys. Indeed, another Australian study, by Harkness (2017), concluded that having neighbours who monitored for unusual activity was a most effective crime prevention measure. Interestingly, the study found the presence of non-residential farm workers could increase opportunities for theft.

Changes in farming and transport infrastructures appear to have increased opportunities for crime. McCall and Homel (2003) have argued that, in Australia, access to rural areas is easier and quicker than it was in the past, and many farms now possess more profitable and portable items (also Sugden, 1998). Many farmers, Gardaí and politicians believe that agricultural theft increased as Ireland improved its motorway infrastructure, which allowed urban gangs to travel further into the countryside (see Carswell, 2017; Dáil Éireann, 2017). Indeed, a review of official data from 562 Gardaí districts found that, on average, there was a 10 per cent 'rise in the burglary rate (or equivalently, five burglaries) in the same year a motorway is placed within 30km' – although burglary rates plateaued after the first year (Agnew, 2020). Indeed, several farmers have informally shared with the author the common belief that most machinery thefts are from within a ten mile radius of cities. The existence of capable guardians has also declined. In Ireland, for example, increasing numbers of farmers are forced to take off-farm employment to supplement incomes. This has reduced the number of people patrolling farmland and reduced time for routine maintenance of basic security measures (see Barclay et al, 2001): essentially target-softening areas.

Farmers' responses to crime

There is some consistency across surveys that farmers tend to be complacent about security and preventive measures are seldom at 'the forefront of the minds of farmers, well, not at least until something happened' (Jones, 2008: 13; also Harkness, 2017). Studies have found that farmers often leave expensive machinery unlocked in remote fields and fail to routinely check stocks (Sugden, 1998; Jobes et al, 2000). Indeed, the Irish Gardaí has reported that one in four tractors are stolen with the keys in them (Gallagher, 2018a). Furthermore, when farmers do employ security measures, they often opt for more traditional options: locks and dogs (Sugden, 1998; George Street Research, 1999; Jones, 2008; Harkness, 2017; Smith and Byrne, 2017; Walsh and Walsh, 2017; Harkness and Larkins, 2020). This situation is not limited to agricultural theft: Hopkins and Tilley (1998) suggest that small businesses (which includes most Irish farms) are often lax about crime prevention because they simply lack time and resources, and are often more concerned with short-term economic survival.

Several studies have suggested that farmers are reticent about reporting theft to the police (McCall and Homel, 2003): two surveys found that 51 per cent (Donnermeyer and Barclay, 2005) and 88 per cent (Mears et al, 2007) failed to report farm crime. However, an Irish survey found that 41 per cent of all theft cases were reported. Machinery and vehicles thefts were the most likely to be reported and all incidents of robbery were reported (Walsh and Walsh, 2017). This said, more recently, the Irish Farmers Association responded to claims that rural crime was falling by suggesting that farmers had simply stopped reporting – partly because they felt abandoned by the state's closure of rural Gardaí stations (Gallagher, 2018b).

There is much consistency between studies as to why farmers fail to report crimes, including beliefs that:

- a certain amount of theft is inevitable (George Street Research, 1999; Jobes et al, 2000);
- the theft would be too difficult to prove and/or uncertainty that anything had been stolen (for example, livestock may have been killed by predators) (Barclay and Donnermeyer, 2002; Mears et al, 2007; Harkness, 2017; Walsh and Walsh, 2017; Harkness and Larkins, 2020);
- too much time had elapsed since the theft because, in large farms, theft may take some time to notice (Jobes et al, 2000; Barclay and Donnermeyer, 2002; Harkness and Larkins, 2020);
- the police can do little and/or do not understand farming (Jobes et al, 2000; Barclay and Donnermeyer, 2002; Walsh and Walsh, 2017; Harkness and Larkins, 2020; Morris et al, 2020);
- the farmer would be penalised for breaking regulatory standards (that is, theft of chemicals which were not properly secured) (Jones, 2008; Harkness, 2017);
- the local community would be angered by a farmer informing on a neighbour to the police, or the farmer may not want to harm the offender's family (Jobes et al, 2000; Barclay and Donnermeyer, 2002; Harkness, 2017; Walsh and Walsh, 2017); and
- there could be retribution from the thief (Harkness, 2017; Walsh and Walsh, 2017; Harkness and Larkins, 2020).

Literature review summary

The available international literature suggests that farms are attractive targets for crime and many farms will be victimised at some point. Farmers are, however, slow to report crimes to the police or spend time and resources on crime prevention. Opportunities for theft from farms can be inflated by a lack of capable guardians, their remoteness and physical terrain, ease of access, relaxed attitudes to security and failure to report theft.

While these studies are important, Irish farms tend to be different from American, Australian and British farms in terms of size, management structure and terrain. The relevance of these studies to the Irish context is, therefore, useful but limited. Furthermore, the studies already cited have almost all been influenced by routine activity theory (Cohen and Felson, 1979), the insights from which are important and likely to be accurate – a lack of capable guardians almost certainly factors in the victimisation of farms, as does proximity to urban areas. A key limitation of all of these studies is, however, the narrow focus on the victim. Looking at agricultural theft from a left realist lens demands a more nuanced and comprehensive contextual assessment and highlights the need for longer-term social prevention.

Left realism

In the 1980s, Young (1986) provided a scathing critique of criminology which formed the foundation of what became left realism, defined as:

> Radical in its criminology and realistic in its appraisal of crime and its causes. Radical, in that crime is seen as an endemic product of the class and patriarchal nature of advanced industrial society … realistic in that it attempts to be faithful to the reality of crime. (Young, 1986: 4)

This section summarises the key arguments of left realism, paying close attention to its two key concepts – the square of crime and relative deprivation. For Young (1992), left realism is composed of four key principles which are summarised here.

First, and most importantly, left realism calls for researchers, policymakers and practitioners to be 'faithful to the nature of crime' (Lea, 2015: 172). That is, all research, theory and practice must acknowledge the precise form that agricultural theft takes and where it takes place; grounded within political and economic context. This must involve all four dimensions of the 'square of crime' (Young, 1992; Lea, 2015; see DeKeseredy and Schwartz, 2018) which, as one of left realisms core concepts, is summarised and applied to agricultural theft in Table 6.1. It is argued that all research, policy and practice must engage all four dimensions.

Table 6.1: Left realist research, policy and practice agenda

Dimension	Actors	Role in agricultural theft
State	• any state agencies, including criminal justice, health, social welfare, education and housing	• define crime / create laws and regulations • enforce regulations on chemicals • gather data on theft • prioritise theft prevention • disruption of theft networks • arrests may deter theft • prevent through target-hardening advice – fund target hardening • pressure machinery companies to improve their security • facilitate organisations that strengthen rural communities • job creation • reduce inequality (improve social welfare, social housing, education and so on)
Public	• communities • the media • NGOs • companies	• improved social efficacy • capable guardians – including community watch but also through looking for sale of stolen goods (that is, *veterinary*, online marketplaces, farmers unions) • reduced fear of crime (that is, responsible media reporting) • victim support • support would-be thieves to transition away from theft – community members acting as mentors / role models and so on • companies design products to prevent theft
Offender	• individuals • organisations	• alter structural factors influencing the decision to steal (that is, reduce relative deprivation) • support desistence from offending
Victim	• individuals • organisations	• alter the situational factors influencing the decision to steal (that is, alter built environment, target hardening) • supported to reduce fear of crime • supported to prevent repeat victimisation • compensation to victims

Second, much criminological theory focuses on one cause (such as strain, social disorganisation), often attentive to just one dimension of the square of crime at the expense of others. Left realists argued that there are often multiple causes at different levels and applied to different dimension of the square of crime. As such, the integration of theories can be advantageous (Young, 1992). This said, while left realists claimed to be open to all applicable theories, anomie-based subcultural theories were given precedence. Drawing from anomie, they identified relative deprivation 'as a major cause of criminal behaviour' (Young, 1992: 33). They argued that absolute poverty is an insufficient explanation for crime. Instead, the motivation for much offending is the inability to achieve the cultural goals dictated by consumer society: that 'experienced injustice in certain limited political situations, is at the root cause of crime' (Young, 1992: 34). In a later article, Young (2003: 389) integrated Mertonian theories of relative deprivation with Katz's seduction of crime thesis to argue that globalisation and neoliberalism have intensified relative deprivation while creating a 'crises of identity' in working-class communities. This 'combination is experienced as unfair, humiliating and threatening' and can result in both instrumental and expressive offending (see Windle, 2021).

Third, not only do different offences have different causes, but different areas experience crime differently (Young, 1992). Thus, blindly adopting theories developed in one context to explain phenomena in another is unlikely to be successful. As crime is experienced differently within different areas and by different people, researchers should assess how different groups are impacted by crime and preventive measures. This calls for narrower geographical inquiries: once we understand the lived realities of specific groups we can tailor preventive measures for that community.

Gauging lived realities requires that those most impacted by agricultural theft be consulted about all policy and practice (see Lynch et al, 2021). Here, local victimisation surveys can be used to measure both local community opinions and the realities of agricultural theft. Once the reality of agricultural theft is understood, the state can allocate resources to where they are most needed (Lea, 2015). In short, farming communities know what has happened and what they want done about it, so ask them.

Fourth, left realists proposed greater emphasis on structural change than policing. They argued that investing in social goods (health, housing, employment and so on) can promote social control, which has a more significant and longer-term impact than criminal justice approaches (Matthews, 1992; Young, 1992). Police and prisons are, however, seen as 'inevitably necessary' but should be minimally used and democratic. That is, police priorities should follow community priorities (Young, 1992: 41). The nuance of left realism is apparent here: preventing agricultural theft in the short term may involve educating potential victims about how theft occurs, target-hardening properties and disrupting theft networks, however, longer-term policies will involve altering the structural factors filling the pool of would-be thieves. Effective agricultural theft prevention will involve multiple agencies within and outside of the criminal justice system, depending on local context. Just as farmers do not use one machine for all jobs (a combine makes a rough job of bailing), policymakers and practitioners should be open to all available preventive tools.

The last two points can conflict, however. Many farmers the author has spoken with over the years have called for stricter law enforcement–based approaches that punish thieves and deter theft. While left realists have been especially critical of zero tolerance and underclass theories (see Matthews, 1992; also Windle, 2021) many farmers would favour such 'common sense' conservative policies over longer-term structural approaches. The Irish Natura and Hill Farmers Association (2020), for example, has lobbied to remove suspended sentences for violent theft, and remove free legal aid and bail from offenders with previous convictions. While left realism demands we listen to communities, what happens when the community rejects the left element of left realism?

Left realism and agricultural theft

While generalising about crime from studies conducted or theories developed in other countries is almost antithetical to the left realist tenant of specificity (Young, 1992), this section proposes that left realism can be a useful approach to reducing agricultural theft. This chapter is not the first to highlight the utility of left realism in a rural setting, DeKeseredy, Schwartz and Donnermeyer have long lobbied for its relevance to a range of issues affecting rural communities (see DeKeseredy and Schwartz, 2018).

If agricultural theft is conducted by people travelling from urban areas, then the subcultural and relative deprivation approaches prioritised by left realists remain important. A number of Irish studies have, for example, shown how decades of neoliberal economic policies, including deindustrialisation and government austerity measures, have widened the gap between the most and least affluent (Hourigan, 2011; Bowden, 2014; Cambridge, 2019). It has been previously argued that increased inequality has been met, in some areas, with subcultural adaptations which have facilitated problematic drug use (Leonard and Windle, 2020) and violence (Windle, 2019, 2021).

Smith and McElwee (2013: 115) have, however, warned against such 'alien conspiracy theories'. They suggest that many 'crimes, such as livestock rustling or theft of farm machinery often require the offender to possess insider knowledge and/or rural social capital to exploit the situation' and that farms are more often victimised by 'rural criminal entrepreneurs' than urban people. While this may be so in parts of the UK, in Ireland many people living in urban areas are familiar with rural life. Many have families living in the countryside (the 'country cousins') and many urban areas are situated close to farmland.

The involvement of organised crime groups in agricultural theft has been identified in other countries, notably in livestock and machinery theft to order (Europol, 2019; Smith and Byrne, 2019; Martin, 2020; Morris et al, 2020). In Ireland, a Gardaí crime prevention officer reported that smaller items are commonly stolen by locals while organised crime groups are involved in machinery theft (Gallagher, 2018a; see also Hourigan et al, 2018). Examples include reports of gangs using drones to identify machinery and livestock (O'Brien, 2020), increased incidents of 'steal-to-order' chemical theft (Farming Independent, 2020) and 'a criminal gang with links to paramilitaries' that transported stolen tractors across Ireland to a mechanic who used the parts in his 'chop shop' tractor sales business (Roche, 2019). More organised offenders may, however, exploit local knowledge. For example, in 2019 a young man living in an economically deprived area on the outskirts of Cork City was imprisoned for burglary, and for stealing tractors and quad bikes. At the trial, Gardaí reported that the defendant was 'was being used for his local knowledge of the area' (Heylin, 2019).

More importantly, subcultural responses to relative deprivation are not uniquely urban phenomena (see DeKeseredy and Schwartz, 2010). Many farms are situated close to small or medium-sized towns that suffer many of the economic hardships and social exclusions of urban areas. Some perpetrators of agricultural theft are likely to come from large urban areas or smaller towns suffering relative deprivation, and agricultural theft probably involves an assortment of amateur opportunists and organised crime groups. The problem is that, in Ireland, there is not a research base of who steals from farms or why, or on the mechanics of theft, to comment with any confidence.

A number of studies have suggested that opportunity theories may be particularly appropriate for the prevention of agricultural theft (Barclay and Donnermeyer, 2002; Donnermeyer and Barclay, 2005; Mears et al, 2007; Harkness and Larkins, 2020) including a study on opium theft (Windle, 2016). The left realists, while critical of opportunity theories' ignorance of structural causes, did acknowledge that some situational measures may be useful as part of a holistic approach. Mears and colleagues (2007: 136), Harkness and Larkins (2020: 235) and Clack (2020) have recommended measures farmers can take to target harden and improve guardianship. These have included, but are not limited to:

- locking chemicals and equipment in secure buildings (preferably close to the main residence) or, hiding or disabling the equipment;
- securely locking gates;
- marking equipment and livestock with identification numbers or using technologies such as ultraviolet etching, microdots or forensic water;
- avoiding overstocking chemicals;
- employing security personal;
- storing machinery, and placing animal pens, away from roads;
- maintaining perimeter fencing and warning signs;
- ensure the farm is permanently occupied, or looks occupied; and
- installing CCTV, security lights, intruder alarms.[4]

While these sound useful, it can be impractical to carry large amounts of chemicals or tools home with you every night and few farmers can afford to buy good locks let alone employ private security or buy expensive technology. For some, the time and financial cost of employing these measures may outweigh the potential cost of theft. Even when farmers can target harden, few thieves will be dissuaded by basic padlocks. Indeed, when Barclay and colleagues (2001) cross-tabulated reported victimisation with 22 common security measures, the only statistically significant measure found to reduce victimisation was a dog – a most capable of guardians – although they acknowledged that the ineffectiveness of security measures may be partly owing to a lack of motivation farmers have to use preventive measures.

Much of the literature has focused on how the potential victim can dissuade the potential offender – two of four dimensions of the square of crime. The third and fourth dimensions have, however, largely been ignored. The government and manufacturers of agricultural goods could make prevention easier for farmers who are often too overworked, and under too much financial stress, to undertake more than basic prevention themselves.

Farrell and Tilley (2020: 1) have argued that as security measures affect quality of life, they should 'preferably be ethical and unobtrusive, aesthetically neutral or pleasing, and the easy-to-use or default option ... inelegant security can fall into disuse even if it prevents crime'. Tractors and mobile agricultural machinery are seldom fitted with immobilisers as standard, let alone alarms. Most do not even provide individually cut keys, with one key fitting all tractors of that make. Research has shown that cars fitted with a combination of central locking, electronic immobiliser and alarm are 'up to 25 times less likely to be stolen than those without security', while tracking devices are 'particularly effective' (Farrell et al, 2011: 21). As such, a simple means of reducing machinery theft is to fit security devices as standard. A similar argument may apply to the computers within most machines – they are easy to steal with minimal security. While this is, in many ways, a victim-focused intervention, it requires farmers, farmers unions and the state to pressure machinery companies, who may be unwilling to pass manufacturing costs to customers or risk reduced profit margins.

Opportunity approaches can only go so far. Reducing agricultural theft requires a response that places the activity within its social and economic context and engages all four corners of the square of crime. Longer-term policies would focus on altering the structural conditions facilitating agricultural theft. The problem is we do not have sufficient evidence of who steals from farms and what motivates them – we can follow the left realist chain and focus on relative deprivation, but this is a hypothesis that needs to be tested. The final section sets out a left realist agricultural theft research agenda.

A left realist research agenda

Young (1986: 62) recommended that left realist criminologists remain sceptical of official crime statistics without a total rejection of quantifying crime. In line with its central concern with a more precise victimology, Young advocated for a detailed mapping of those at risk and specifying the impact of crime on their lives. He also proposed avoiding unfocused crime surveys that provide national averages. The limitations of official statistics are well known (for Ireland, see Windle, 2018) while unfocused national victimisation surveys often overlook the most vulnerable and marginalised. Many farmers fail to report agricultural theft to the police, and those made vulnerable by age or income are even less likely to report to the police. Furthermore, the Irish government does not collect national estimates of agricultural theft but classifies simply as theft.

Localised victimisation surveys were proposed by left realists as the most effective means of measuring victimisation within an area, especially surveys that can gather the opinions of those who may not report crimes to the police (Lea, 2015): farmers in this case. There are, however, challenges to conducting such research with farmers. This section will explore those challenges.

First, as farmers are notoriously reticent about talking to researchers, being known to the local community can be helpful (Sugden, 1999). The author has spoken to farmers over the years about whether they would participate in research and many felt that they would be slow to discuss their experiences of victimisation with strangers. Any large-scale victimisation survey would, therefore, need to be supported by a trusted politician, trade union or agricultural co-op, and/or be conducted by an insider-researcher.

Second, farmers work unpredictable schedules dictated by the unpredictability of livestock, machinery and weather. As such, door-to-door surveys may prove difficult, as might face-to-face interviews for, unless the researcher lives close-by, they could find themselves racking up many miles driving across the country to find farmers cancelling at the last minute. This is why several studies have interviewed farmers over the telephone (Barclay et al, 2001). Involving a local agricultural co-op, where the researcher could meet farmers when they came to buy supplies or sell goods, would speak to both the first and second limitation.

Third, the lack of an agricultural research base may limit the development of a survey instrument. A smaller pilot, employing semi-structured interviews and using a grounded theory approach, would give farmers an opportunity to discuss victimisation in their own words. This would allow for the development of questionnaires based upon these interviews at a later stage. Alternatively, the left realist surveys of the 1980s began with focus groups in which local communities, including police and politicians, were asked what they wanted included in the survey (Lea, 2015). A note regarding quantitative surveys: while the use of online surveys is cost effective compared with postal and face-to-face surveys, they present challenges in rural settings such as, for example, access to reliable internet connectivity (see Harkness et al, 2022 in press).

Fourth, and credit for this goes to this author's mother-in-law: the research must balance the perspective of men and women, young and old. If we focus predominantly on male farmers then we omit the view of their female partners. Not only are many women equal partners in the running of farms, but they are often in precarious situations. They may be home alone for long periods or driving out to isolated fields and farms to deliver machine parts and/or dinners. The partners will provide important alternative perspectives.

Finally, while the left realists argued that all research must involve all four dimensions of the square of crime, they then proposed victimisations surveys that focus on just one dimension. To fully understand agricultural theft in Ireland, and how to counter it from all dimensions of the square of crime, we need knowledge of offender motivation and decision-making. That is, a holistic research project will survey local communities about their experience and interview active or former offenders about why and how they stole.

Conclusion

It is time to rejuvenate left realism as much of the context within which the theory emerged is apparent today in many countries. Considering Ireland specifically, there is a move within Irish critical criminology to return to the left idealist cornerstone of abolitionism (O'Keeffe and Swirak, 2020) and Ireland has fully embraced neoliberalism, reducing positive state intervention and the safety net of welfare to a minimum. This has ensured a widening of the gap between the richest and poorest. All these are issues that motivated the original left realists to action (see Young and Matthews, 1992).

There is a tendency among some to either downplay farm theft (a moral panic) or exaggerate (we're all doomed!). Fear of agricultural theft is not irrational. But the perceived threat of violent crime is heightened by media reporting. Young's (1986) advice that being 'realistic about crime as a problem is not an easy task' applies today. The Irish media distort the reality of crime and crime control (see Black, 2016; Windle, 2019; Windle and Murphy, 2021). A left realist approach demands that we listen to farming communities, and take their concerns and experiences seriously. This does not mean we uncritically accept common perceptions, which can represent media-driven distortions. Rather, researchers can appraise rural people's fears and experiences of crime through victimisation surveys. Not only does this give affected communities a voice, but it may quell some anxieties about the true extent of crime while directing resources to where they are most needed. Indeed, left realists proposed that all data be made available to the local community so that they could develop proposals, hold local government and police to account, and lobby for policies and strategies the community need (Lea, 2015): armed with evidence, farming communities are a formidable force.

A solid evidence base is the foundation to effective preventive policy and intervention. This chapter has attempted to take a first step towards establishing an evidence base by exploring some conceptual, theoretical and methodological issues, through a left realist lens. The next step will be to conduct local victimisation surveys. Many of the recommendations reviewed in the first half of this chapter can sensibly be assumed to have some effectiveness, but there is little evidence of success in rural settings globally (Barclay and Donnermeyer, 2011) let alone in Ireland.

Research also needs to prioritise who the offenders are, where they come from, what motivates them to steal from farms, and why they target particular farms. Speaking to thieves will provide insight into which theories can best explain farm theft at different levels. Can routine activity theory explain increased theft because new motorways, alongside profitable global markets for machinery, produced new opportunities to steal machinery? Or did decades of neoliberalism inflate inequality across Ireland, a situation exaggerated by the Great Recession and prolonged austerity? It is possible that both are true, but the scarcity of systematic research evidence means that any attempt at causal explanation will quickly become speculation. Once we get a sense of causes then we can develop longer-term policies – which may involve reducing opportunities through targeting hardening and developing guardianship in the short term while tackling inequalities in the longer-term.

Notes

[1] While 1,100 incidents of farm theft may not seem significant internationally, these are simply those reported to the Gardaí and need to take into account that the population of the Republic of Ireland is less than five million.

[2] Of 710 respondents to Walsh and Walsh (2017), 91 reported not insuring some assets because it was too expensive or they were unable to secure insurance.

[3] Machinery included trailers, parts for machinery and equipment, computer and other information technology – all of which can be profitable. It is relatively quick to steal (often very expensive) machinery parts or computers, and trailers are commonly stolen. There is also a large market for quad bikes, chainsaws and hand tools: 119 quad bikes were stolen from Irish farms in 2019 (Moran, 2020).

[4] Bowden and Pytlarz (2020) and Naomi Smith (2020: 81) highlight the potential for text alert schemes and social media apps as preventive devices to widen guardianship, alert communities, provide crime prevention information and also 'help establish a more responsive style of policing that is awake to community concerns before they become systematic issues', a sentiment in line with left realisms focus on democratic policing. Bowden and Pytlarz (2020) do, however, caution that such technologies can heighten anxiety and fear of crime.

References

Agnew, K. (2020) 'Crime highways: the effect of motorway expansion on burglary rates', *Journal of Regional Science*, 60(5): 995–1024.

Barclay, E. and Donnermeyer, J.F. (2002) 'Property crime and crime prevention on farms in Australia', *Crime Prevention and Community Safety*, 4(4): 47–61.

Barclay, E. and Donnermeyer, J.F. (2011) 'Crime and security on agricultural operations', *Security Journal*, 24(1): 1–18.

Barclay, E., Donnermeyer, J.F., Doyle, B.P. and Talary, D. (2001) *Property Crime Victimisation and Crime Prevention on Farms*, Armidale, NSW: University of New England.

Black, L. (2016) 'Media, public attitudes and crime', in D. Healey, C. Hamilton, Y. Daly and M. Butler (eds) *The Routledge Handbook of Irish Criminology*, Abingdon: Routledge, pp 399–416.

Bowden, M. (2014) *Crime, Disorder and Symbolic Violence: Governing the Urban Periphery*, Basingstoke: Palgrave Macmillan.

Bowden, M. and Pytlarz, A. (2020) 'The development of rational models of crime prevention: a critique of situationist common sense in rural context', in A. Harkness (ed) *Rural Crime Prevention: Theory, Tactics and Techniques*, Abingdon: Routledge, pp 30–42.

Cambridge, G. (2019) '"Seeking peace of mind": understanding desistance as a journey into recovery and out of chaos', PhD thesis, Cork: University College Cork.

Carswell, S. (2017) 'Farmers "carrying shotguns" in fear of rural crime: Garda taskforce to tackle gangs roaming along motorway network in midlands', *Irish Times*, 13 November. Available from: https://www.irishtimes.com/news/crime-and-law/farmers-carrying-shotguns-in-fear-of-rural-crime-1.3289208 [Accessed 4 March 2022].

Clack, W. (2020) 'Livestock theft prevention', in A. Harkness (ed) *Rural Crime Prevention: Theory, Tactics and Techniques*, Abingdon: Routledge, pp 205–19.

Cohen, L.E. and Felson, M. (1979) 'Social change and crime rate trends: a routine activity approach', *American Sociological Review*, 44(4): 588–608.

Dáil Éireann (2017) 'Rural crime: motion', Dáil Éireann Debate, 21 November, Vol 961, No 7. Available from: https://www.oireachtas.ie/en/debates/debate/dail/2017-11-21/40/ [Accessed 11 October 2020].

Danaher, D. (2019) '"I'm very lonely and living in fear, but I have got used to it"', Farming Independent [Ireland], 25 November. Available from: https://www.independent.ie/business/farming/rural-life/im-very-lonely-and-living-in-fear-but-i-have-got-used-to-it-one-bachelor-farmer-tells-his-story-of-rural-isolation-38722577.html [Accessed 4 March 2022].

DeKeseredy, W.S. and Schwartz, M.D. (2010) 'Friedman economic policies, social exclusion, and crime: toward a gendered left realist subcultural theory', *Crime, Law and Social Change*, 54(2): 159–70.

DeKeseredy, W.S. and Schwartz, M.D. (2018) 'Left realism: a new look', in W.S. DeKeseredy and M. Dragiewicz (eds) *Routledge Handbook of Critical Criminology* (2nd edn), Abingdon: Routledge, pp 30–42.

Donnermeyer, J.F. and Barclay, E. (2005) 'The policing of farm crime', *Police Practice and Research*, 6(1): 3–17.

Europol (2019) 'String of tractor satnav thefts brought to an end by France and Lithuania', Europol Media and Press, 29 November. Available from: https://www.europol.europa.eu/newsroom/news/string-of-trac tor-satnav-thefts-brought-to-end-france-and-lithuania [Accessed 11 October 2020].

Farming Independent (2020) 'Public warning after theft of liquid nitrogen from farm', Farming Independent [Ireland], 6 May. Available from: https:// www.independent.ie/business/farming/news/rural-crime/public-warn ing-after-theft-of-liquid-nitrogen-from-farm-39185275.html [Accessed 4 March 2022].

Farrell, G. and Tilley, N. (2020) 'Elegant security: concept, evidence and implications', *European Journal of Criminology*, ahead of print. Available from: https://doi.org/10.1177/1477370820932107 [Accessed 4 March 2022].

Farrell, G., Tseloni, A. and Tilley, N. (2011) 'The effectiveness of vehicle security devices and their role in the crime drop', *Criminology and Criminal Justice*, 11(1): 21–35.

Gallagher, C. (2018a) 'Lock up your tractors, gardaí warn, as one in four is stolen with key in it', Irish Times, 18 September. Available from: https:// www.irishtimes.com/news/ireland/irish-news/lock-up-your-tractors-garda%C3%AD-warn-as-one-in-four-is-stolen-with-key-in-it-1.3633464 [Accessed 4 March 2022].

Gallagher, C. (2018b) 'Farmers' group rejects Garda view that rural crime is falling', *Irish Times*, 17 October. Available from: https://www.irishtimes. com/news/crime-and-law/farmers-group-rejects-garda-view-that-rural-crime-is-falling-1.3666625 [Accessed 4 March 2022].

George Street Research (1999) *Crime and the Farming Community: The Scottish Farm Crime Survey, 1998*, Edinburgh: Scottish Office.

Hamilton, A. (2019) 'Farmer sleeps with loaded gun in his bedroom as crime leaves a community on the edge', Farming Independent [Ireland], 10 December. Available from: https://www.independent.ie/business/farm ing/news/rural-crime/farmer-sleeps-with-loaded-gun-in-his-bedroom-as-crime-leaves-a-community-on-the-edge-38767294.html [Accessed 4 March 2022].

Harkness, A. (2017) 'Crime prevention on farms: experiences from Victoria, Australia', *International Journal of Rural Criminology*, 3(2): 131–56.

Harkness, A. and Larkins, J. (2019) 'Farmer satisfaction with policing in rural Victoria, Australia', *International Journal of Rural Criminology*, 5(1): 47–68.

Harkness, A. and Larkins, J. (2020) 'Technological approaches to preventing theft from farms', in A. Harkness (ed) *Rural Crime Prevention: Theory, Tactics and Techniques*, Abingdon: Routledge, pp 226–44.

Harkness, A., Mulrooney, K. and Donnermeyer, J. (2022, in press) 'Surveying in rural settings', in R. Weisheit, J. Peterson and A. Pytlarz (eds) *Research Methods for Rural Criminologists*, Abingdon: Routledge.

Heylin, L. (2019) 'Man stole tractors and cars four days after being released from prison, court hears', Irish Examiner, 28 June. Available from: https://www.irishexaminer.com/news/arid 30933619.html [Accessed 4 March 2022].

Hopkins, M. and Tilley, N. (1998) 'Commercial crime, crime prevention and community safety: a study of three streets in Camden, north London', in M. Gill (ed) *Crime at Work, Volume II: Increasing the Risk for Offenders*, London: Palgrave, pp 51–65.

Hourigan, N. (2011) *Understanding Limerick: Social Exclusion and Change*, Cork: Cork University Press.

Hourigan, N., Morrison, J.F., Windle, J. and Silke, A. (2018) 'Crime in Ireland north and south: feuding gangs and profiteering paramilitaries', *Trends in Organized Crime*, 21(2): 126–46.

Irish Natura and Hill Farmers Association (2020) The Irish Farmers Guide, 4. Available from: http://www.inhfa.ie/Issue%204%20-%20Spring%202020.pdf [Accessed 11 October 2020].

Jobes, P.C., Barclay, E., Donnermeyer, J.F. and Weinand, H. (2000) *A Qualitative and Quantitative Analysis of the Relationship Between Community Cohesiveness and Rural Crime*, Armidale, NSW: University of New England.

Jones, J. (2008) 'Farm crime on Anglesey: local partners and organisations' views on the issues', unpublished report presented to Anglesey Joint Action Group Committee, University of Chester.

Jones, J. (2012) 'Looking beyond the "rural idyll": Some recent trends in rural crime', *Criminal Justice Matters*, 89(1): 8–9.

Lea, J. (2015) 'Jock Young and the development of left realist criminology', *Critical Criminology*, 23(2): 165–77.

Leonard, J. and Windle, J. (2020) '"I could have went down a different path": talking to people who used drugs problematically and service providers about Irish drug policy alternatives', *International Journal of Drug Policy*, 84: art 102891. Available from: https://doi.org/10.1016/j.drugpo.2020.102891 [Accessed 4 March 2022].

Lynch, O., Ahmed, Y., Russell, H. and Hosford, K. (2020) *Reflections on Irish Criminology: Conversations with Criminologists*, Cham: Palgrave.

Lynch, O., Windle, J. and Ahmed, Y. (2021) *Giving Voice to Diversity in Criminological Research: 'Nothing About Us Without Us'*, Bristol: Policy Press.

Martin, R. (2020) 'Livestock theft rises by nearly 20% as rustlers raid UK farms', *Agriland*. Available from: https://www.agriland.co.uk/farming-news/livestock-theft-rises-by-nearly-20-as-rustlers-raid-uk-farms/ [Accessed 4 March 2022].

Matthews, R. (1992) 'Replacing "broken windows": crime, incivilities and urban change', in R. Matthews and J. Young (eds) *Issues in Realist Criminology*, London: Sage, pp 19–50.

McCall, M. and Homel, P. (2003) 'Preventing crime on Australian farms: issues, current initiatives and future directions', Australian Institute of Criminology Trends & Issues in Crime and Criminal Justice, No 268, Canberra: Australian Institute of Criminology. Available from: https://www.aic.gov.au/publications/tandi/tandi268 [Accessed 5 March 2022].

Mears, D.P., Scott, M.L., Bhati, A.S., Roman, J., Chalfin, A. and Jannetta, J. (2007) *Process and Impact Evaluation of the Agricultural Crime, Technology, Information, and Operations Network (ACTION) Program*, NCJ No 217906, Washington, DC: Urban Institute.

Moran, C. (2020) 'Kildare and Meath farmers most at risk of quad thefts', Farming Independent [Ireland], 5 May. Available from: https://www.independent.ie/business/farming/news/rural-crime/kildare-and-meath-farmers-most-at-risk-of-quad-thefts-39179712.html [Accessed 4 March 2022].

Morris, W., Norris, G. and Dowell, D. (2020) 'The business of farm crime: evaluating trust in the police and reporting of offences', *Crime Prevention and Community Safety*, 22(1): 17–32.

Mulrooney, K.J.D. (2021) 'New South Wales farm crime survey 2020', University of New England, Centre for Rural Criminology. Available from: https://spark.adobe.com/page/zsV05pknxXl7N/ [Accessed 15 August 2021].

O'Brien, D. (2020) 'Rural crime gangs using drones and online mapping apps to case out farms', Farming Independent [Ireland], 12 May. Available from: https://www.independent.ie/business/farming/news/rural-crime/rural-crime-gangs-using-drones-and-online-mapping-apps-to-case-out-farms-39196957.html [Accessed 5 March 2022].

O'Keefe, T. and Swirak, K. (2020) 'Is police abolition relevant to Ireland?' RTÉ Brainstorm. Available from: https://www.rte.ie/brainstorm/2020/0727/1155802-police-abolition-defunding-ireland-garda/ [Accessed 11 October 2020].

Roche, B. (2019) 'Man jailed for two years for running "a chop shop" in Cork'. *Irish Times*, 15 February. Available from: https://www.irishtimes.com/news/ireland/irish-news/man-jailed-for-two-years-for-running-a-chop-shop-in-cork-1.3795263 [Accessed 5 March 2022].

Smith, K. (2020) 'Desolation in the countryside: how agricultural crime impacts the mental health of British farmers', *Journal of Rural Studies*, 80: 522–31.

Smith, K. and Byrne, R. (2017) 'Farm crime in England and Wales: a preliminary scoping study examining farmer attitudes', *International Journal of Rural Criminology*, 3(2): 191–223.

Smith, K. and Byrne, R. (2019) 'Horizon scanning rural crime in England', *Crime Prevention and Community Safety*, 21(3): 231–45.

Smith, N. (2020) 'Social media, rural communities and crime prevention', in A. Harkness (ed) *Rural Crime Prevention: Theory, Tactics and Techniques*, Abingdon: Routledge, pp 73–83.

Smith, R. and McElwee, G. (2013) 'Confronting social constructions of rural criminality: a case story on "illegal pluriactivity" in the farming community', *Sociologia Ruralis*, 53(1): 112–34.

Sugden, G. (1998) 'In defence of farms: an agrarian crime prevention audit in Rutland', in M. Gill (ed) *Crime at Work, Volume II: Increasing the Risk for Offenders*, London: Palgrave, pp 83–94.

Sugden, G. (1999) 'Farm crime: out of sight, out of mind – a study of crime on farms in the county of Rutland, England', *Crime Prevention and Community Safety*, 1(3): 29–36.

Teagasc (Agriculture and Food Development Authority) (2020) 'Agriculture in Ireland', Teagasc. Available from: https://www.teagasc.ie/rural-econ omy/rural-economy/agri-food-business/agriculture-in-ireland/ [Accessed 9 March 2020].

Walsh, K.M. and Walsh, L. (2017) 'Agricultural crime in Ireland, Report 3: agricultural crime reporting to gardaí and crime prevention employed by farmers in Ireland', 30 September. Waterford: Waterford Institute of Technology. Available from: https://icsaireland.ie/wp-content/uploads/ 2017/11/ICSA-WIT-Agricultural-Crime-Survey-Report-3.pdf [Accessed 5 March 2022].

Windle, J. (2016) 'Preventing the diversion of Turkish opium', *Security Journal*, 29(2): 213–27.

Windle, J. (2018) 'The impact of the Great Recession on the Irish drug market', *Criminology and Criminal Justice*, 18(5): 548–67.

Windle, J. (2019) 'The causes and consequences of gangland violence in the Republic of Ireland', in R.M. Lombardo (ed) *Organized Crime: Causes and Consequences*, Toronto: Nova, pp 60–72.

Windle, J. (2021) 'Reconsidering the 1991 Blackbird Leys rioters as an underclass: an insider perspective', in O. Lynch, J. Windle and Y. Ahmed (eds) *Giving Voice to Diversity in Criminological Research: 'Nothing About Us Without Us'*, Bristol: Policy Press, pp 133–48.

Windle, J. and Murphy, P. (2021) 'How a moral panic influenced the world's first blanket ban on new psychoactive substances', *Drugs: Education, Prevention and Policy*, ahead of print. Available from: https://doi.org/10.1080/09687637.2021.1902480 [Accessed 5 March 2022].

Young, J. (1986) 'The failure of criminology: the need for a radical realism', in R. Matthews and J. Young (eds), *Confronting Crime*, London: Sage, pp 4–30.

Young, J. (1992) 'Ten points of realism', in R. Matthews and J. Young (eds) *Rethinking Criminology: The Realist Debate*, London: Sage, pp 24–68.

Young, J. (2003) 'Merton with energy, Katz with structure: the sociology of vindictiveness and the criminology of transgression', *Theoretical Criminology*, 7(3): 389–414.

Young, J. and Matthews, R. (1992) *Rethinking Criminology: The Realist Debate*, London: Sage.

7

Climate Change and
the Geographies of Ecocide

Rob White

Introduction

Climate change continues to be the most significant and urgent matter of
our time. Rapid global warming characteristic of this era is not 'natural'. It is
human made. The resultant climate change is distorting what used to be the
familiar patterns of weather and disrupting long-established climate patterns
(IPCC, 2014, 2021). All of this is entirely due to the continued collusion
of national and state/provincial leaders with the fossil fuel industries and
other degraders of the environment and generalised support for the growth
agenda of global capitalism (van der Velden and White, 2021).

Yet even in the face of these contemporary changes, the Earth continues
to be a battleground where plundering of resources and pollution of the
planet is rampant and inexorably moving towards an even more radically
altered ecological state. Prominent world leaders are diminishing emission
controls and environmental protections, burning forests and fracking oils,
and actively encouraging violence against Indigenous peoples and local
farmers. Much of this occurs in so-called rural and remote locations, away
from prying media eyes and governmental purview.

The geographies of ecocide provide insight into how crimes of the
powerful are perpetrated and communities victimised. This chapter considers
questions of eco-justice from the point of view of place and 'sights unseen'.
It considers how climate change is impacting upon the metropole and
periphery, and how ecological destruction linked to climate change is based
upon exploitation of humans and natural resources in predominantly rural
and remote settings.

Climate change – trends and issues

The rapidity and intensity of climate change is substantial and having tremendous impact across the globe. The consequences of climate change are evident in major disasters and high-impact events worldwide. The 2020–21 fires in Siberia, California, eastern Australia, the Brazilian Amazon, Turkey and Greece, and other places, are visible effects of extreme temperatures, moisture-draining droughts and unprecedented heat domes. Simultaneously, excessive amounts of rain, in very short periods of time, have created floods in Germany, the UK and elsewhere. The unseasonal is becoming the ordinary.

Things will only get worse. Greenhouse gas emissions (carbon dioxide, methane, nitrous oxide) continue to rise, as do global temperatures (IPCC, 2013, 2014, 2018, 2021; WMO, 2020a). The warmest years on record are the most recent years, as the oceans absorb record levels of heat content. All the key indicators – temperature, greenhouse gases, oceans, marine heatwaves, sea levels, ocean acidification, and changes in the cryosphere, sea ice and the Greenland ice sheet – are going in the wrong direction. This is resulting in high-impact events that are geographically specific but universally experienced. These kinds of climate disruptions include heat and cold waves, unusually low and high precipitation amounts, heavy rainfalls and floods, severe storms, wildfires and drought.

Climate-related risks and impacts

The damage caused by global warming is also being felt in the form of increased competition for dwindling natural resources (such as potable water), outbreaks of disease and viral infections (witness the COVID-19 pandemic), and further extinctions of species (IPBES, 2019; Portner et al, 2021). Social inequality and environmental injustice will undoubtedly be the drivers of continuous social conflicts for many years to come, as the most dispossessed and marginalised of the world's population suffer the brunt of food shortages, undrinkable water, climate-induced migration and general hardship in their day-to-day lives.

Those most vulnerable to the consequences of climate change live in specific geographical and political locations. For instance, rising seas are disproportionately affecting low-lying countries, such as the Pacific islands and those in the Indian Ocean, and present as an immediate existential threat. Where you live does count from a geophysical point of view. So too, however, does the developmental, population, technological and economic status of the country in question. For example, Bangladesh and the Netherlands are both low-level countries subject to potential flooding from rising seas. The former, however, does not have the financial and infrastructural capacity to build protective sea walls.

The distributions of climate-related risk are thus not socially neutral. This is evident in the prevalence and intensity of harm in particular countries, stemming from high-impact events such as cyclones, floods and fires (for example, the 2021 earthquake in Haiti). It is also demonstrated in the variable capacity, depending upon national resources, to meet people's needs in the aftermath of such events (for example, access to medical staff, hospitals and emergency services). More fundamental to long-term human health and well-being are the disparities and vulnerabilities related to reduced soil quality, water supply and arable land.

Issues of food security and population displacement due to climate variability and extreme weather are substantial and growing, and again the effects are disproportionately affecting those in less-developed countries, as noted by the World Meteorological Organization:

> Between 2006 and 2016, agriculture (crops, livestock, forestry, fisheries and aquaculture) in developing countries accounted for an estimated 26% of total loss and damage incurred during medium- and large-scale climate-related disasters. While about two-thirds of loss of and damage to crops was associated with floods, almost 90% of loss and damage in the livestock sector was attributable to drought. (WMO, 2020a: 28)

Indeed, it has been pointed out that the key risks to the United Nations Sustainable Development Goals include rising poverty, food insecurity, health issues, water scarcity, damaged infrastructure, rising inequalities, displacement, ecosystem collapse, biodiversity loss and conflict – all of which are in some way associated with or compounded by climate change (WMO, 2020b). For example, the phenomenon of ocean acidification has implications for fishing and therefore the food supply for many peoples worldwide reliant upon sea-derived protein. Rises in sea levels affect many organisms and ecosystem services, threatening food security by endangering fisheries and aquaculture. It also affects coastal protection by weakening coral reefs, which shield coastlines.

In 2020–21, disruption to the agricultural sector by COVID-19 exacerbated weather impacts along the entire food supply chain, further elevating levels of food insecurity. This is a pattern which the World Meteorological Organization notes is not short-term or transient:

> After decades of decline, the recent increase in food insecurity since 2014 is being driven by conflict and economic slowdown as well as climate variability and extreme weather events. Nearly 690 million people, or 9% of the world population, were undernourished, and about 750 million, or nearly 10%, were exposed to severe levels of food insecurity in 2019. (WMO, 2020b: 38–9)

There are thus compounding effects of climate-related disasters affecting food supply and quality, such as floods, droughts and storms. The main burden of these falls on vulnerable areas and population groups, and this occurs differentially depending upon location and country. The lack of value attached to these people, these countries and these locations is highlighted in how the pleas of Pacific Island heads of state for climate action have largely been ignored by the wealthier nation states such as Australia over the past decade (O'Malley et al, 2020).

Untimely inaction

Indeed, for political leaders of the hegemonic nation states, time has *not* been of the essence when it comes to climate responses. The United Nations Environment Programme (UNEP, 2019) reports that greenhouse gas emissions continue to rise, despite scientific warnings and political commitments, and that 'Fossil CO_2 emissions from energy use and industry, which dominate total greenhouse gas emissions, grew 2.0 per cent in 2018, reaching a record 37.5 $GtCO_2$ per year' (UNEP, 2019: xiv). Yet, delays in reducing greenhouse gases mean that even deeper cuts are needed as each year goes by. And the timeline for preventive, mitigating action has now shrunk to less than one decade (IPCC, 2021). More needs to be done, and more quickly, but there is neither the required transformational policy shift or the needed urgency.

Inaction and inadequate responses relate to the dominance of global capitalism and its growth and globalisation climate endgame. This is the key stumbling block of our age, one that hinges on state–corporate collusion in environmental destruction (van der Velden and White, 2021). The main losers in this battle for the planet are those living in remote, rural and less-developed areas. This is especially manifest in the poverty and inequality apparent in regional Africa and South America, as well as in metropole countries such as Australia, the US and Canada. It is the Global South, geographically and metaphorically, that is paying the price for inaction. Threats to biodiversity and rises in global heating are combining to accelerate the downward economic, ecological and political spiral, which is first and foremost affecting the most vulnerable, marginalised and dispossessed of global society.

As the United Nations Human Rights Council has pointed out, while the problems are epic and urgent, the response has been totally inadequate and indeed appalling. The main culprits are nation states and companies, especially those that continue to produce the greatest contributions to global carbon emissions (Heede, 2014; UNEP, 2019; WMO, 2020a). In its summary statement for the Climate Change and Poverty report, the Council critically observed that:

In Brazil, President Bolsonaro has promised to open up the Amazon rainforest for mining, end demarcation of indigenous lands and weaken environmental agencies and protections. China is moving to end reliance on coal, while exporting coal-fired power plants abroad and failing to implement its regulations for methane emissions at home. In the United States of America, until recently the world's biggest producer of global emissions, [then] President Trump has placed former lobbyists in oversight roles, adopted industry talking points, presided over an aggressive rollback of environmental regulations and is actively silencing and obfuscating climate science. (UNHRC, 2019: 9–10)

The net result has been a continued tendency in government administration to move further away from the public interest in favour of specific private industry and firm interests. This goes to the heart of the problem. Environmental degradation and carbon emissions are essentially associated with exploitation of natural resources that bring profit to powerful companies (both privately owned and state-owned). The science of biodiversity, of climate change, and of pollution and contamination tells us that the environment cannot bear the weight of these exploitations any longer (Portner et al, 2021). However, as the planet burns, it is sectional self-interest that is preventing the application of appropriate, necessary and equitable responses. This is happening in Biden's America as it did in Trump's (Bokat-Lindell, 2021). Meanwhile, the carbon emission status quo remains intact in countries such as Australia (Morgan and Long, 2020) and Canada (Heydon, 2020) where resource extraction continues to reign supreme.

Ecocide and climate change

As a broad generalisation, ecocide can be defined first and foremost by the destruction, degradation and demolition of ecosystems and specific environments, with harmful consequences for the living creatures to which they are home. Those who wield significant power, especially governments and corporations, are particularly responsible for ecocide, as they are better placed to make a difference if they change their behaviour (White, 2018a, 2018b; Kramer, 2020; Whyte, 2020). They are the lynchpins of both ecological well-being and social justice.

An anthropocentric conception of ecocide sees protection of human rights as paramount and extends to protections pertaining to the human living environment. Thus, the demise of environmental amenity and security is considered a derogation of this duty to protect and enhance human rights, including the right to ecosystem services upon which human populations rely (White, 2018a). Ecocide is also premised on and linked to the idea of Earth stewardship. Ecocide in this instance is closely aligned with the concept of ecocentrism that views the environment as having value for its own sake, apart from any instrumental or utilitarian value to humans. Ecocentrism views non-human animals, plants and rivers as rights holders and/or as objects warranting a duty of care on the part of humans (Schlosberg, 2007; White, 2018c). Ecocide, in this view, is a crime not only against humans but against non-human environmental entities.

Ecocide can be described, therefore, as the causing of widespread long-term and severe damage to the natural environment. The concept has been used to refer to the extensive damage to, or destruction or loss of, ecosystems of a given territory, and includes both natural (for example, pest infestation of an ecosystem) and anthropogenic (that is, as a result of human activity) causes for the harm (Higgins, 2012; Higgins et al, 2013). Recently the concept has also been applied to the global scale insofar as the consequences of climate change are planet-wide, transformative and catastrophic (White, 2018b). Climate change and the gross exploitation of natural resources are leading to our general demise. Eventually everyone on the planet will be affected by processes that undermine existing ecosystems and habitats. This is the essence of ecocide.

Those least responsible for, and least able to remedy the effects of climate change, are the worst affected by it (Shiva, 2008; Bulkeley and Newell, 2010; Baatz, 2013). Ecocide is not socially (or, indeed, ecologically and species) neutral. It is the poor, the marginalised, the dispossessed and the vulnerable that bear the brunt of environmental destruction. In this sense, the victims are human and non-human, living and non-living, as human rights are ignored and landscapes devastated. For example, Indigenous people reliant upon clean water and arable lands for their livelihoods suffer greatly when large industrial projects – such as the Alberta Tar Sands project in Canada – negatively affect their forests, rivers and soils (Heydon, 2020). In this particular example, the project also happens to be the largest single contributor to the increase of global warming pollution in Canada (Klare, 2012).

Geography – place and location

Different geographical levels lend themselves to different issues: some are of a planetary scale (such as global warming), others regional (such as oceans and fisheries), some are national in geographical location (such as droughts in particular African countries), while others are local (such as specific oil spills). At the country level, different kinds of crimes and harms are linked to specific national contexts and particular geographical regions. For example, threats to biodiversity have been associated with illegal logging and deforestation in the Atlantic Forest of Brazil; illegal wildlife hunting and trade in Chiapas,

Mexico; commercial-scale illegal logging, and shipment of illegal logs, in Papua Province, Indonesia; and illegal fishing with dynamite and cyanide in Palawan, the Philippines (Akella and Cannon, 2004). Threats to biodiversity are also produced through *legal* activities such as the production of palm oil in Colombia (Mol, 2017). There is, as well, cross-over between legal and illegal activities, with significant harms resulting from mining, shale gas extraction and timber harvesting, regardless of legality, in places such as Latin America, Mexico and Vietnam (Cao, 2017; Goyes et al, 2017; Arroyo-Quiroz and Wyatt, 2018; Goyes, 2019).

The geographies of ecocide, while pertinent to global dilemmas, likewise stem from and are related to specific types of exploitation of the environment and of humans. There are interrelated factors that together combine to disguise or make disappear the harms associated with climate change ecocide. The following section briefly explores these.

Out of sight, out of mind

How the world is representationally presented has implications for empathy, security, protection of human rights, and basic knowledge of others. For instance, most world maps used in the northern hemisphere centre the world somewhere in the Atlantic Ocean. In this representation, countries like Australia and New Zealand are situated on the periphery – there on the edges, on the lower right-hand side of the map. Conversely, an Asia/ Australia-centred map features Australia in the middle of the map, and it is countries like the UK that are positioned on the periphery, as relatively small islands positioned near the top left-hand corner of the map.

Maps are important since they provide a glimpse into how different people situated differently on the planet might also see the world around them. They also reveal knowledge, or lack thereof, of those with whom we are not familiar. For example, many Americans do not know where countries such as Iraq or Afghanistan actually are, at least not from the point of view of a map presence. Ignorance of 'the other' is fostered not only by lack of geographical place awareness, but by the emphasis on the centrality of one's own place. If not for tourism, one wonders about contemporary public knowledge of people and events 'elsewhere'. Saving the planet demands a modicum of knowing where things are on the planet.

Where individuals are personally positioned in the world also influences concepts of remoteness and isolation. That is, remoteness is itself socially constructed relative to the position of the observer. For the Yanomami people living in the forests of the Amazon, for example, they live in and with nature in close proximity to each other and to what matters in their lives. They are not 'remote'. They do not experience a sense of separation from the hubs of civilisation. They are centred, self-sufficient and resilient if and when left to their own devices. For the Yanomami, it is Americans who are remote, who are foreign to them, and who present as strange and alien.

Yet geographical location nonetheless does count. For while the Yanomami people do not experience their homes as remote, where they live is far from the public eye of world attention. Insofar as they are 'out of sight' to a global audience, what happens in their territories remains 'out of mind' for those outside their region. Unless and until strategic media action is taken (such as press conferences with international rock stars), for many Indigenous people these kinds of remote areas escape close public scrutiny. As such, they are perfect places for corporate exploitation, environmental pillaging and human rights violations.

Notions such as 'remote' and 'isolated' reinforce the worthlessness and lack of apparent value of particular places. These same places, however, are frequently worth much to those wishing to exploit natural resources. Here there is also often a dynamic related to scarcity. As natural resources worldwide get used up and diminish in quantity (for example, trees, minerals, food sources), there is enhanced profit in accessing ever more 'remote' parts of the planet. The discourses of 'wilderness' and 'backwardness' obscure the exploitative nature of first world interventions in these areas. Interestingly, the only continent that is not home to ancient Indigenous civilisations is Antarctica. But the tundra, tropical forests and the deserts continue to be framed as 'empty' and ripe for corporate colonisation.

Thus, the world is shrinking as resources dry up and new 'green fields' for exploitation are sought, and as Gedicks observes:

> Multinational mining, oil, and logging corporations, for example, are now using advanced exploration technology, including remote sensing and satellite photography, to identify resources in the most isolated and previously inaccessible parts of the world's tropical rain forests, mountains, deserts, and frozen tundras. What the satellites don't reveal is the fact that native peoples occupy much of the land containing these resources. (Gedicks, 2005: 168)

In this corporate 'race for what's left', traditional and Indigenous people worldwide are especially vulnerable (Klare, 2012). In Canada, for example, governments have allowed extraction industries to enter into and fully work lands occupied by Indigenous peoples, regardless of the wishes of the local people, as particularly evidenced by the exploitation of the Alberta Tar Sands (Smandych and Kueneman, 2010; Heydon, 2020). More recently, the pipeline battles on Wet'suwet'en land in northern British Columbia have seen local Indigenous people and their allies at loggerheads with Canadian governments and business interests (Morin, 2020).

Cartographies of catastrophe

Maps are also useful in giving representational weight to historical processes, including the march and withdrawal of imperialism (European and Asian in particular). The carve-up of Africa by the European powers (for example, Britain, Germany, Italy, Belgium, the Netherlands, France) occurred in a relatively short space of time – between 1880 and 1914 (Lenin, 1917). Formal decolonisation took most of the twentieth century but, like the Middle East, the withdrawal of direct European control was accompanied by new borders, the pushing together of rival ethnic and cultural groups, and failures to guarantee or establish stable transitions and rule.

This is important since the presence of social conflict and civil war have also been integral to the exploitation of resources in Africa (Brisman et al, 2015). Markets in Europe and North America are there for the woods, minerals, diamonds and other resources used to fund territorial contests and internecine struggles. Instability can be good for business even if disastrous for the local people. From the point of view of the final consumer, what counts is the commodity, not the blood that went into its production. The 'heart of darkness', the novel idea of Joseph Conrad, still influences Western thinking and perceptions. The land is unknown and mysterious, its inhabitants foreign in spirit and ways, the continent a place where famine and danger are rampant (yet entirely socially constructed). It is a place to 'take from'.

The colonial project also manifests in other ways. In Amazonia, the land is presumed 'there for the taking' on the part of the unscrupulous, the corrupt and the ruthless. Consistent with the general pattern of environmental injustice, it is the most vulnerable who are likely to suffer from both takeover of land and radical alterations to existing land uses (Boekhout van Solinge, 2010; Boekhout van Solinge and Kuijpers, 2013; Borras et al, 2013). To some degree, in some places such endeavour is tacitly if not explicitly supported by central governments. Illegal logging, land grabs, modification of environments to plant commercial 'flex crops', illegal mining and so on are based on violence. But the violence is 'out there' not in the urban centres and the loungerooms of the world citizen. The same occurs in Central America, where in Honduras dissent and activism are met with killing and silencing; their brothers and sisters in the Philippines experiencing a similar fate (Global Witness, 2017, 2019). In many places around the globe where minority or Indigenous peoples live, oil, timber, plants and minerals are extracted in ways that devastate local ecosystems and destroy traditional cultures and livelihoods (Tekayak, 2016; Goyes et al, 2017; Mol, 2017; Goyes, 2019). And lives are lost.

Indeed, the history of the modern world is based precisely upon resource extraction and conflicts over natural resources, as seen in the processes of colonisation, a phenomenon that has affected many different Indigenous peoples in places such as South America, North America and Australasia, as well as the native inhabitants of Africa, Asia and beyond (White, 2011; Tekayak, 2016; Goyes, 2019). In countries such as Australia, Indigenous territories were considered frontier lands that were unowned, underutilised and therefore open to exploitation. The prior ownership rights, interests and knowledge of Indigenous inhabitants were treated as irrelevant by the European invaders. Environmental victimisation of this sort is central to dispossession and maltreatment of Indigenous peoples across many continents and over a period of several centuries. Who is most negatively affected by resource colonisation is partly a function of what can be exploited, where it is located, and how much resistance is likely to be encountered. As indicated, this is not just a thing of the past; it describes the present as well.

The universalisation of the capitalist mode of production is not only an assault on the relationship between 'country' and Indigenous people (in part due to the privatisation of land as well as the intrusions on to their land). It also undermines basic ecological requirements for sustainable human–environment relations:

> The diversity of Native cultures and kinds of social organizations which developed through time represent a high degree of social/political complexity and are varied according to the demands and necessities of the environment. For example, American Indian nations organized at the band level of social/political development have used effective strategies to take advantage of marginal habitats such as the Arctic and deserts of the Americas where resources are limited. (Robyn, 2002: 198–9)

Importantly, such systems are usually decentralised, communal and self-reliant: 'These societies live closely with and depend on the life contained in that particular ecosystem. This way of living enabled Indigenous communities to live for thousands of years in continuous sustainability' (Robyn, 2002: 199). Furthermore, such methods and modes of living do not contribute to global processes, such as climate change; the environmental footprint is limited and appropriate to scale.

Disconnect of production and consumption

The exploitation of environments and humans occurs in a relative social and geographical vacuum for those not directly affected. Those who ought to know are shielded from knowing due to the disconnect between production and consumption (O'Brien, 2008). This is evident in the furore over 'fast fashion'. The issues are dramatic and dire. Major European fashion houses premise their sales model on rapid turnover of styles and stock. To facilitate this, they commission external providers, for example, workers in villages in India, to prepare clothing materials using a variety of toxic and highly polluting processes. Customers buy cheaply and frequently. Local communities suffer greatly and persistently. Without recent media coverage, no one would be the wiser.

Contributions to global warming are disguised and distorted by similar processes of disconnect. For example, research into the association between per capita carbon dioxide emissions and exports to the US examined the relationship between per capita carbon dioxide emissions and exports for 169 countries (Stretesky and Lynch, 2009). The findings of the study indicated that US consumption practices have important implications for world production of carbon dioxide, and that preventing environmental harm arising from such pollution will require significant efforts to reduce emissions abroad as well as within the US. To put it differently, while American consumers thought that their carbon emissions were, relatively speaking, less than that outside the US, it was their importation of goods produced elsewhere that increased the global emissions substantially.

A similar observation is made by the United Nations Environment Programme which points out that: 'Consumption-based emission estimates, also known as a carbon footprint, that adjust the standard territorial emissions for imports and exports, provide policymakers with a deeper insight into the role of consumption, trade and the interconnectedness of countries' (UNEP, 2019: xv). It was found that the net flow of embodied carbon is from developing to developed countries. Thus, even as developed countries reduce their territorial emissions this effect is being partially offset by importing embodied carbon, implying for example that EU per capita emissions are higher than Chinese when consumption-based emissions are included. According to the UNEP (2019), the US has the highest per capita 'territorial' and 'territorial' plus 'consumption' carbon dioxide emissions.

Not only is 'dirty' production externalised to non-metropole countries, but these are also the places most likely to carry out a wide range of other extraction activities, including mining, logging, fishing and harvesting of wild animals (such as pangolin, turtles and parrots) (Goyes, 2019; Zabyelina and van Uhm, 2020). New technologies, such as smartphones, also require new components, and thus mining of rare earth materials (in particular, lithium) has boomed in places such as the 'remote' mountains of Peru.

This search for increasingly scarce natural resources is taking companies to new frontiers of extraction. This is seen, for instance, in regard to mineral and gas exploration and technical exploitation, carrying with it obvious environmental risks. For instance, there are hazards and dangers associated with activities such as drilling in deep offshore locations (as evidenced by the demise of the BP oil rig in the Gulf of Mexico); that is, new methods of extraction carry with them new dangers and new potential harms (Bradshaw, 2015). Second, the more remote and marginal the areas that are exploited, and the more reliant on mining those communities become for their local economy, the less likely that there will be adequate regulation of mining activities (Zabyelina and van Uhm, 2020). In either case, issues pertaining to extensive production of greenhouse gas emissions remain of major concern.

Disconnect of consumption and waste

As extensive work on specific incidents and patterns of victimisation demonstrates, some people are more likely to be disadvantaged by environmental problems than others. This is evident with respect to the location of toxic waste dumps, extreme air pollution, chemical accidents, access to safe clean drinking water and so on (Bisschop, 2015; Brisman et al, 2018). It is the poor and disadvantaged who suffer disproportionately from such environmental inequalities, regardless of geographical location. Moreover, it is these communities that also suffer most from the extraction of natural resources.

The shifting of waste and contamination to so-called third world countries (of which 'fast fashion' is the latest contributor) has long been a central concern of green criminology (White and Heckenberg, 2014; Bisschop, 2015). It represents not only the 'disappearance' of waste materials and liquids from the metropole countries, but the perpetuation of environmental racism on a global scale. From Nigeria to China, Vietnam to Somalia, the surreptitious transfer of hazardous waste has done extensive damage to human and ecological health wherever it has occurred. The sheer arrogance of the trafficking perpetrator has been matched by the audacious ignorance of the mass consumer. Again, an instance of 'out of sight, out of mind'.

This extends to the unclaimed spaces of the planetary 'commons' as well. Oceans have become communal sewers for industry and urbanity. Five huge ocean gyres offer a site for congregation of vast amounts of plastic and other waste, while microplastics litter the ocean floor and permeate the water environs. This is space that is both common and 'not ours'. No one is held responsible, and no one is charged with cleaning up the catastrophic mess. Meanwhile, up above, near-Earth space is filling up with junk and more junk, as satellites go past their use-by date and every billionaire and their dog races into the outer reaches of the planet. Remote these places might be, but how they are treated affect everyone, everywhere.

Regardless of land ownership, shared commons or national interests, the production of global environmental harm is partly determined through complex processes of transference (White and Heckenberg, 2014). In other words, regardless of origin, harm moves from one place to another.

The transformation of environments, and the interplay between water, air and land, means that risk and harm have to be viewed in dynamic rather than fixed terms. It may originate in a specific location, but due to natural processes of water and air movement and flow, environmental harm can spread to other parts of a city, region, country or continent. A localised problem thus contains the seeds of a global dilemma.

Environmental harm – such as dioxins in water – is both temporal and spatial in nature. That is, the harm itself actually moves across time and space, covering wide areas and with long-lasting effects. Moreover, toxins accumulate over time. In other words, there is a cumulative impact on waterways and aquatic life, and small amounts of poison may eventually lead to great concentrations of toxicity in fish and other living creatures of the water, with major social consequences for fishers and human consumers of fish (White, 2008). In the context of wider climatic changes affecting ocean temperatures and thereby the creatures of the sea, water pollution is yet another contributor to human misery and the increasingly desperate scramble for survival.

Conclusion

Viewed from space, the world is a wonderous, circumscribed place. It is made up of water, land and air. It is home to millions of species. It features rivers and mountains, forests and glaciers. It teems with life.

Yet, the Earth, our home, is under threat. The biggest of these threats are climate change and the diminishment of biodiversity. These are intertwined in complex ways, but resilience in the face of the former depends on the abundance of the latter. But both these trends are accelerating, leading to increased social dislocation and conflict, and even potential collapse of civilisation.

Much of the destructive activity is targeted at and especially affects those living in so-called remote and rural parts of the globe. This is what makes it of central concern to rural criminology as the field continues to expand its conceptual reach and topical scope. As this chapter has discussed, the geographical location of environmental vandalism plays no small part in why and how that vandalism occurs. This stems from the vulnerability of the people so victimised and the fragility yet richness of the environments within which they live. It also relates to the relative invisibility, even though they live in plain sight, of those subject to exploitation by the powerful.

Issues of visibility and value are intertwined. The othering of the marginalised and dispossessed is indispensable to global profits. Securing advantage and placating consumers through exploitative practices is self-fulfilling to the detriment of all else. The result is the demise of both environment and humanity.

References

Akella, A.S. and Cannon, J.B. (2004) *Strengthening the Weakest Links: Strategies for Improving the Enforcement of Environmental Laws Globally*, Washington, DC: Center for Conservation and Government.

Arroyo-Quiroz, A. and Wyatt, T. (eds) (2018) *Green Crime in Mexico: A Collection of Case Studies*, London: Palgrave Macmillan.

Baatz, C. (2013) 'Responsibility for the past? Some thoughts on compensating those vulnerable to climate change in developing countries', *Ethics, Policy and Environment*, 16(1): 94–110.

Bisschop, L. (2015) *Governance of the Illegal Trade in E-Waste and Tropical Timber: Case Studies on Transnational Environmental Crime*, Farnham Ashgate.

Boekhout van Solinge, T. (2010) 'Equatorial deforestation as a harmful practice and a criminological issue', in R. White (ed) *Global Environmental Harm: Criminological Perspectives*, Cullompton: Willan, pp 20–36.

Boekhout van Solinge, T. and Kuijpers, K. (2013) 'The Amazon rainforest: a green criminological perspective', in N. South and A. Brisman (eds) *Routledge International Handbook of Green Criminology*, New York: Routledge, pp 199–213.

Bokat-Lindell, S. (2021) 'Where is Biden's climate change "revolution"?', *New York Times*, 22 July. Available from: https://www.nytimes.com/2021/07/22/opinion/biden-climate-change.html [Accessed 6 March 2022].

Borras, S.M. Jr, Franco, J.C. and Wang, C. (2013) 'The challenge of global governance of land grabbing: changing international agricultural context and competing political views and strategies', *Globalizations*, 10(1): 161–79.

Bradshaw, E.A. (2015) '"Obviously, we're all oil industry": the criminogenic structure of the offshore oil industry', *Theoretical Criminology*, 19(3): 376–95.

Brisman, A., South, N. and White, R. (eds) (2015) *Environmental Crime and Social Conflict: Contemporary and Emerging Issues*, Farnham: Ashgate.

Brisman, A., McClanahan, B., South, N. and Walters, R. (2018) *Water, Crime and Security in the 21st Century: Too Dirty, Too Little, Too Much*, London: Palgrave.

Bulkeley, H. and Newell, P. (2010) *Governing Climate Change*, Abingdon: Routledge.

Cao, N. (2017) *Timber Trafficking in Vietnam: Crime, Security and the Environment*, Cham: Palgrave Macmillan.

Gedicks, A. (2005) 'Resource wars against native peoples', in R. Bullard (ed) *The Quest for Environmental Justice: Human Rights and the Politics of Pollution*, San Francisco: Sierra Club Books, pp 168–87.

Global Witness (2017) *Honduras: The Deadliest Country in the World for Environmental Activism*, London: Global Witness. Available from: https://www.globalwitness.org/en/campaigns/environmental-activists/honduras-deadliest-country-world-environmental-activism/ [Accessed 6 March 2022].

Global Witness (2019) *Defending the Philippines: How Broken Promises Are Leaving Land and Environmental Defenders at the Mercy of Business at All Costs,* London: Global Witness. Available from: https://www.globalwitness.org/en/campaigns/environmental-activists/defending-philippines/ [Accessed 6 March 2022].

Goyes, D.R. (2019) *Southern Green Criminology: A Science to End Ecological Discrimination,* Bingley: Emerald.

Goyes, D.R., Mol, H., Brisman, A. and South, N. (2017) *Environmental Crime in Latin America: The Theft of Nature and the Poisoning of the Land,* London: Palgrave.

Heede, R. (2014) 'Tracing anthropogenic carbon dioxide and methane emissions to fossil fuel and cement producers, 1854–2010', *Climate Change,* 122(1/2): 229–41.

Heydon, J. (2020) *Sustainable Development as Environmental Harm: Rights, Regulation, and Injustice in the Canadian Oil Sands,* New York: Routledge.

Higgins, P. (2012) *Earth Is Our Business: Changing the Rules of the Game,* London: Shepheard-Walwyn.

Higgins, P., Short, D. and South, N. (2013) 'Protecting the planet: a proposal for a law of ecocide', *Crime, Law and Social Change,* 59(3): 251–66.

IPBES (Intergovernmental Science-Policy Platform on Biodiversity and Ecosystem Services) (2019) *The IPBES Global Assessment Report on Biodiversity and Ecosystem Services,* Paris: IPBES. Available from: https://www.ipbes.net/global-assessment [Accessed 6 March 2022].

IPCC (Intergovernmental Panel on Climate Change) (2013) *Working Group I Contribution to the IPCC Fifth Assessment Report Climate Change 2013: The Physical Science Basis, Summary for Policymakers,* Geneva: IPCC. Available from: https://www.ipcc.ch/site/assets/uploads/2018/02/WG1AR5_SPM_FINAL.pdf [Accessed 6 March 2022].

IPCC (Intergovernmental Panel on Climate Change) (2014) *Climate Change 2014 Synthesis Report, Summary for Policymakers,* Geneva: IPCC. Available from: https://www.ipcc.ch/site/assets/uploads/2018/02/AR5_SYR_FINAL_SPM.pdf [Accessed 6 March 2022].

IPCC (Intergovernmental Panel on Climate Change) (2018) *Special Report: Global Warming of 1.5°C, Summary for Policymakers,* Geneva: IPCC. Available from: https://www.ipcc.ch/sr15/chapter/spm/ [Accessed 6 March 2022].

IPCC (Intergovernmental Panel on Climate Change) (2021) *Climate Change 2021: The Physical Basis,* Geneva: IPCC. Available from: https://www.ipcc.ch/report/sixth-assessment-report-working-group-i/ [Accessed 6 March 2022].

Klare, M.T. (2012) *The Race for What's Left: The Global Scramble for the World's Last Resources,* New York: Metropolitan Books.

Kramer, R.C. (2020) *Carbon Criminals, Climate Crimes*, New Brunswick, NJ: Rutgers University Press.

Lenin, V.I. (1917) *Imperialism: The Highest Stage of Capitalism*, Moscow: Progress.

Mol, H. (2017) *The Politics of Palm Oil Harm: A Green Criminological Perspective*, Cham: Palgrave Macmillan.

Morgan, E. and Long, S. (2020) 'Coronavirus economic recovery committee looks set to push Australia towards a gas-fired future', *ABC New Analysis*, 12 May. Available from: https://www.abc.net.au/news/2020-05-13/coronavirus-recovery-to-push-australia-towards-gas-future/12239978 [Accessed 6 March 2022].

Morin, B. (2020) 'Canada at "tipping point" over Wet'suwet'en land dispute', *Aljazeera*, 22 February. Available from: https://www.aljazeera.com/news/2020/2/21/canada-at-tipping-point-over-wetsuweten-land-dispute [Accessed 6 March 2022].

O'Brien, M. (2008) 'Criminal degradation of consumer culture', in R. Sollund (ed) *Global Harms: Ecological Crime and Speciesism*, New York: Nova Science, pp 35–50.

O'Malley, N., Shields, B. and Crowe, D. (2020) ' "Sacrificial canary": Fiji warns Australia not to let Pacific sink', *Sydney Morning Herald*, 11 December. Available from: https://www.smh.com.au/environment/climate-change/sacrificial-canary-fiji-warns-australia-not-to-let-pacific-sink-20201211-p56mtv.html [Accessed 6 March 2022].

Portner, H., Scholes, R. et al (2021) *IPBES-IPCC Co-sponsored Workshop Report on Biodiversity and Climate Change*, Paris: IPBES, 24 June. Available from: https://zenodo.org/record/5101133#.YiSky5anyUk [Accessed 28 August 2021].

Robyn, L. (2002) 'Indigenous knowledge and technology', *American Indian Quarterly*, 26(2): 198–220.

Schlosberg, D. (2007) *Defining Environmental Justice: Theories, Movements, and Nature*, Oxford: Oxford University Press.

Shiva, V. (2008) *Soil Not Oil: Environmental Justice in an Age of Climate Crisis*, Brooklyn, NY: South End Press.

Smandych, R. and Kueneman, R. (2010) 'The Canadian-Alberta tar sands: a case study of state-corporate environmental crime', in R. White (ed) *Global Environmental Harm: Criminological Perspectives*, Cullompton: Willan, pp 87–109.

Stretesky, P. and Lynch, M. (2009) 'A cross-national study of the association between per capita carbon dioxide emissions and exports to the United States', *Social Science Research*, 38(1): 239–50.

Tekayak, D. (2016) 'Protecting earth rights and the rights of indigenous peoples: towards an international crime of ecocide', *Fourth World Journal*, 14(2): 5–13.

UNEP (United Nations Environment Programme) (2019) *Emissions Gap Report 2019*, Geneva: UNEP. Available from: https://www.unep.org/resour ces/emissions-gap-report-2019 [Accessed 6 March 2022].

UNHRC (United Nations Human Rights Council) (2019) *Climate Change and Poverty: Report of the Special Rapporteur on Extreme Poverty and Human Rights*, A/HRC/41/39, 24 June–12 July 2019, Agenda item 3. Available from: https://www.ohchr.org/EN/HRBodies/HRC/RegularSessions/ Session41/Documents/A_HRC_41_39.docx [Accessed 6 March 2022].

van der Velden, J. and White, R. (2021) *The Extinction Curve: Growth and Globalisation in the Climate Endgame*, Bingley: Emerald.

White, R. (2008) *Crimes Against Nature: Environmental Criminology and Ecological Justice*, Cullompton: Willan.

White, R. (2011) *Transnational Environmental Crime: Toward an Eco-global Criminology*, Abingdon: Routledge.

White, R. (2018a) 'Ecocide and the carbon crimes of the powerful', *University of Tasmania Law Review*, 37(2): 95–115.

White, R. (2018b) *Climate Change Criminology*, Bristol: Bristol University Press.

White, R. (2018c) 'Ecocentrism and criminal justice', *Theoretical Criminology*, 22(3): 342–62.

White, R. and Heckenberg, D. (2014) *Green Criminology: An Introduction to the Study of Environmental Harm*, Abingdon: Routledge.

Whyte, D. (2020) *Ecocide: Kill the Corporation Before It Kills Us*, Manchester: Manchester University Press.

WMO (World Meteorological Organization) (2020a) *WMO Provisional Statement on the State of the Global Climate in 2019*, Geneva: WMO. Available from: https://library.wmo.int/index.php?lvl=notice_display&id=21626#. YiSqCpanyUk [Accessed 6 March 2022].

WMO (World Meteorological Organization) (2020b) *State of the Global Climate 2020*, Geneva: WMO. Available from: https://public.wmo.int/en/ our-mandate/climate/wmo-statement-state-of-global-climate [Accessed 6 March 2022].

Zabyelina, Y. and van Uhm, D. (eds) (2020) *Illegal Mining: Organized Crime, Corruption, and Ecocide in a Resource-Scarce World*, Cham: Palgrave Macmillan.

8

Critical Perspectives on Rural Policing in Times of Change: Cops, Communication and Context

Andrew Wooff

Introduction

Rural environments remain under-represented in the criminological and policing literature, though there is a significant emerging scholarship in this area (see, for example, recent books by Mawby and Yarwood, 2011; Donnermeyer, 2016; Harkness, 2020; numerous special journal issues; and the formation of the Division of Rural Criminology within the American Society of Criminology and the International Society for the Study of Rural Crime).

While much of the recent focus has been on the spatial complexities and tactics required to police rural spaces (Harkness, 2020), far less consideration has been given to the conceptualisation of 'the rural' and the impact of large-scale police reform on the relationships between the police and community. Much has been written about the complexities of understanding 'the rural' and 'rurality' more generally, yet theorising the spatiality of rural locations remains relatively absent (Wooff, 2016, 2017).

Drawing on evidence from two rural case studies, this chapter seeks to add to debates in this area by considering the interaction and relationships between the police, rural communities and key stakeholders in rural Scotland against the backdrop of substantial police organisational change. Considering established understanding of the importance of local knowledge, context and communication in rural policing, this chapter will utilise theoretical insights by Halfacree (2006) on the ways rural communities are represented and by Terpstra et al (2019) on the impact of 'abstract' policing, to argue that police–community relationships are of key importance when considering trust and confidence in the police. Finally, the chapter will draw on emerging findings of the impact of COVID-19 on these relationships and consider the implications for rural policing research, policy and practice.

Theorising rural spaces

The relationships between the police, key stakeholders and rural communities is important for both enhancing trust and preventing crime through partnership working. With society changing rapidly, consideration of the critical and conceptual framing of rural policing is imperative. The concept of the 'rural idyll' is important for considering policing in rural locations. Rural representations are developed through the staging of different performances; both in the ways that the rural is represented for tourists and visitors through representations in text and performance, and as Woods (2010: 837) highlights, in the 'less-staged manner in the everyday inactions of people who live and/ or work in the countryside'. This everyday enaction – 'performance' – of the everyday routine of those in both communities plays a large part in the lived experience of those living and working in rural communities (Halfacree, 2006). For the police, this is an important consideration because understanding the way(s) that the rural is staged and performed can help shape interactions with the public. Importantly it can also elucidate what is important to that particular rural community and therefore what the police should focus their attention on.

However, as Halfacree (2006) highlights, representations of the rural only make up one aspect of the 'totality of rural space'. In order to fully consider the context of the 'rural' and police–community interactions, it is useful to also consider the other facets of rural space interact: rural localities; formal representations of the rural; and everyday lives of the rural.

This threefold model is based on Lefebvre's (1991 [1974]) understanding of spatiality, where spatial practices, representations of space and spaces of representations combine to form a three-part dialectic where space is perceived, conceived and lived. This model provides a useful basis for examining and conceptualising rural space because it allows for analysis at the local scale and provides a basis for contextualising the response of the police in rural Scotland. It allows for difference between rural communities to be considered and consideration of the impact of policing styles on different types of community. Conceptually, it enables us to consider rural space in a multifaceted and complex way, beyond some of the monolithic representations of 'the rural'. Furthermore, when considering the ways in which police officers interact with communities, understanding rural space and rural policing styles is important (Wooff, 2017).

External factors are of key importance when considering the impact of rural policing on different communities. Policing in Scotland underwent a seismic shift in 2013 with the amalgamation of eight territorial regional police forces and two national organisations (Scottish Crime and Drug Enforcement Agency; Scottish Police Services Authority) in to a single organisation, Police Scotland (Fyfe, 2014). Although Police Scotland claimed that community policing lay at the heart of the new organisational structure, work has highlighted deficiencies in this claim (Henry et al, 2019). As Yarwood and Wooff (2016) observe, following the formation of a single police force in Scotland, there was a loss of local democratic accountability, keenly felt in rural locations. In particular, by centralising decision-making, as Fyfe (2014) notes, the distribution of power moved to the centre with a sense that Police Scotland reflected less of the local policing agenda rural communities had become accustomed to.

This organisational backdrop formed the basis of Terpstra et al's (2019) conceptualisation of the changing dynamic of policing across a number of countries. They argue that over recent years, both internally and externally, the police have 'become more at a distance, more impersonal and formal, less direct and more decontextualized' (Terpstra et al, 2019: 340). This is what they term the 'abstract police' and is typified by large-scale police reform, as witnessed in Scotland. Terpstra et al (2019) focus on the internal and external impacts of the shift to the abstract police who are less dependent on personal knowledge, which, they argue, has been replaced by 'system knowledge, framed within the logic and categorisation of computer data systems' (2019: 340). As rural scholars have described, relationships between police and communities are particularly important in rural locations where backup may be a long way away and where officers are often 'in and of the community', living and working in the same place (Yarwood, 2011; Fenwick, 2015; Wooff, 2015; Harris, 2020; Souhami, 2020). The notion of abstract policing, therefore, has potentially serious implications for rural police–community relationships, particularly in light of Halfacree's model and the importance of taking account of the rural locality and lives of the rural.

Drawing on both these theoretical strands, this chapter seeks to use data collected following the implementation of Police Scotland to examine the extent to which relationships between police, community and partners have altered and what that might highlight for policing in other rural contexts. Amalgamation and centralisation are happening across the world and, combined with recovery after COVID-19, it is important to think about the disproportionate impact these events have on rural communities. Taking account of the knowledge of the community that police officers utilise to make decisions and the network of partners involved in decision-making, this chapter draws on data collected in 2017–18, four years after the introduction of Police Scotland. This chapter is based on two case studies in rural Scotland encompassing different 'representations of the rural', and it will focus on the way(s) the impact of centralisation on knowledge of the communities and perceptions of partners and communities on policing post-implementation of Police Scotland. The chapter will conclude by highlighting lessons learned in Scotland that may be applicable to other broader conceptualisations of policing rural communities.

Sketching the rural context: two contrasting case studies in rural Scotland

Funded research was carried out in 2017–18 and undertaken in two contrasting rural Police Scotland local policing areas. The project, entitled 'Rural Policing in Scotland: Measuring and Improving Public Confidence', sought to understand the experiences of police–community–partner relationships following the introduction of Police Scotland. Undertaking the study four years after the introduction of Police Scotland allowed the project team to take account of the 'bedding in' of organisational change and examine whether the outcome of the changes had adversely impacted policing in two different rural case study locations. The project was designed in conjunction with a divisional commander who had recently been appointed to a large rural policing area, having previously been a commander in a city. The team identified some challenges particularly around loss of trust and confidence in the police in some rural communities, and this study sought to explore this and critically assess the extent to which policing styles and understandings of rural contexts might impact on police–community relationships.

Explored, in particular, was the loss of localism and the impact this had on trust and confidence in the police in two rural communities. Two case studies were selected based on contrasting socio-demographic characteristics and scales of rurality: one with high socio-economic deprivation, classed as a small rural town (denoted by CS1); the other with socio-economic deprivation and classed as remote rural (denoted by CS2). This allowed for an understanding of the differences in public confidence in different types of rural community and across a range of stakeholders. The study makes use of a qualitative methodology, involving 'ride-alongs' with local community police officers (n = 20 hours) and focus groups with community members (n = 8). Semi-structured interviews were conducted with police officers and community stakeholders (n = 8). The data was transcribed and systematically analysed by the researchers, allowing themes to develop. The remainder of this chapter will explore some of the impact of centralisation of policing on relationships between police and community and partners in the case study locations, the 'rural space' in its three dimensions, and the degree to which abstract policing is a useful conceptualisation of experiences brought about by Police Scotland in rural Scotland.

Knowing the community: the importance of communication in rural relationships

Many rural communities project an image, often imagined, about what is important. Notwithstanding the considerable scholarship that highlights that 'the rural' is made up of many complex groups, where power and hiddenness, marginalisation and subordination make up the lived experience of many people living in rural communities (for example Bell, 2006; Short, 2006; Neal and Walters, 2008), rural communities often also prominently display representations about what is important to them.

With the introduction of Police Scotland and the centralisation of many of the services, including police officers being moved around divisions more readily and out of community-facing roles, there was a feeling in both case study locations that it was important for police officers to be able to 'speak the language' in order to connect with the community. Police officers knowing the community and vice versa was identified as key and interestingly this was articulated by police officers by talking about 'local customs'.

As one police officer described it, "understanding the local customs and culture enables you as a cop to tap in to the important information" (PC, CS2). This theme was particularly apparent in the remote rural location, where most of the officers had lived in the location for a substantial amount of time and therefore felt able to connect with people and 'speak their language':

'I'll speak at them at their level, and I don't mean talk down to them. I mean, their level. We've got a real, [name of person], I can walk into that house and among a load of people going mental, and I can speak to them so they trust and understand what I'm saying. But by the same token you go and speak to maybe some nice old man or woman who's never seen the Police in their life, you don't go in and say, right who broke in. It's all about speaking their language, you know people when you live in a small place and how to speak to them.' (PC, CS1)

Speaking the language can mean a number of different things in different contexts, but in the case of policing in this rural community, it meant 'tapping into' the everyday lives of those living here and being able to speak to people on their level and with the appropriate language. This is knowledge built up over time, knowing the lives of those in the community and what is appropriate for which context. This officer (PC, CS1) highlights the importance of knowing community members and using different approaches with different people. In a sense, by applying his knowledge of the intersection between the rural locality and the lives of those that live in the case study, this officer decides on the best approach to communication with the particular community member.

Communication, therefore, appeared at the heart of much of the discussion around the context of rural policing in the case study locations. This manifests itself in a number of ways, both at the structural and personal level with the concept of communication from and with local police an ongoing reference point when discussing trust and confidence with participants. This notion of trust and confidence in the police being founded on communication between the police and the public is supported in the wider academic literature with authors such as Rosenbaum and Lawrence (2017) arguing that effective police engagement with the public on a daily basis is at the heart of delivering good policing at the local level. Tyler and Fagan (2008: 254) also discuss the importance of the 'quality of police performance' – that is, the manner in which these engagements take place can be associated with the wider concepts of procedural justice in terms of how the characteristics of those interactions shape the public's confidence and trust of the police and, importantly, their willingness to obey the law. It is through the work of authors such as Sunshine and Tyler (2003), Bottoms and Tankebe (2012) and Jackson et al (2012) that we have become aware of the importance not only of police public encounters but how these encounters have been perceived by the public. Communication is a key part of this, particularly the way the police communicate with members of the community.

Beyond the police communicating at the 'right level', the importance of effective communication was acknowledged by frontline police officers and their senior managers who took part in this project:

> 'Communication is 95% of this job ... because as long as you can talk ... you need to speak to people on their level, that's the easiest way ... you need to be able to go in and say, find out what's going on, don't patronise them. And I think that's something that only comes, perhaps, with experience.' (Sergeant, CS1)

This is particularly true when engaging with remote rural communities, where a bad encounter was considered to have a disproportionately negative impact on police–community relationships:

> 'One thing I've noticed moving here from [nearby large town], everyone talks and if something doesn't pan out as well as it might, you know an arrest or something, everyone in the town knows about it. So we need to be more careful here about how we get perceived.' (PC, CS2)

They explain that incidents which, from a policing perspective are relatively low key, can in rural communities undermine trust in the organisation very quickly:

'We had one case, like it was nothing really on the face of it, low-level antisocial behaviour with young people hanging about in [name of street], but there was a perception in the community that we weren't dealing with it and I was surprised by the anger towards the police.' (PC, CS2)

While communication is important in these examples, taking the rural context into account is also crucial (Wooff, 2015), where it is argued that the police need to have a clear understanding of the context of the community in order to effectively engage and communicate. Beyond the physical context, though, an interesting dimension to emerge in CS1 related to the local dialect. Speaking the 'local way', with the local accent, was something which the police highlighted as an issue in this case study.

Once Police Scotland was introduced in 2013, officers tended to be more routinely moved between divisions and roles. Being able to speak the local dialect was something used by members of the rural case study as a proxy to gauge how local the officer was believed to be. By extension, this was linked to the officer's perceived competency and therefore perceptions of how effective they would be at understanding and resolving issues in the local community:

M1:   We had a Glaswegian community cop, well I think that's where he was from, come to the class and he said didn't understand what we were saying because the lilt [sic] here
        [Laughter]
M2:   That's it eh, when we asked him, said he'd just been moved here
M1:   So how's he going to know the issues here. (FG1, CS1)

The distinctive local accent ('lilt') in CS1 was highlighted in this quote as an important marker of local knowledge and understanding of the community. The accent of the police officer here represents something different, 'an incomer', to this rural community. This symbolised a lack of understanding of the local context deemed to be so important by members of this case study. The insider/outsider dichotomy, represented by this form of the rural, was reinforced in another interview when the participant quipped "it can take 50 years to be considered a local" (CS1).

This is significant in the context of the totality of rural space because, as Halfacree (2006) argues, there are clear links between the rural locality, representations of the rural and the lives of those living in those community. If the perception is that police officers do not have the intricate knowledge of the rural locality or the lives of those in these communities, then they are only getting a partial view of those rural spaces. As Police Scotland as an organisation has centralised services, the role of the individual officer becomes even more important for bridging the perceived (and in some cases actual) distance between the organisation and the rural communities.

The next section will explore the ways that the practical and perceived impacts of the structural changes instigated by Police Scotland decontextualised and lessened the ability to make local decisions. This impacted on partners, community members and local police officers, leading to discussions around the importance of local knowledge.

Understanding the rural locality: the importance of local knowledge in an era of abstract policing

The introduction of Police Scotland arguably impacted on the policing of rural space and rural communities in a more fundamental way, with Terpstra et al (2019) arguing that policing organisations have become increasingly 'abstract' from communities, line managers and external partner agencies. They argue that although officers can still have a local focus, as outlined in the community policing focus, this has increasingly become decontextualised with a focus on centralised targets and decision-making. Terpstra et al (2019: 355) argue that the increasingly abstract nature of the police means that 'communities will feel the police are less accessible and will have less confidence that the police have a good understanding of local problems'. The decontextualisation associated with abstract policing in rural communities is particularly important given that the local context of rural communities, where Wooff (2015) argues for the importance of contextualised policing responses.

Findings from this study reinforce the importance for rural police–community relationships of understanding local context, local community focus and the impact national decisions can have on rural localities. Of importance to participants in this study, the centralisation of police control rooms was used as an exemplar of the impact of the removal of local decision-making on both police officers and community members living in the case study locations.

One of the outcomes of centralised control centres was the introduction of the 101 number, a centralised non-emergency 24-hour telephone line. Although it was meant to make contacting the police quicker and easier, reducing pressure on the 999 emergency system, rural participants noted that the introduction of this new telephone line had created some unintended consequences on their ability to access local officers:

'public confidence ... is down. It's gone down quite a bit and that comes from the 101 number, where they cannot get through. I cannot even get bloody through and I'm a cop.' (PC, CS1)

'I think it's the whole 101 thing and you know the whole centralisation that you phone up and they don't know who you are talking about or you know that kind of thing.' (Partner agency, CS2)

'I think when folk phoned [local police force] you felt you dealing with someone who lived in the area and was interested in this area, when you get through to a switchboard and you get the feeling, I'm talking to somebody goodness knows where, it's just not quite the same.' (Teacher, CS1)

These quotes underline the feeling that by replacing a local contact number with a national, non-specific control room, the rural locality is perceived to be less of a concern to the organisation. The police are seen as more abstract and removed, and this impacts on the lives of those in rural communities in both a lived way and in symbolic ways. In terms of the lived experience of having centralised, remote call centres, rural police officers regularly noted the impact on their job. With a lack of knowledge of the local geography, dispatchers were making resourcing decisions that seemed nonsensical to those working in the remote rural parts of the case studies:

'Police Scotland obviously sat down with a map and started doing, this is where the call volume is, but that is not the whole picture. And that is a bug bear of mine, because they're not taking into account the geography. It looks a short distance as the crow flies, but they had me the other day driving all over the countryside not realising how long it takes to drive 20 miles on these roads. Never used to be like this.' (Sgt, CS1)

This highlights what Terpstra et al (2019: 343) call the 'abstractness of police in the changing internal relation', where local officers no longer know the dispatching teams by name and are concerned that knowledge of the rural locality has been lost. Not only does this impact on policing efficiency, but there are numerous accounts of poor decision-making by call centre staff abstracted from the local division to the centre of Police Scotland, some of which have had tragic consequences (see the report by HMICS, 2015 into a delayed response of police officers to a car accident in July 2015).

As Wooff (2015, 2016) has argued elsewhere, understanding the nature and context of local communities is a key part of being a rural police officer. The abstract nature of the 101 call centre means that there is a (perceived) loss of local knowledge of the lives of those living in rural environments. A key factor in being able to police rural environments effectively is using knowledge of local policing contexts. This importantly includes the relationships developed through living and working in rural communities (Yarwood and Mawby,

2011) and the application of 'softer' policing techniques (Wooff, 2017). The notion of being 'abstract' from the community impacts on this to a degree, where discretion and relationships are impacted when the police are less 'in and of the community' (Fenwick, 2015), even if that abstracted nature is more imagined than the reality of doing rural policing.

Rural policing often requires working and living in the community and being accessible outside of 'normal' working hours. Even since the introduction of Police Scotland and more abstract policing, there was a sense among policing participants that rural policing continues despite organisational challenges:

> 'Living and working in [name of town], well let's say you become known quickly that you're the local cop. They'll come and speak to me, because they know and that comes from just being local and being a known face. The same with the community council. They walk in, they know, there's continuity.' (Sergeant, CS2)

An inspector put it even more strongly, arguing that there is something fundamentally important and different in the way that policing in these contexts occurs, linked to living and working in the communities, with families and roots:

> 'It's an old, kind of principle, you know, we are the community and the community are us. That's what it should be like. Down here that's one of the strengths we've got, because of the job, if you're the police and you're still essentially being policed by and large by the same boys and girls that were being policed before Police Scotland. They're [police officers] people that stay in the communities. They're people that live there. Their families are connected. They've got roots there. You know, that hasn't changed. There's always been a pride, in the local officers here, that are from the region, brought up in the region. I live in the region, my family are committed to the region and I'm delivering this for and with the region.' (Inspector, CS1)

Much of the rural community policing happening in these case study locations broadly mirrors pre-Police Scotland policing, with local officers frequently living and working in the same community and having dual roles of being 'in and of the community'. The abstract policing conceptualised by Terpstra et al (2019) in this example appears to relate to the internal decision-making and structural impact of amalgamation rather than the experience of community police officers on the ground.

That is not to say that the impact of the structural reform has not impacted on the delivery of rural policing and the sense that, at least symbolically, the police are more remote than they were before Police Scotland. A number of community members highlighted that remote call centres did give worse service, with one participant in CS2 stating:

'[Y]ou ring somebody in Aberdeen or in Glasgow or somewhere, they haven't got a clue … I think the 101 doesn't give people that confidence that people [police officers] are going to come out straightaway.' (Community member, CS1)

Despite call centre handling times improving following the introduction of Police Scotland's 101 number, the removal of a locally accessible number to call gave the perception that these rural locations are less of a focus for local policing. Thus, it appears to be the symbolism of people calling an anonymous, unknown call centre located out of the region that serves as an ongoing reminder to community members that policing has become more abstracted and removed from the rural locality, rather than a reality always borne out of experience.

For external policing partners in these case studies, however, the internal organisational changes brought about by the introduction of Police Scotland have had an impact. That is to say that with the 'loss of local engagement activities' highlighted by Hail (2016), local partnerships have felt increasingly disconnected from the relevant decision-makers within Police Scotland. The loss of local orientation witnessed by the introduction of Police Scotland was a result of the organisational focus in the first few years being about ensuring national parity, decision-making, processes and flavour to policing. As others have highlighted (Fyfe and Scott, 2013; Fyfe, 2014; Hail, 2016; Henry et al, 2019; Terpstra et al, 2019), one of the impacts of moving to Police Scotland was less engagement activity in rural communities and a more enforcement-style policing. This, combined with financial cutbacks, strained existing partnership relationships across Scotland (Hail, 2016). This is something that was also clear in these rural case studies, where representatives of partner organisations highlighted how the introduction of Police Scotland had made local partnership working much more complicated:

'[It] can be very difficult with staff moving around and a focus on using the 101 number and not officers' direct numbers which they do not always share with partners … but the communication between Police Scotland and this office I would say is really bad.' (Partner, CS2)

In one case a partner highlighted how problematic the situation had become. As a children's reporter in a rural area, there is often a requirement to be able to get police representation at short notice, something this participant noted had become significantly more difficult since the introduction of Police Scotland:

'It used to be that I would know most of the Police Officers involved in our business and I would just be able to pick up the phone and say you know what about this. ... Nowadays I would say that that is almost non-existent and part of that is you can't even phone the Police. Sometimes it will be the case that when I'm preparing for a Children's Hearing I feel that we must have a Police presence to maintain order in the room and in the past I would have picked up the phone on the morning of the Hearing to the Duty Sergeant and said *I've got a Children's Hearing running today and I'm going to need a Police officer.* Nowadays, I would have no confidence that I would even be able to get the Duty Sergeant because if you phone 101 and ask for the Duty Sergeant they will say *well who is the Duty Sergeant, well I don't know who the Duty Sergeant is today, how would I possibly have that information?* This isn't a joke, we now write a letter and we walk it across the road to the Police Station and put it in the front counter.' (Partner, CS1)

The impact of increasingly abstract internal policing structures, therefore, appears to be affecting the partnership arrangements in rural communities. As has been explored in the rural literature, partner agencies are often more required to support the police in order to support the delivery of services (Wooff, 2015), but this often utilises informal networks where key people in one organisation know those in the other. Thus, even although the number of police officers has not reduced, and frontline officers have not therefore become any less 'abstract' in that sense, the internal machinations and organisational structural changes have essentially made police officers less easily contactable and identifiable. Alongside the obvious frustration around the local processes involved with partnership working, these challenges have also had the impact of making police officers and the organisation appear more abstract from partners. In rural communities this can have a more profound impact due to the challenges around service delivery in these contexts.

The next section of this chapter will bring together these findings, and discuss conceptually how rural space and abstract policing in rural communities are helpful ways to conceptualise rural communities, particularly as we look towards learning lessons from the policing of the COVID-19 pandemic.

Conceptualising rural space

The rural environment is an important space of analysis when considering rural policing. As an increasing body of work highlights, the policing of rural environments requires a distinctive set of skills. Not only are geographic distances a challenge for rural police officers, but there are often limited options for backup, support and specialist interventions (Yarwood and Cozens, 2004; Mawby and Yarwood, 2011; Slade, 2013; Wooff, 2015; Ruddell and Jones, 2020). Furthermore, as a result of the isolated nature of these communities, the role of police officers in these communities tends to be broad, where officers are expected to cover many other tasks than they would in urban communities. This emerges as a result of often living and working in the community, described as being both in and of the community, but also because officers frequently live and work in the community, and so are on hand to support and use their skills more readily than in other policing contexts. These observations have been made in a wide range of rural policing settings, but it is helpful to examine the extent to which they remain in place in the face of complete organisational change as was the case with the introduction of Police Scotland.

Understanding the totality of rural space as a complex interweaving of the locality, representations of the rural and the lives of those living in these communities (Halfacree, 2006) is important when thinking about the way that the police interact with rural communities. These rural spaces are not monolithic or uniform, and considering the complex intertwining of police–community relations helps elucidate the changing power dynamics in rural communities. Drawing on Halfacree's work alongside Terpstra et al's (2019) conceptualisation of 'abstract policing', this chapter has sought to highlight the way(s) that police–community relationships in two remote rural communities in Scotland were impacted by the once-in-a-generation reform of policing in Scotland.

Arguing that some of the familiar themes from the rural policing literature remained constant with the large-scale centralisation of policing in Scotland, the chapter has sought to highlight the degree to which elements of internal organisational change have impacted the totality of policing rural space. Evidence in this chapter highlights the importance of communication and local context and culture in maintaining trust in the police. It underlines the importance of police officers 'talking the talk' and being able to communicate in a way that the community felt was in keeping with the norms of the area. With the introduction of a more abstract organisational structure and footprint, where many police buildings have been sold off and officers therefore need to travel from centralised locations to rural policing beats, this chapter has shown that these changes have not gone unnoticed by members of community in the case study locations.

In particular, frustration among community members and partner agencies was almost universal at the introduction of the national 101 number. The frustration of the partners here was born out of the reality of trying to get police officers engaged in partnership processes where communication with

Police Scotland was less accessible because of the use of 'anonymous' call centres. In this sense Police Scotland has becoming increasingly abstract from partners. For members of the community, the issue was more symbolic. The introduction of the 101 non-emergency call system has improved response times, so for community members the frustration of 101 (in the main) was symbolised through a loss of localism and understanding of the local context rather than a lived reality of a poorer service.

The 'abstract nature' of policing here, then, is intimately related to the perception that there is a loss of policing the rural locality, leading to a greater distance between the community and partners and therefore a (perceived) loss of understanding by Police Scotland over the lives of those living in these communities. Simply put, the organisational development of Police Scotland has led to the internal structures being centralised, abstracted from these rural communities. This has led therefore to a policing service which is less equipped to deal with the local context and where local knowledge to inform police decision-making is less apparent. Centralisation appears to have had less of an impact on urban communities because most of the services being centralised (call centres, for example) have been moved to urban locations and the urban policing norm has not significantly changed. Thus, it tends to be rural communities that have lost elements of institutional knowledge that are important for policing effectively in rural space.

While this chapter has focused on two case study contexts in Scotland, it is of conceptual significance for the rural criminology subfield because the learning from Scotland can be considered in other contexts where policing centralisation is happening. As Ricciardelli (2018) notes, budgets are constrained across policing in different contexts; innovative learning and practice need to be shared. The formulation of Police Scotland has certainly saved money, with projected savings of £2.2 billion (US$3.12 billion) by 2026 (double the initial business case) over the existing policing structures (Police Scotland, 2020). The Netherlands, along with a number of other European countries, are also centralising policing structures (Fyfe et al, 2013) and this chapter highlights some of the significant implications for rural policing in this agenda, in particular around police–community relationships in rural locations and context-dependent policing that rural communities value (Wooff, 2015).

COVID-19 has also proven to have been a step change in the way that police and communities interact. Emerging work suggests that relationships between the police and community have been impacted by the draconian laws introduced globally in response to the pandemic (Reicher and Stott, 2020). As Nix et al (2021) demonstrate, however, public confidence in the police has been broadly maintained by those police organisations who applied the principles of procedural justice when enforcing COVID-19 restrictions and, importantly, maintained visible policing in communities. Emerging evidence in Scotland suggests that the pandemic has impacted on the physical visibility of police officers, with many spaces of police–community interaction (for example, community council or youth groups) unable to run in the pandemic (Wooff et al, forthcoming). Early findings from this study therefore suggest that COVID-19 has compounded the abstracted nature of policing in rural communities and will reinforce the challenges described in this chapter for rural police–community relationships. With the pandemic affecting countries across the globe, it is therefore vitally important to consider the impact of police–community relationships in rural locations.

Conclusion

Consideration of the critical and conceptual framing of rural policing is particularly important in the post-pandemic world. This chapter has sought to provide one way of framing the conceptual and theoretical challenges of large-scale organisational change. Bringing together Halfacree's theoretical model with understandings of 'abstract policing', this chapter has sought to highlight the complex intertwining of rural space (and all that it encompasses) with the organisational change that encompasses the rural policing backdrop in Scotland.

Understanding some of the complex interactions between the representations of these rural communities, how they have impacted on the rural locality and the everyday lives of people in these communities, helps to underline how broader organisational changes to policing in Scotland impacts disproportionately on those living rurally. Although based on the specific experiences in Scotland, there are important lessons to consider in other countries undertaking centralisation, particularly in a post-COVID-19 recovery. Understanding the community context is key for developing understandings of rural policing and social control in Scotland, because by taking account of this, legitimacy and procedural justice in the police can be maintained. In light of COVID-19, this is especially important.

References

Bell, D. (2006) 'Variations on the rural idyll', in P. Cloke, T. Marsden and P. Mooney (eds) *Handbook of Rural Studies*, London: Sage, pp 149–60.

Bottoms, A. and Tankebe, J. (2012) 'Criminology beyond procedural justice: a dialogic approach to legitimacy', *Journal of Criminal Law and Criminology*, 102(1): 119–70.

Donnermeyer, J.F. (ed) (2016) *The Routledge International Handbook of Rural Criminology*, Abingdon: Routledge.

Fenwick, T. (2015) 'Learning policing in rural spaces: "Covering 12 foot rooms with 8 foot carpets"', *Policing: A Journal of Policy and Practice*, 9(3): 234–41.

Fyfe, N. (2014) 'Observations on police reform in Scotland', *British Society of Criminology Newsletter*, 74: 8–12. Available from: http://britsoccrim.org/new/newdocs/bscn-74-2014_Fyfe.pdf [Accessed 6 March 2022].

Fyfe, N. and Scott, K. (2013) 'In search of sustainable policing? Creating a national police force in Scotland', in N. Fyfe, J. Terpstra and P. Tops (eds) *Comparative Perspectives on Contemporary Police Reform in Northern and Western Europe*, The Hague: Eleven International, pp 119–35.

Fyfe, N., Terpstra, J. and Tops, P. (2013) *Centralizing Forces? Comparative Perspectives on Contemporary Police Reform in Northern and Western Europe*, The Hague: Eleven International.

Hail, Y. (2016) 'Local policing in transition: examining the impacts and implications of police reform in Scotland', PhD thesis, Dundee: University of Dundee. Available from: https://discovery.dundee.ac.uk/en/studentTheses/local-policing-in-transition [Accessed 6 March 2022].

Halfacree, K. (2006) 'Rural space: constructing a three-fold architecture', in P. Cloke, T. Marsden and H. Mooney (eds), *Handbook of Rural Studies*, London: Sage, pp 44–62.

Harkness, A. (ed) (2020) *Rural Crime Prevention: Theory, Tactics and Techniques*, Abingdon: Routledge.

Harris, B. (2020) 'Social crime prevention: theory, community and the "rural idyll"', in A. Harkness (ed) *Rural Crime Prevention: Theory, Tactics and Techniques*, Abingdon: Routledge, pp 43–57.

Henry, A., Malik, A. and Aydın-Aitchison, A. (2019) 'Local governance in the new Police Scotland: renegotiating power, recognition and responsiveness', *European Journal of Criminology*, 16(5): 1–38.

HMICS (Her Majesty's Inspectorate of Constabulary in Scotland) (2015) *Independent Assurance Review Police Scotland: Call Handling Final Report*, Edinburgh: HMICS. Available from: https://www.hmics.scot/publications/independent-assurance-review-police-scotland-call-handling-final-report [Accessed 6 March 2022].

Jackson, J., Bradford, B., Hough, M., Myhill, A., Quinton, P. and Tyler, T. (2012) 'Why do people comply with the law? Legitimacy and the influence of legal institutions', *British Journal of Criminology*, 52(6): 1051–71.

Lefebvre, H. (1991) [1974] *The Production of Space*, trans D. Nicholson-Smith, Oxford: Basil Blackwell.

Mawby, R.I. and Yarwood, R. (2011) *Rural Policing and Policing the Rural: A Constable Countryside?*, Farnham: Ashgate.

Neal, S. and Walters, S. (2008) 'Rural be/longing and rural social organizations: conviviality and community-making in the English countryside', *Sociology*, 42(2): 279–97.

Nix, J., Ivanov, S. and Pickett, J.T. (2021) 'What does the public want police to do during pandemics? A national experiment', *Criminology and Public Policy*, 20(3): 545–71.

Police Scotland (2020) *Justice Sub-committee on Policing*, Edinburgh: Police Scotland.

Reicher, S. and Stott, C. (2020) 'On order and disorder during the COVID-19 pandemic', *British Journal of Social Psychology*, 59(3): 694–702.

Ricciardelli, R. (2018) '"Risk it out, risk it out": occupational and organizational stresses in rural policing', *Police Quarterly*, 21(4): 415–39.

Rosenbaum, D. and Lawrence, D. (2017) 'Teaching procedural justice and communication skills during police–community encounters: results of a randomized control trial with police recruits', *Journal of Experimental Criminology*, 13(3): 293–319.

Ruddell, R. and Jones, N.A. (2020) 'Policing the "middle of nowhere": officer working strategies in isolated communities', *Policing: A Journal of Policy and Practice*, 14(2): 414–27.

Short, B. (2006) 'Idyllic ruralities', in P. Cloke, T. Marsden and P. Mooney (eds) *Handbook of Rural Studies*, London: Sage, pp 133–48.

Slade, B. (2013) 'Professional learning in rural practice: a sociomaterial analysis', *Journal of Workplace Learning*, 25(2): 114–24.

Souhami, A. (2020) Understanding Police Work in the Remote Northern Isles of Scotland: The Extraordinary Ordinariness of Island Policing, Edinburgh School of Law Research Paper No 2020/17.

Sunshine, J. and Tyler, T.R. (2003) 'The role of procedural justice and legitimacy in shaping public support for policing', *Law and Society Review*, 37(3): 513–48.

Terpstra, J., Fyfe, N.R. and Salet, R. (2019) 'The abstract police: a conceptual exploration of unintended changes of police organisations', *The Police Journal: Theory, Practice and Principles*, 92(4): 339–59.

Tyler, T.R. and Fagan, J. (2008) 'Legitimacy and cooperation: why do people help the police fight crime in their communities?', *Ohio State Journal of Criminal Law*, 6(1): 231–75.

Woods, M. (2010) 'Performing rurality and practising rural geography', *Progress in Human Geography*, 34(6): 835–46.

Wooff, A. (2015) 'Relationships and responses: policing anti-social behaviour in rural Scotland', *Journal of Rural Studies*, 39: 287–95.

Wooff, A. (2016) 'The importance of context: understanding the nature of anti-social behaviour in rural Scotland', in J.F. Donnermeyer (ed) *International Handbook of Rural Criminology*, Abingdon: Routledge.

Wooff, A. (2017) '"Soft" policing in rural Scotland', *Policing: A Journal of Policy and Practice*, 11(2): 123–31.

Wooff, A., Hogan, S. and Tatnell, A. (forthcoming) *Rural Policing in the Pandemic: A Scottish Case Study*, Edinburgh: Scottish Institute of Policing Research.

Yarwood, R. (2011) 'Voluntary sector geographies, intraorganisational difference, and the professionalisation of volunteering: a study of land search and rescue organisations in New Zealand', *Environment and Planning C: Government and Policy*, 29(3): 457–72.

Yarwood, R. and Cozens, C. (2004) 'Constable countryside? Policing perspectives on rural Britain', in L. Holloway and M. Kneafsey (eds) *Geographies of Rural Cultures and Societies*, Aldershot: Ashgate, pp 145–72.

Yarwood, R. and Mawby, R.I. (2011) 'W(h)ither rural policing? An afterword', in R.I. Mawby and R. Yarwood (eds) *Rural Policing and Policing the Rural: A Constable Countryside?*, Farnham: Ashgate, pp 217–21.

Yarwood, R. and Wooff, A. (2016) 'Policing the countryside in a devolving United Kingdom', in J.F. Donnermeyer (ed) *International Handbook of Rural Criminology*, Abingdon: Routledge, pp 375–86.

9

Rural Policing: Spaces of Coherence and Fragmentation

Susanne Stenbacka

Introduction

Several researchers engaged in rural areas as a site for crime and policing have stated that this combination of the themes of coherence and fragmentation has not undergone as careful investigation as many other social or economic processes prevalent in the rural (Hayward, 2012; Mawby and Yarwood, 2016). Those who usually provide society with knowledge of rural living conditions – often geographers or sociologists – have to a lesser extent paid attention to rural localities and contemporary transformation in relation to crime and policing. Geographers have focused more upon who are being 'policed' and how this impacts the rural society, while criminologists have focused upon those who are doing the 'policing', such as the police themselves (Mawby and Yarwood, 2016: 1).

What is needed, then, is increased knowledge on how the diversity of rural actors – and their social and material embeddedness – interrelate and form a basis for safety and security in rural areas. This volume, aimed at contributing to theoretical understandings and addressing conceptual challenges facing the research field, in the intersection of rurality and criminology studies, provides an appropriate forum to present an analytical framework with a potential to emphasising rurality and the police–society link. Such an intention involves a need for a relational approach, since any and all spaces or places are 'precarious achievements made up of relations between multiple entities' (Anderson, 2008: 230).

This chapter has two main aims: to scrutinise how structural factors and representations of the rural intersect with everyday police work; and to consider how police work in rural areas interrelates with and impacts other sectors in society, and how transformation occurs in several dimensions. It seeks to contribute to the broader field of rural policing within the Swedish context, to draw from this specific national context and to identify lessons that can contribute to the development of the field of research. In addition, there is a hope that the chapter should add to the development of theories initiated in various studies considered later. Drawing from literature on spatial power relations and the threefold modelling of rural space, this chapter will also connect to the strand of research involving rural–urban power relations including spatial inequalities and outcomes.

Rural policing in scholarly context

A review of Swedish police research for the years 2010–17, published by the Swedish National Council for Crime Prevention (BRÅ, 2018), identifies five themes:

- police methods and working practices;
- organisation, governance and leadership;
- work environment and health;
- police training and police students; and
- use of force among police officers.

Studies dealing with local police work are focused on demonstrators, security creation and gang crime in urban environments. Another review including Scandinavia (Høigård, 2011) identifies in turn three themes that characterise police research:

- practices and culture within the police;
- new ways of working within the police; and
- police violence and other forms of misconduct.

Neither of these reviews tries to identify or include a spatial perspective; policing is understood as primarily being performed in urban areas, and conditions for police work in rural and sparsely populated contexts do not seem to have been the subject of research.

A reason for this might be that police research in Sweden has not paid, to an overwhelming extent, attention to rural conditions. However, there are important studies that map police accessibility (Stassen and Ceccato, 2021), make visible aspects of crime and safety (Ceccato, 2016), and pay attention to the spatial distribution of police officers in relation to development of crime and population distribution (Lindström, 2015). A recently published study examines how geographical conditions such as remoteness impact on the work of police investigators in Northern Sweden. The authors identify a conflict between the routines and regulations available for criminal investigation and the contextual factors relating to the rural location (Rantatalo et al, 2021).

Wooff (2015) offers a theorisation of rural policing using a threefold model of production of space aiming at understanding the key practices that structure the response of the police to antisocial behaviour in rural Scotland. He concludes that discretion is vital primarily for two reasons: because of local knowledge of family circumstances and individuals they are able to respond in a less formalised manner; and because the everyday lives are affected by different localities creating diverse bureaucratic challenges for the police. Wooff clarifies how, in a fundamental way, the rural context impacts on policing responses and how the police–community relationship is mirrored in the prevalent policing styles. While Wooff's study illuminates the specific skills involved in rural policing, Smith (2010: 373) pays attention to the closure of rural police stations and decreased police presence which have led to 'a deskilling of the archetypal "country bobby"' in a UK context.

Yarwood (2015) is one of the geography scholars who have contributed to enriching the rural–policing–crime field of research by applying a relational approach. In so doing, he presents an understanding of how networks of different actors affect change in particular places, with a case study on search dogs, thereby shedding light on how non-human agency is part of this spectrum. He effectively illustrates how policing is co-constructed by different actors across different spaces and places. This is not to dismiss community-centred approaches or neglect civil society activities, but rather it emphasises that rural policing is much more, and thus its organisation needs to be analysed with an extended tool box.

Theorising rural policing

Bringing a geographical mindset into a theoretical framing of rural criminology might be fruitful, according to Hayward (2012: 443), who refers to the field of cultural geography as vibrant: 'In this body of work, space is understood almost as if it were a living thing, a multi-layered congress of cultural, political and spatial dynamics'. It is by acknowledging space as diverse and relational, and imbedded in social and power relations, that it will be possible to develop meaningful policies and practices (Hayward, 2012: 459).

Hayward (2012: 449) lists the shortcomings in contemporary criminology as failure to consider 'the intricate nature of space and the complexity of human actions within space'; spatial aspects of power and meaning; and late-modern socio-economic and cultural transformations. The new cultural geography, he argues, will help criminology address these shortcomings. He admits that cultural geography and associated concepts do not subsume existing criminological methods, but that such approaches might play a role as a 'background hum, asking questions of style, form, technique and method' (Lorimer, 2008, cited in Hayward, 2012: 443). Hopefully this work, as well as others embracing human and cultural geographical approaches, will be convincing as contributing to theoretical development and empirical insights rather than merely acting as a 'background hum'.

Mawby and Yarwood (2011: 1) define rural policing as 'how the police, public and other agencies regulate themselves and each other according to the dominant ideals of society. This can be formally, perhaps through the ever-growing spectrum of policing partnerships in neo-liberal countries, or informally through the performance and enforcement of moral codes and values'. Wooff (2015) argues that 'rural policing' is a preferable conceptualisation of the distinct challenges facing rural officers compared to 'policing in rural areas'. Rural policing, he argues, is a term that contributes to examining rural society and the role the police play. Reiner (2000) distinguishes between the police as a social institution, and policing, as a set of processes with social functions. These arguments, as developed by Barton et al (2016), include that policing is constituted by actions that embrace the police authority as well as tasks performed by a wider range of actors such as medical authorities, social welfare services and informal services. A geographical understanding of these processes, or governance of the rural, is crucial as we can expect to find local variations regarding the distribution of power (Woods and Goodwin, 2006; Barton et al, 2016).

The interpretation offered in this chapter is that while the term 'policing the rural' implies that policing is a demarcated practice, implemented in multiple contexts – for certain acknowledging spatial specific crimes – 'rural policing' emphasises the meaning of the spatial context in how policing is experienced and practised. While the focus here is set upon formal police work, such a focus will necessarily extend to include how public and other agencies regulate themselves and each other – this is not necessarily about 'neo-liberal partnerships' (Mawby and Yarwood, 2011), but rather about how formal police work is organised and redefined on different levels. In addition, formal police work in rural areas cannot be understood and interpreted without recognising its informal aspects. This is in line with the study by Rantatalo et al (2021) who found that police investigators operating in a rural context in Northern Sweden alternated between 'rural investigations', a decentralised approach to casework, and 'investigating the rural', implicating a centralised model of investigation. This work will illuminate the tensions arising in rural areas as a result of the encounter of policing the rural and rural policing.

By examining rural policing, it is possible to discern knowledge on the transformation of several functions in rural societies, how they work and how their status affects the minds and identity formation of those living in sparsely populated areas. It is also of importance to shed light on how rural police officers experience their situation in rural municipalities, considering their organisation and place embeddedness – by studying rural policing we are informed about several aspects of rural society (Mawby and Yarwood, 2011), including spatial hierarchies and power relations.

Exploring rural policing within a Swedish context

The organisation of police services in Sweden has undergone a transformation since the mid-2010s. The reasons for this were that the existing structure, with 21 police authorities of varying size, was considered to be an obstacle to increased cost efficiency, increased flexibility and higher quality. The police authorities were considered too small to be able to achieve efficiency and quality of all functions. The change should promote clear and efficient management of police operations (SOU, 2012: 13). With the reorganisation completed in 2018, the Police Authority has introduced seven regional command centres (RLC), shutting down 19 regional command centres. These centres can manage resources over larger geographical areas, which gives the organisation greater flexibility and the ability to concentrate police resources if needed (Statskontoret, 2018: 18). The northern region, the focus of this chapter, consists of four police districts organised into 12 local police areas.

Rather than investigating the police organisation in full, or the broader judicial system, this chapter offers a departure from everyday police work and police experiences, and in addition experiences from professionals in adjacent sectors. However, it is not possible nor wanted to avoid references towards the national organisation of the police. The reorganisation of policing in Sweden figures as a recurrent reference in understanding and analysing the data and is an important source for knowledge. The reorganisation has attracted a great deal of attention in Swedish media, in the police organisation itself and it has also been critically evaluated (Statskontoret, 2018: 18). It has been debated and criticised by researchers, for example regarding a redistribution of resources, favouring the region's core business and reducing the national unit (Holgersson, 2018). It has also had an impact on job satisfaction among police officers in external service, with fewer opportunities for development within the organisation (Huss, 2019). Certain local outcomes have been the subject of review in critical media reporting.

For rural and remote areas, this change was supposed to increase police presence in the countryside and better the conditions for police work. However, investigations confirm that the reform did not lead to an increased police presence locally but, on the contrary, in many cases to a reduced presence. This is especially true in those sparsely populated parts of the country (SOU, 2017: 1). The transformation of the police authority can thus be described as resulting in decreased police presence and growing challenges regarding, for example, a low number of police stations with limited opening hours, increasing distances for serving patrols and extended driving hours. In addition, many areas are characterised by a limited physical and social infrastructure (road quality, internet access, phone connections and provision of healthcare).

The empirical basis consists of in-depth interviews with 20 respondents active mainly on local level in one municipality in Norrbotten County and three actors active at regional and national levels. The actors represent the police authority (internal service police officers working as investigators or external uniformed service officers, managers, safety representatives), schools, social services, municipal council, civil society (Neighbourhood Watch; the women's shelter), the county administrative board, the rescue service, ambulance service, a Sami village and Lantbrukarnas Riksförbund (LRF, a Swedish farmer cooperative). The interviews focused on the spatial context and local conditions affecting how to pursue the police profession or other professions dependent upon police work, in a sparsely populated part of the country. Interview themes were developed around the peculiarities of rural areas, preventive or facilitating aspects of the rural as well as perceptions of the rural – public or individual – in relation to access to police services.

Peripheralisation and a threefold production of space

In Sweden, as in the rest of the world, we can identify spatial processes that mean that places get their status and their confirmation in relation to other places, and where a spatial integration in the form of flows of people, goods and ideas are found in parallel with a spatial separation, where individuals, groups and places occupy positions that include both spatial and social distances (Stenbacka and Heldt Cassel, 2020). Spatial power relations can be understood by using the dichotomy or conceptual pair centre–periphery, including spatial inequalities and outcomes. When examining such processes of spatial power geometries, peripheralisation is a relevant concept. Peripheralisation means, following Kühn (2015: 368), 'dynamic processes through which peripheries actually emerge'. These processes may involve a combination of political, social, economic and/or communicative processes. Peripheries are being made and remade when some spatial units (regions, municipalities, suburbs and so on) achieve an unfavourable position compared to others, a 'demotion or downgrading of a socio-spatial unit in relation to other socio-spatial units' (Kühn, 2015: 374). To avoid falling into an approach where conditions are implicitly considered static, a self-evident categorisation of places or regions, we should, rather, speak of peripheralisation.

Social relations are thus understood as what actually creates spatial conditions, instead of assuming such conditions as a result of an absolute localisation (Ehrlich et al, 2012). Processes of peripheralisation are important in concrete situations as they can affect which places or groups are allocated resources and for what reasons. The location of a head office or an administrative unit affects the spatial relationships with other places. The processes affect the actions of both those who hold central positions and those who hold peripheral positions (Stenbacka, 2020).

The political, social, economic and/or communicative processes that together constitute peripheralisation and thereby producing spaces and spatial attributes (such as relative remoteness, physical and social distance and/or hierarchical positions) operate in several dimensions. To unfold these dimensions, let us turn to the model of rural space as introduced by Keith Halfacree (2004, 2007), and thereafter assayed in relation to diverse rural issues (see for example Munkejord, 2009; Rye and Gunnerud Berg, 2011; Bygdell, 2014; Wooff, 2015).

Handling spatial complexity is what geographers do – including the endeavour to bring clarity while celebrating complexity. The transformation of the rural, now acknowledged as a continuous condition, takes place in several layers. It is shaped and reshaped in the restructuring of industries, in our everyday speech, and in the composition of the population and individual practice. A model that has been found useful in explaining rural space and rural life is the theory of the threefold production of space as presented by Halfacree. This theory is based upon the understanding of space as a conceptual triad consisting of: spatial practice or perceived material space; representations of space or conceived, imagined mental space; and spaces of representation or lived space (Elden, 2007). Halfacree (2004) departs from Lefebvre's (1991 [1974]) theory of the threefold production of space and suggests a model of rural space including the three dimensions, emphasising how they influence and have constant contact with each other, at the same time as they might be disconnected and even compete over the right and scope to define the rural.

When we speak about the rural as a material, specific locality, we acknowledge that it is being seen as 'constantly produced, reproduced and (potentially) transformed' (Halfacree, 2006: 45). Material space includes spatial practices such as inscribed routine activities; such spatial practices (material and social) bear similarities with the concept of locality (Halfacree, 2007: 126). Halfacree promotes a theoretically reflexive approach to the understanding of localities as 'relatively enduring spaces inscribed by social processes or, less passively, both inscribed and used by social processes; product and means of production' (Halfacree, 2006: 45).

The material distinctiveness of the rural involves one, or a combination, of 'agriculture and other primary productive activities; low population density and physical inaccessibility; and consumption behaviour' (Halfacree, 2006: 47). This is in contrast to the social representation of space, where 'an imagined rural geography of landscape aesthetics and "community"' (Halfacree, 2006: 47) is contrasted to other spaces, often the urban. These definitions are interwoven, and they intersect in practice (Halfacree, 2006: 47). The imagined space will be active in producing symbolic constructions or discourses. They play a crucial role in how public and private understandings of rurality take shape. The notion of a non-homogenous rural might be self-evident, but nevertheless it needs to be stressed since tendencies to speak of 'the rural' or 'the countryside people' prevail and lead to, for example, othering processes, increased tensions and a disturbed knowledge production. One road to acknowledging diversity, and at the same time trace sources for potential conflict, is to discern the rural local place in terms of parallel dimensions.

Rural localities, formal representations and everyday lives

In line with Halfacree (2006), this chapter treats the rural as a compound space, consisting of materialities, representations and practices. The rural is a place with a material, social and economic characteristic (locality). It is a place where people, such as police officers and representatives of other sectors in society, develop an understanding of what rural policing means (representations). It is a place where individuals such as police officers and other key professionals live and practise their everyday life.

Rural localities – material space

Of most relevance in this section is materiality in terms of low population density, physical inaccessibility and the organisation of the police that has been developed to correspond to population density and expected needs. In relation to the range of the areas that are supposed to be covered, the number of police stations and uniformed officers are low and the decimated police force in rural areas does not correspond to the development of crime (Lindström, 2015). Each police unit is responsible for a large area, long distances increase even more when a patrol needs to start from 'one corner' in the region. Limited presence also means fewer opportunities for getting to know places and people. One of the local police areas has a catchment the size of Denmark and when these working circumstances (one police car covering a large area) were taken to court as working environment risk, the Court of Appeal states that in terms of working environment, one police car at night in this area is sufficient (Polistidningen, 2017).

Locality is both perceived and *practised*, and practices are associated with everyday perceptions of space: 'They structure our everyday reality, while at the same time being rooted within that reality. As such, spatial practices can also be traced to rules and norms, and to space as lived' (Halfacree, 2006: 50). In the following, rules and norms related to informal cooperation or formal 'mutual agreements' will be discussed. The tasks for the police include to assist rescue services, ambulance services and social services. If a situation is considered serious and the emergency call centre operator knows that it is not possible to send a police car, the alarm might instead become a matter for the ambulance. One informant, representing the ambulance service, relates that duties are transformed in relation to police scarcity and reflects upon differences in access to police services:

'For example, we had an incident this summer where we had a person who walked around with an axe and would kill people around the community. The patrol was in [the town], about an hour away so they sent out the ambulance.' (Ambulance service, Norrbotten County, #10)

The formal label of such mutual agreements – where formal 'blue-light actors' initiate each other's assignments – are so-called IVP-alarms (*I väntan på*, or While Waiting For). It may be the case that the rescue service gives first assistance at an accident while waiting for the ambulance (IVP alarm). One of the respondents provided an example of how police work is planned to be restructured to better answer towards materiality, in this case suggesting that rescue services are the first to answer a call:

'[B]ecause there are so few police in the northern part of Jämtland ... and the police ... there are some ... but no more than that. Then you want to send the rescue service instead ... send them on the first call. In any case, it is better for an adult to come in uniform than for no one to come at all.' (Police service, regional level, Norrbotten County, #1)

In the interviews, it is also emphasised that such solutions might put some professionals in situations they are not trained for – like meeting a person with a weapon, a person who might view any official person as a threat. This solution is labelled IVPP (*I Väntan På Polis*, or While Waiting for the Police). Another solution or adjustment is how to assess the seriousness of a call. One police officer at the regional level explained how operators located in the regional centre might assess situations that arise:

'They themselves say that they have a different level of assessment of the alarms in sparsely populated areas versus coastal cities where there are round-the-clock police. ... And then if someone is calling for help, it's not a death threat, but next to it, huh. Then it is added to a lower assessment level in sparsely populated areas. Because there is no patrol to send. And if you have a lower assessment level for that, then you cannot demand that they send a patrol. So, in the system it is a built-in error. Which is somehow accepted. To agree to this lower level of policing.' (Police service, regional level, Norrbotten County, #1)

An interpretation of the use of such steering mechanisms is that they contribute to improving the measurable outcomes in rural areas. These problematics have also been highlighted by Holgersson and Wieslander (2017: 1) who argue that 'an aim of looking good can have a negative impact on how an organization will work and evolve' and that the Swedish Police efforts to 'look good' have increased (Forsell and Ivarsson Westerberg, 2014; Holgersson, 2014). With regard to the formalisation of mutual agreements among several actors, it has been shown that to get the most out of such collaboration, more emphasis should be put on building common platforms, where the different organisations and actors can communicate and share experiences. Today such interaction is rare (Weinholt, 2015).

Aspects of autonomy and dependency are crucial when the organisation of the police is considered. In a large organisation such as the police authority, decisions on one level will impact the next. One police officer speaks about 'the frustration that is starting to erode me' (Police service, local level, Norrbotten County, #6). He means that managers do not take responsibility for the municipality where he works, but they should, considering their function and area of responsibility. A somewhat sharp wording would be that interest decreases as distance increases. Another officer points to the prioritising practices that will happen when resources are scarce and there are not enough police officers. Should anyone intervene in these smaller and more remote places then they will go from a town one or several hours away. The smaller municipalities and villages thus compete with the larger towns in the region, illuminating an unfavourable position that can be described as a process of peripheralisation, where the distanced and increasingly rural will lose in favour of the closer and urban:

'So, no one is going to these places. Which is devastating for the smaller municipalities ... this disassembling has been going on for a long time, and with the will and acceptance of the managers ... it is ongoing with the aim to save money, and an agreement that this saving goes on, that reductions take place.' (Police service, regional level, Norrbotten County, #1)

As will be demonstrated in the following section, the rural locality interacts with the representations being made and it will impact the experiences of everyday lives.

Formal representations of the rural

In June 2015, the Swedish Government decided to appoint a parliamentary committee with the task of submitting proposals for a cohesive policy for long-term sustainable development in Sweden's rural areas. The aim of this policy was to foster optimism and faith in future rural development across the whole of Sweden. Part of the background, the committee states, is that rural development has for a long time headed in a direction that counteracts the ambition to provide the same conditions to develop all over Sweden and provide the people who live and work in rural areas with equal opportunities to live good lives. The police presence is part of being able to fulfil this ambition: 'The Committee wishes to emphasise that the impoverishment of the police presence in rural areas that have been going on for a long time must have an end' (SOU, 2017: 177). The second dimension, labelled 'representations of space', constitutes 'formal' conceptions of space; that is, formal representations of the rural, as articulated by capitalist interests, cultural arbiters, planners or politicians (Halfacree, 2006, 2007). They are abstract and expressed through, for example, plans, blueprints, jargon and codification. Here, the focus is set upon representations in policy documents, written in relation to Swedish rural policy and the recent reorganisation of the police. A statement from the governmental investigation (SOU, 2017: 1) might illustrate the aims with a rural coherence policy:

> In order for citizens to have confidence in state authorities, the Committee believes that the state must be present throughout the country, even in rural areas with a relatively small population. In order for people to feel safe in their everyday lives, it is necessary for the police to have a local presence and be able to intervene when crimes have been committed.

In the governmental investigation (SOU, 2012: 13) as to how to reach cohesion within the police authority, rural areas are mentioned once, in an argument meaning that the planned reorganisation will allow for an increased police presence, not least in neighbouring policing areas. The evaluation of the new organisation made by Statskontoret (the Swedish Agency for Public Management) does not distinguish explicitly between police operating in rural versus urban areas. However, the report discusses levels, and the local level is mentioned in relation to doubts about the development in the aftermath of the reorganisation.

One conclusion is that in such a large organisation, flexibility increases, but the local risks became lower priority (Statskontoret, 2018: 96). Above all, it is stated that the operational flexibility of national and regional level increased due to the reorganisation; events that require extensive police resources or specialists are handled in a better way. However, it is not as obvious that flexibility has increased locally. It is not always the case that decisions made at the central level leads to local change (Statskontoret, 2018: 86). In general, the reorganisation has not improved accessibility; police visibility has not increased and response and processing times have not been shortened. In addition, many representatives of the social services experience a deterioration in the availability of the police (Statskontoret, 2018: 88).

Concepts that are supposed to make visible the local conditions for policing and outcomes of the reorganisation are thus degrees of flexibility and availability. The concept that should shed light on how to reach a coherent rural policy including police cohesion is 'greater responsibility'. With Halfacree's understanding, representations of space are conceived and abstract, and the examples given earlier can be understood within this framework. An exception is a formulation from the governmental investigation (SOU, 2017: 1) about a cohesive rural development policy, where it is possible to find a more concrete suggestion for how to improve spatial cohesion in relation to police presence: the state must become more present throughout the country and the state, as an employer, must take greater responsibility for rural development. 'The state is physically present in rural areas with jobs, government services and police' (SOU, 2017: 1).

The blame in statements from operational police officers laid at the door of the current police organisation can be discerned in the representations identified in the policy reports, although they are expressed as a concern rather than real criticism. In the report from Statskontoret assessing the new organisation, criticism is more pronounced.

Everyday lives of the rural

The third dimension, everyday lives of the rural, highlights the significance of what people experience in their everyday lives, how they exist in a place-specific context and incorporate individual and social elements in their interpretation and negotiation (Halfacree, 2006: 51). The experiences revealed here testify to the impact of materiality on access to welfare.

This section will focus upon individual experiences from several sectors in society; how they interact and how these everyday lives are developed in relation to the rural or peripheral location, and how their position in a network of places is evaluated. A structuring factor is thus the rural–peripheral perspective including limited police presence, low population density and distance. Rural space is lived in terms of a continuous transformation of responsibilities and cooperation. The actors, representing diverse contexts where dependence on a police presence infuses their work, engage in different ways to handle situations by widening their own definition of what their work tasks should be, when it should be performed (off-work times) and whom to approach in acute situations. Local networks are crucial for dealing with sudden events, for example when police officers in a town 93 kilometres away (an hour's drive) are called upon by SOS alarm, they might call the ambulance nurse directly, rather than responding by going there:

'For example, if a person seems to be intoxicated, they might not drive to here from [town], we are supposed to do their assessment ... but it is not by the book.' (Ambulance service, Norrbotten County, #10)

Social services are dependent upon police support, for example in accordance with LVU (Lag med särskilda bestämmelser om Vård av Unga [laws with special provisions on the care of young people]). The requirement is that there is risk of significant harm to the child's health or development due to abuse or lack of care. It might also be that laws with special provisions on the care of addicts presumes police support:

'There have been situations, several situations where we have been faced with custody, where we have had to postpone custody because there have been no police. Where we have needed police assistance. It affects the third person quite properly. I do say all situations, but that can be quite serious.' (Social services, Norrbotten county, #16, 17, 18)

All kinds of spaces need to be understood with regard to how they relate to other spaces, and the power relations that are infusing these relations. We need to pay attention to the way 'that places fit together in the dynamic production of space' (Corbett, 2016: 145). Everyday experiences are interpreted in the light of the formal representations, meaning that other spaces and spatial relations are present in these interpretations and meaning-making. The situation in their own municipality is compared to what would be expected in other places, and in an extended reasoning this leads to an assessment of the relationship between the individual and the state:

'In another municipality, you can sell drugs outside ICA [grocery store]. And it has to do with the fact that everyone knows that there are no police here. You can drive drunk, drive a scooter drunk, everyone in the community knows who sells drugs and where to buy them.' (Social services, Norrbotten county, #16, 17, 18)

Another informant touches upon the same reasoning and believes that the absence of the police leads to a view of the town as 'free' in a negative sense, that one can stretch boundaries without risking being prosecuted:

'It gets kind of lawless, you can do what you like, it's a bit of no man's land, I was about to say, when you take away too much police resources. ...

I mean, the state, it's the police, among other things. And if the state is not represented, then you may lose some trust in the state. I mean, we pay at least as much tax, we pay more tax than many others, and they have all the social resources to use. So, I think there is a risk that you lose a little trust in the state, that's it.' (Ambulance service, Norrbotten County, #10)

Materiality goes together with lived life and experiences of working as a police officer:

'It eats one up from within ... the darkening, the self-glorification and "look how good we are" when we are really shitty at certain things. Above all, on transparency and on following our own rules that we have set up, our own guidelines, strategies, goals, we do not even follow them.' (Police service, local level, Norrbotten County, #23)

People do inhabit space but are also active in creating and transforming their lived spaces. Interpretation of situations and embodied action are transforming these places, the embedded local social relations and the creation of meaning related to place hierarchies, including spatial identities in relation to the urban–rural power asymmetry. Different professional groups handle the materiality (distances, climate, organisational structures) together, which means that cohesion at the local level is strengthened. At the same time, the so-called gap that has been identified between different parts of the country risks increasing, partly due to increasing differences in access to services (SOU, 2017: 1, Stenbacka, 2020).

How the police organisation is structured, and police practices performed, is understood within a centre–periphery framework. The process of peripheralisation, thus becomes part of understanding and organising everyday lives. In line with the threefold model of space, formal representations of the rural strive to dominate the everyday life experiences. In this case, it is possible to identify a coherence between the formal representations and lived life, and that materiality strives to change the conditions for this coherence.

The rural as a particular socio-spatiality

Yarwood (2015) raises a concern for using the community rhetoric on rural policing; community usually refers to the kind of partnership that is presented as a solution and a suitable outcome, to practise policing as a cooperation among, for example, state, voluntary and private agencies. The idea of community, he argues, exposes the risk of shifting responsibility for policing away from the state at the same time as it presumes 'place' as something delimited or insular. This is a valid concern, and why this chapter had adopted the threefold analytical model of policing to uncover shifting responsibilities within public welfare services.

From the results presented here, we learn that professionals adapt to the prevailing circumstances and solve problems as they arise. While doing this, however, they simultaneously deviate from and follow existing structural regulations. The experiences revealed here imply that the contemporary structure does not succeed in providing the necessary resources.

One solution is to invent new structural elements that blur the imprint of this nonconformity. One such element is how reported crime is prioritised, since the same crime would be given a different priority depending on where the crime is reported; an adaptation to an unequal distribution of resources involving an intentional or unintentional impact on the results of operations. The assessment of a crime's degree and the urgency of sending a patrol is thus relative, depending on access to the police. Informal agreements and social networking are important for upholding a certain level of safety and security, but responsibilities are transferred from the police authority to the ambulance or rescue services. A conclusion is that structural change, such as reformulation or introduction of new practices, are implemented to alter the context for and the outcome of local police work.

The threefold model of rural space constitutes in this chapter a tool for understanding rural policing as produced in a specific materiality, in social representations and in lived life. The first dimension, material space, is in this case the prevalent structure that constitutes the police organisation; its construction and content that form the basis for carrying out police work. The second dimension is about how rural policing is presented and understood in official documents directed towards rural cohesion and rural development, respectively towards the organisation of policing. The third dimension refers to the everyday lives of individuals who are dependent on an available police authority.

Within these dimensions, it is shown how 'rural' is a relative location, understood as distinct from the urban or the centre. Material rural spaces deviate in terms of distance and population density, and in structure and organisation. Representations of rural space state the peculiarity of the rural area and describe an associated problematic. The third dimension, in the words of Halfacree (2006: 51), 'incorporate[s] individual and social elements ('culture') in [its] cognitive interpretation and negotiation', and in this case such an element is how the place is perceived in relation to a hierarchy of places and an adherent distribution of power, and the meaning incorporated in this.

While separating the three dimensions is a fruitful way of ordering rich empirical material, it should also be acknowledged that they influence and have constant contact with each other. A question following upon the use of the threefold model of production of space is whether these dimensions – localities, representations and everyday lives of the rural – correspond or present a united front. If so, according to Halfacree, there is a condition of rural coherence. In the work presented here, a result is that two dimensions – representations and everyday lives – are united in stating the importance of the presence of state authority for security and safety reasons. But there is a parallel incoherence with regards to the opporunities to pursue this within the contemporary materiality; a materiality including the contemporary organisation and the physical context.

The inability, among national governments, to deal with the problems associated with rural areas, has led to disillusionment in many rural places (Woods, 2016: 627) and to some extent disillusionment and resignation are also present in the understanding of the situation in the area investigated in this chapter. The development of welfare services related to safety and security is viewed as a long-term issue or distress, not primarily as something new caused by the new organisation, even though this is often referred to.

It could be reasonable to argue that stability would be the result of the identified coherence among representations – official views – and lived lives. But the occurrence of coherence does not affect the experiences in a straightforward manner, so that increased coherence means stability and agreement on how to manage. This follows from an insight that the problematic is acknowledged but that measures are absent and change is perceived as an illusion. In addition, it is difficult to hold a debate against an established centre of power, that acknowledges and describes conditions in a similar way to those affected by policy.

Conclusion

Rural physical space, in this case meaning covering large distances, constitutes a specific working environment. Combined with a police organisation with a low number of police stations and limited patrolling, rural policing to an increasing extent means that responsibility for what were previously defined as police duties is transferred to other professions. Thus, adjustment towards physical and organisational materiality transform rural policing in a broader sense, impacting several professional categories, Meanwhile, frustration and disappointment with leadership and policy formulation grow.

Governmental reports covering rural policing are supportive when presenting the needs of rural areas as well as recording doubts regarding the police organisation's ability to meet those needs: thus, the case of the critics of the contemporary organisation is strengthened. At the same time, the level of abstraction makes it difficult to discern concrete outcomes and solutions to the ongoing disintegration of the service provided by the police. For example, 'increased flexibility' and 'greater responsibility' do not say anything about spatial coverage of, and access to, police services. A consequence regarding the formal representations of rural policing, such as governmental investigations, is that they will be regarded as empty of meaning and that they have little opportunity to influence rural policing in practice.

Rural policing as lived experience involves adjustment, a need for rapid assessments and an emphasis on what is going on here and now; on measures where the local is part of both the problem and the solution. An outcome is strengthened networks in the local context involving mutual trust and understanding of each other's work situation. A voice on the phone from a well-known police officer is viewed as positive support in a challenging situation, since physical presence might be expected within hours. Another outcome is weakened trust for national politics and the ability to create spatial cohesion.

Earlier research has found that a limited or scarce presence of, and access to, institutions that work with judiciary issues, affects individuals' perception of justice in a broader sense (George and Harris, 2014; Neilson and Renou, 2015). Finally, it should thus be stressed that research on rural policing should not be seen as solely adding information on policing geographies alternative to the urban. In many contexts, there are reasons for discussing the rural situation relative to its urban counterparts. This is true also when rural policing is the subject of study, partly because rural policing takes place and develop in relation to urban ideas of policing (Owen and Carrington, 2015; Rantatalo et al, 2021). However, it also needs to be stressed that studying rural space and processes of transformation is important as it can contribute to conceptual development and understanding of spatial theory. As shown in this chapter, investigating rural space enriches an understanding of spatial networks of power that includes both rural *and* urban spaces, and all the variations included in these rather blunt categories.

The absence – or the limited presence – of the police is about far more than emptied or lively police stations and the reduced risks of, say, getting caught while driving drunk. It is about people's perception of their value; of the value of their living environment. Local cohesion can benefit when different professions are forced to cover for each other, while regional cohesion suffers. The meaning of the rural, as expressed in the lived lives of rural inhabitants, the key informants in this study, illuminates spatial processes of power. These processes involve experienced unequal access to welfare services, stretched area of responsibility and contain a conflation of rural and peripheral. Since 'peripheral' is infused with a certain (missing) value, the rural is situated in an unfavourable position.

References

Anderson, B. (2008) 'For Space (2005): Doreen Massey', in P. Hubbard, R. Kitchin and G. Valentine (eds) Key Texts in Human Geography, London: Sage, pp 227–35.

Barton, A., Storey, D. and Palmer, C. (2016) 'A trip in the country? Policing drug use in rural settings', in R. Mawby and R. Yarwood (eds) Rural Policing and Policing the Rural: A Constable Countryside?, Abingdon: Routledge, pp 147–67.

BRÅ (Brottsförebyggande Rådet) [Swedish National Council for Crime Prevention] (2018) Polisforskning i Sverige: En sammanställning över publicerad polisforskning i Sverige 2010–2017 [Police Research in Sweden: A Compilation of Published Police Research in Sweden 2010–2017], Stockholm: Brottsförebyggande Rådet. Available from: https://bra.se/publikationer/arkiv/publikationer/2018-10-01-polisforskning-i-sverige.html [Accessed 7 March 2022].

Bygdell, C. (2014) 'Omsorgsfylld landsbygd: Rumsliga perspektiv på åldrande och omsorg på den svenska landsbygden' [The caring countryside: spatial perspectives on ageing and care in Swedish rural areas], Upplands fornminnesförenings tidskrift, 56: 9–216.

Ceccato, V. (2016) Rural Crime and Community Safety, Abingdon: Routledge.

Corbett, M. (2016) 'Reading Lefebvre from the periphery: thinking globally about the rural', in A. Schulte and B. Walker-Gibbs (eds) Self-Studies in Rural Teacher Education, Self-Study of Teaching and Teacher Education Practices, Cham: Springer, pp 141–56.

Ehrlich, K., Kriszan, A. and Lang, T. (2012) 'Urban development in Central and Eastern Europe: between peripheralization and centralization?', disP: The Planning Review, 48(2): 77–92.

Elden, S. (2007) 'There is a politics of space because space is political: Henri Lefebvre and the production of space', Radical Philosophy Review, 10(2): 101–16.

Forsell, A. and Ivarsson Westerberg, A. (2014) Administrationssamhället [The Society of Administration], Lund: Studentlitteratur.

George, A. and Harris, B. (2014) Landscapes of Violence: Women Surviving Family Violence in Regional and Rural Victoria, Geelong, Vic: Deakin University.

Halfacree, K. (2004) 'Rethinking "rurality"', in T. Chapman and G. Hugo (eds) New Forms of Urbanization: Beyond the Urban–Rural Dichotomy, Aldershot: Ashgate, pp 285–304.

Halfacree, K. (2006) 'Rural space: constructing a three-fold architecture', in P. Cloke, T. Marsden and P. Mooney (eds), *Handbook of Rural Studies*, London: Sage, pp 44–62.

Halfacree, K. (2007) 'Trial by space for a "radical rural": introducing alternative localities, representations and lives', *Journal of Rural Studies*, 23(2): 125–41.

Hayward, K.J. (2012) 'Five spaces of cultural criminology', *British Journal of Criminology*, 52(3): 441–62.

Høigård, C. (2011) 'Policing the north', *Crime and Justice*, 40: 265–348.

Holgersson, S. (2014) Polisen bakom kulisserna [The police behind the scenes], Åby: Åby PC System.

Holgersson, S. (2018) *Ursäkta, men vi är faktiskt POLISEN och vi står över lagen!* [Sorry, but we are actually the POLICE and we are above the law!], Center for Advanced Research in Emergency Response (CARER), Linköping: Linköping University Electronic Press.

Holgersson, S. and Wieslander, M. (2017) 'How aims of "looking good" may limit the possibilities of "being good": the case of the Swedish Police', presented at the 33rd EGOS Colloquium, The Good Organization, 6–8 July, Copenhagen. Available from: https://static1.squarespace.com/static/5437a800e4b0137bd4ed4b13/t/5a5ad61b8165f521dd4a9f6d/1515902497934/EGOS+SH+MW+Swedish+Police.pdf [Accessed 7 March 2022].

Huss, J. (2019) 'En omorganisations påverkan på arbetstillfredsställelsen hos poliser i yttre tjänst: En fenomenologisk studie' [The impact of a reorganisation on job satisfaction among police officers in external service: a phenomenological study], Masteruppsats, Avdelningen för pedagogik, Sociologiska Institutionen, Lunds universitet [master's thesis, Department of Education, Department of Sociology, Lund University]. Available from: https://lup.lub.lu.se/student-papers/search/publication/8990795 [Accessed 7 March 2022].

Kühn, M. (2015) 'Peripheralization: theoretical concepts explaining socio-spatial inequalities', *European Planning Studies*, 23(2): 367–78.

Lefebvre, H. (1991) [1974] *The Production of Space*, trans D. Nicholson-Smith, Oxford: Basil Blackwell.

Lindström, P. (2015) 'Police and crime in small Swedish municipalities', *Journal of Rural Studies*, 39: 271–7.

Mawby, R.I. and Yarwood, R. (2016) 'Introduction', in R.I. Mawby and R. Yarwood (eds) *Rural Policing and Policing the Rural: A Constable Countryside?*, Abingdon: Routledge, pp 1–8.

Munkejord, M.C. (2009) 'Hjemme i Nord: En analyse av stedsopplevelser med utgangspunkt i kvinnelige og mannlige innflytteres fortellinger om hverdagsliv I Havøysund og Vadsø, Finnmark' [Home in the North: An analysis of place experiences based on female and male immigrants' stories about everyday life in Havøysund and Vadsø, Finnmark], dissertation thesis, Tromsø University, Tromsø. Available from: https://www.academia.edu/1599847/Hjemme_i_nord [7 March 2022].

Neilson, C. and Renou, B. (2015) 'Regional women advocate for justice reform', *DVRCV Advocate*, 2: 35–8. Available from: https://search.informit.org/doi/10.3316/INFORMIT.780986487266265 [Accessed 7 March 2022].

Owen, S. and Carrington, K. (2015) 'Domestic violence (DV) service provision and the architecture of rural life: an Australian case study', *Journal of Rural Studies*, 39. 290–38.

Polistidningen, Tidningen för polisförbundets medlemmar [Newspaper for police union members] (2017) 'En ensam patrull på yta stor som Danmark' [A lone patrol of an area as large as Denmark], 18 October. Available from: https://polistidningen.se/2017/10/en-ensam-patrull-pa-yta-stor-som-danmark/ [Accessed 7 March 2022].

Rantatalo, O., Lindberg, O. and Hällgren, M. (2021) 'Criminal investigation in rural areas: how police detectives manage remoteness and resource scarcity', *Policing: A Journal of Policy and Practice*, 15(2): 1352–66.

Reiner, R. (2000) *The Politics of the Police* (3rd edn), Oxford: Oxford University Press.

Rye, J.F. and Gunnerud Berg, N. (2011) 'The second home phenomenon and Norwegian rurality', *Norsk Geografisk Tidsskrift* [Norwegian Journal of Geography], 65(3): 126–36.

Smith, R. (2010) 'Policing the changing landscape of rural crime: a case study from Scotland', *International Journal of Police Science and Management*, 12(3): 373–87.

SOU (Official Reports of the Swedish Government) (2012) En sammanhållen svensk polis [A unified Swedish police service], Betänkande av Polisorganisationskommittén [Report of the Police Organisation Committee], 13, Stockholm. Available from: https://www.regeringen.se/rattsliga-dokument/statens-offentliga-utredningar/2012/03/sou-201213/ [Accessed 7 March 2022].

SOU (Official Reports of the Swedish Government) (2017) För Sveriges landsbygder – en sammanhållen politik för arbete, hållbar tillväxt och välfärd [For rural Sweden: a coherent rural policy for work, sustainable growth and welfare], Slutbetänkande av Parlamentariska landsbygdskommittén [Final report of the Parliamentary Committee on Rural Affairs], 1, Stockholm. Available from: https://www.regeringen.se/rattsliga-dokument/statens-offentliga-utredningar/2017/01/sou-20171/ [Accessed 7 March 2022].

Stassen, R. and Ceccato, V. (2021) 'Police accessibility in Sweden: an analysis of the spatial arrangement of police services', *Policing: A Journal of Policy and Practice*, 15(2): 896–911.

Statskontoret (2018) Ombildningen till en sammanhållen polismyndighet [The transformation into a cohesive police authority], Slutrapport [final report], 18. Available from: https://docplayer.se/104791230-Ombildnin gen-till-en-sammanhallen-polismyndighet.html [Accessed 7 March 2022].

Stenbacka, S. (2020) 'Polisfrånvaro och periferialisering' [Police absence and peripheralisation], in S. Stenbacka and S. Heldt Cassel (eds) *Periferi som process* [Periphery as process], *Ymer*, Årgång 140, Svenska Sällskapet för Antropologi och Geografi [The Swedish Society for Anthropology and Geography], Stockholm, pp 109–30.

Stenbacka, S. and Heldt Cassel, S. (2020) 'Introduktion: Periferier och periferialisering' [Introduction: peripheries and peripheralization], in S. Stenbacka and S. Heldt Cassel (eds), *Periferi som process* [Periphery as process], *Ymer*, Årgång 140, Svenska Sällskapet för Antropologi och Geografi [The Swedish Society for Anthropology and Geography], Stockholm, pp 7–24.

Weinholt, Å. (2015) Exploring Collaboration Between the Fire and Rescue Service and New Actors: Cost Efficiency and Adaptation, Licentiatavhandling [Licentiate thesis], Linköping University Electronic Press. Available from: https://www.dissertations.se/dissertation/c9d0180 cfb/ [Accessed 7 March 2022].

Woods, M. (2016) 'Confronting globalisation? Rural protest, resistance and social movements', in M. Shucksmith and D.L. Brown (eds) *Routledge International Handbook of Rural Studies*, New York: Routledge, pp 626–37.

Woods, M. and Goodwin, M. (2006) 'Applying the rural: governance and policy in rural areas', in P. Cloke (ed) *Country Visions*, Harlow: Pearson, pp 245–62.

Wooff, A. (2015) 'Relationships and responses: policing anti-social behaviour in rural Scotland', *Journal of Rural Studies*, 39: 287–95.

Yarwood, R. (2015) 'Lost and hound: the more-than-human networks of rural policing', *Journal of Rural Studies*, 39: 278–86.

10

Punishment, Politics and the Realities of Rurality

Rachel Hale, Alistair Harkness and Kyle Mulrooney

Introduction

Punishment is a complex, nuanced and multifaceted socio-cultural phenomenon, with a significant body of knowledge having been accrued about punishment generally, so much so that it is now considered a specific area of study in criminology. The 'geography' of punishment, however, is relatively under-researched (Hogg, 2016) with scarce extant analyses of the ways in which punishment is negotiated by and experienced in rural, regional and remote (RRR) communities; and considering that the nature of rural punishment is critical to shining a light on the unequal and detrimental impacts of punishment in places and spaces that are often beyond the conscious consideration of the public and policymakers alike.

This chapter focuses on the provision of punishment in rural settings, using prisons as a primary example to examine the roles of politics and populism in the delivery of justice outcomes and the impacts on rural communities. It explores the politics of punishment through analysis of three key areas: rural public sentiments and punitive attitudes; the political and socio-economic influences on prisons siting in rural areas; and rural prison and post-release challenges.

First, although rural communities are by no means homogenous, rural attitudes and sentiments towards crime and punishment tend to be more punitive, which can serve to reinforce penal responses to crime. Second, with land cheaper and more abundant outside cities, the locating of prisons in rural settings can be a temptation without objection. Justification is made to rural communities by decision-makers based on promises of financial investment and job creation, although this is not often actualised. Third, there exist significant impacts brought about by the tyranny of distance for those incarcerated in rural prisons, as well as challenges accessing post-release support in rural communities.

Drawing on these themes, the chapter concludes with a discussion of the complexities and nuances regarding punishment and prisons in rural spaces, highlighting the need for further scholarship and engagement with the issues raised, with particular attention to the intersecting impact of disadvantage and access to justice issues felt by rural communities.

Dimensions of penality

Let us begin with a brief contemplation of the development of punishment, as both a focus of study as well as a means of societal control. 'Punishment is not a behavior', Binder (2002: 321) asserts, 'but an institution', with a central importance in both political and moral spheres. Punishment is central to how societies and governments maintain social order, and the history of punishment and prisons is a profoundly political business with no unitary trajectory, as the purpose and shape of punishment shifts according to time and place.

In pre-Enlightenment times, punishment was largely delivered in retaliatory, retributive terms ('an eye for an eye'). Ultimately, though, responsibility for punishment came to rest with the nation state. In the eighteenth century, the moral philosopher Immanuel Kant argued that retribution necessitated and justified punishment in accord with 'just deserts' (Koritansky, 2005), a popular view of the time and still found among some communities. Michel Foucault, in his seminal work *Discipline and Punish: The Birth of the Prison* (1977), examined the shift from punishment of the 'body' to the 'mind' across nineteenth-century Europe. He positioned incarceration as a mechanism for constant surveillance serving as a means of discipline, creating 'docile bodies' that can be controlled and exploited; and it is through the ever-expanding carceral society – a vast network of panoptic institutions and practices – that domination is achieved. In essence, then, prison is retained because of its failures – high recidivism rates – rather than in spite of them.

Contemporary scholarship has highlighted the centrality of prisons to economies internationally, referred to as the 'prison industrial complex', where government and industry profit from punishing the marginalised (Davis, 2003). A so-called 'new punitiveness' (Pratt et al, 2005) is believed to have emerged, characterised by longer prison sentences under harsher conditions, the re-emergence of historical forms of punishment (for example, shaming), and pervasive technology-facilitated surveillance: this punitivity, though, is perhaps not so 'new' if considering the colonial periphery (Moore, 2014). In the context of British imperial history, Moore explains that this idea of an 'enhanced punitiveness' witnessed in the metropole is not an 'aberration', but rather a 'continuation of well-established British penal traditions ... underpinned and legitimised by the philosophy of liberalism' (Moore, 2014: 32).

Critical scholars position mass incarceration as a mechanism of control and oppression based on gender, sexuality, class, ability, indigeneity and race (Reiman, 2007; Alexander, 2010), with abolitionists calling for non-carceral, preventive responses. Connected to critical criminology, left realists purport that prisons will always exist in some form, and that some interventions (including those that take place in the prison environment) can have a positive impact if designed effectively, albeit limited by unchanged broader social conditions (Currie, 2010). Regardless of one's position, prison is generally understood as a 'total institution' that involves a period of enforced detention; the summit of an ascending scale of penalties of supposed last resort (in Western liberal democracies, at least). Prison represents the reality and symbol of state social control over lawbreakers.[1]

Alongside denunciation, retribution, deterrence and reform, a key sentencing principle is incapacitation for a set period locked behind bars – or with capital punishment (often preceded by many years on death row) as the ultimate permanent incapacitation. Imprisonment, though, also serves as a means of displacing many of society's problems, such as illiteracy, drug addiction, homelessness, unemployment and trauma (Reiman, 2007; Wacquant, 2009): therefore, even when providing temporary community protection, prisons do not necessarily guarantee long-term community safety,[2] as most imprisoned persons will eventually return to the community (Vera, 2021).

Perceptions of and approaches to punishment differ across place, with attitudes towards crime and punishment constituting the penal culture of a given jurisdiction, with recent research suggesting that there may be considerable 'penal diversity' at a micro level across states within a country, not just across nations (Tubex et al, 2015). When considering imprisonment with rural contextualisation, we therefore need to grapple with how the principles and actuality of punishment sit in the minds of rural residents.

Public sentiments and punitive attitudes

Understanding public attitudes towards punishment provides insight into the broader cultural norms associated with crime control in particular societies and, more specifically, to the prevailing perceptions around the question of what is to be done about criminal offending.

Scant research explores the spatial dimensions of punitive attitudes and specifically on urban and rural variations. Yet, considering that the multitude of factors associated with locational context and cultural geography, place and space no doubt impacts upon understandings of crime and its control. The limited available research suggests that those who live in rural areas are, in general, less tolerant of many offences and more likely to support strongly punitive law and order approaches than people from metropolitan areas (Weisheit et al, 2006; Gelb, 2011; Donnermeyer and DeKeseredy, 2014).

Mulrooney and Wise (2019) examined punitive attitudes across rural and urban geographical areas in Canada, specifically employing a multidimensional measurement of punitiveness, which considered: attitudes towards the goals of punishment; support for specified forms of penal sanctions; and support for the intensity of penal sanctions. They found that across all dimensions, residents of 'the rural' held significantly more punitive attitudes than those of 'the urban'. Regarding goals of punishment, the rural favoured punishing violent young offenders significantly more than the urban. While both classifications favoured limiting the rights of offenders to address offending (intensity of penal sanctions), rural support was significantly greater than that of urban residents. Rural support in Canada for the death penalty was also significantly greater than for urban classifications. Notably, while there was a significant trend towards a decrease in punitive attitudes in Canada as a whole, no significant trend appeared in the rural. Subsequently, as the urban is driving reductions in punitive attitudes, the gap between the rural and urban appears to be growing (Mulrooney and Wise, 2019).

There exists, though, limited empirical understanding of why 'the rural' is more likely to strongly support punitive approaches to issues of law and order, yet there are some theoretical perspectives in the 'sociology of punishment' on which we may hypothesise. In the extant literature, a number of key variables have been correlated with punitive attitudes and punitiveness: for instance, high levels of fear of crime, the perception that crime is increasing and a lack of confidence in the criminal justice system have all been linked to increased punitivity (Jones and Weatherburn, 2010; Garland, 2013; Armborst, 2017).

Let's consider two other examples through a rural criminological lens. First, following a Durkheimian perspective, trust and solidarity have been shown to shape punitive attitudes (for example, Karstedt, 2015). Specifically, punishment serves to affirm social solidarity in times of 'flux', as the criminal justice system is used to define and reaffirm core values that are under the threat of socio-economic and/or cultural change (Kennedy, 2000). Here we can consider the dramatically changing nature of local rural economies and well as the threat posed by cultural change both at a values level (such as gender roles) and demographic composition.

Second, closely associated to elements of social solidarity is the theoretical approach of 'minority threat', which holds that changes in the size of minority groups, and associated resource competition, threaten long-standing social relationships (Jacobs and Wood, 1999). In response to these real or imagined threats, powerful groups may support coercive and punitive crime control policies as a means of maintaining social position (see Brown and

Piscitelli, 2016). Rural communities are inclined to associate crime with outsiders; in externalising the crime problem, an image is maintained of the cohesive rural community. As identities often solidify and harden in the face of threats (such as economic decline), crimes may be met with exemplary force to ensure the exclusion of such offenders and outsiders and assist in the promotion of internal social order (solidarity).

Politics and ideology are paramount in considerations of how to control and respond to crime (Jacobs and Helms, 1996; Loader and Sparks, 2016). Specifically, punitive approaches to crime tend to be associated with conservative politics and ideology, especially relevant to the rural context when considering that the rural–urban divide is one of the greatest political fault lines in contemporary politics. The public is highly influential in guiding crime policy, as many politicians believe that penal policies should follow the public's view (Green, 2008). Public attitudes towards responses to crime, thus, become particularly important in shaping policy and strategies to address crime, and punitive attitudes play a key role in the form and expression of punishment in rural spaces – including the place and role of prisons.

The politics of punishment and the role of rural prisons

A prison boom across many Western industrialised nations from the late 1970s to early 2000s – most notably in the US, and marked by a pessimistic 'nothing works' critique (Martinson, 1974) – constitutes a period of mass incarceration wherein the number of prisons and prisoners expanded greatly (Sakoda and Simes, 2021). With an expanding prisoner population and land cheaper and more plentiful in rural areas, the siting of prisons has become another vexed, complex and nuanced debate replete with political dimensions.

Eason (2008) posits that while prison placement in rural areas does not in and of itself produce inequality, it is the result of the heightened disadvantage in many of these areas. He describes how the stigma associated with 'rural ghettos' can influence a town to seek prison development for the benefits it brings. The desirability of prison development to rural communities can therefore be conceptualised as a consequence or product of the disadvantage experienced by rural communities. With limited options for economic development 'a prison becomes the best of the worst options available for struggling communities' (Eason, 2019).

Economic arguments for rural prison siting

Hogg (2016: 134) notes that pragmatic economic factors have often led to the closure of ageing inner-city prisons owing to escalating urban land values and sub-development opportunities, and 'a growing belief in the potential of new prisons to revive flagging rural economies and address poverty and disadvantage in rural areas suffering long-term population and employment decline'. Because of these economic factors, much of prison construction in Australia has been in rural areas, and a similar trend has occurred in the US. The expected economic benefits of prisons, though, are often overstated with 'negligible, or perhaps negative impact on economic development in rural communities' (Tootle, 2004: 2).

Preferences for the location of 'locally undesirable land uses' (such as homeless shelters, drug or alcohol treatment places, waste disposal facilities and prisons) differ, and places where residents may work at such a facility are more accepting of these land uses than in other settings (Been, 1993). The construction and operation of prisons in rural locations is perceived to provide significant (often unionised) employment opportunities, increased collective efficacy by 'maintaining community stability and order by generating well-paid positions with benefits for otherwise low-wage, low-skill workers' (Eason, 2008: 20), and may increase a community's tax base leading to improved public infrastructure (Yanarella and Blankenship, 2008). In rural prison towns, the local economy can benefit from the essential services required by correctional employees who utilise local businesses, either when they move into the town or in travelling to work through surrounding areas (Eason, 2008). Prisoner visitors may also generate a form of de facto tourism, utilising the services of local accommodation and restaurants when visiting.

Prisons in many jurisdictions have become a normal – indeed, perhaps, an essential – part of the economy of nation states and local communities within. In neoliberal capitalist economies, the management of many prisons has been outsourced to the private sector, as governments retreat from hands-on daily operations of hitherto state-owned and operated infrastructure. Australia, for example, has the highest proportion of persons incarcerated in privately run prisons in the world (O'Neil et al, 2020). But with this comes an array of flow-on effects, not least of all diminishing levels of public accountability and defences of 'commercial in confidence' provisions, and in some jurisdictions the exploitation of prisoners for manual labour dovetailed not in the least with skill development and rehabilitative functions.

There exist partisan political machinations, too, when decision-makers determine prison siting based on deriving electoral benefit from locating a prison in a certain area. In a US context, electoral districts might be drawn around the location of an existing prison to increase electoral representation. Prisoners cannot vote, but get counted in census figures and thus 'represented' within what has become a gerrymandered constituency (see Prison Policy Initiative, 2021), shifting political power away from cities that perhaps comprised larger concentrations of liberal or progressive voters and transferred to predominantly conservative rural locations. Huling (2002: 197) observes that: 'this massive penetration of prisons into rural America portends dramatic consequences for the entire nation as huge numbers of inmates from urban areas become rural residents for the purposes of Census-based formulas used to allocate government dollars and political representation'.

With a rural lens, we can ask whether political pressure might be brought to bear on rural communities, oftentimes more vulnerable to exploitation – especially in circumstances where reliance on a single industry has been disrupted, such as through the closure of coal mining or forestry operations, fruit canneries and so on. Job losses in rural communities are also often accompanied by an increase in drug use and abuse, including opioids and methamphetamine (Thomas et al, 2020).

In examining disadvantaged communities in America's rural north-west, Bonds (2009) highlights the ways in which the criminalisation of poverty legitimises investment in rural prison development while simultaneously camouflaging the erosion of the welfare state. In the context of a decline in economic benefits and employment opportunities from 'traditional' rural industries, a shift to less desirable industries – such as prisons – has occurred, which offer rural communities the opportunity to survive and thrive, as is expected of them under a neoliberal framework based on individual choice and autonomy. The individualisation of poverty, drug use and mental illness diverts attention away from the macro, systemic roots of disadvantage, placing responsibility in the hands of the individual – if they cannot address their 'issues', then a criminal justice system will. This neoliberal rhetoric of individual responsibilisation and associated criminalisation feeds prison expansion, which, in turn, sustains the economic health of rural communities who are constantly in competition for resources, funding and employment opportunities.

Community support for rural-based prisons

Support for prison construction and expansion, regardless of motivation, implies that prisons are both acceptable and desirable, bolstering the political 'law and order' rhetoric characterised by tough-on-crime policies, of which prisons are the cornerstone. Therefore, rural communities, when supporting prison development – albeit unintentionally – contribute to the normativity of prisons as a panacea to solve wider social and economic issues.

Prison siting in rural communities elicits both longing and loathing, positioning rural prisons as 'neither entirely pariah nor panacea' (Eason, 2017: 1). Polarised community views concerning rural prison siting have been witnessed in Ararat Rural City to the west of Melbourne in Victoria, Australia. The town has long been the home of state-run institutions, with the Aradale Mental Hospital operating from 1865 to 1998, and the establishment of the Ararat Prison in 1967 – now the Hopkins Correctional Centre, a medium security protection prison (Corrections Victoria, 2021). In 2010, a transitional facility – Corella Place – was established close to the prison to monitor post-sentence sex offenders who were deemed to remain an unacceptable risk to the community. The facility, located on the site of the former Commonwealth Games village, is referred to colloquially as the 'village of the damned' (Edwards, 2017).

Despite Ararat's legacy as a prison town, the residential facility has elicited concern and fear among community members, owing to the type of offender – understandable, given that numerous detainees absconded from the site despite being electronically monitored. Community consternation peaked in 2016 when the tenth escape occurred, warranting a community meeting facilitated by police. More recent insights, however, indicate support for continued prison development in the area (Cowan, 2017). This is probably influenced by the fact that Corrections Victoria is a primary employer of residents, for whom working in the industry may be a family tradition given Ararat's history as a 'prison town' with 'a culture of corrections' (Cowan, 2017). One local resident noted that: "The prison pays a lot of mortgages. A lot of businesses make a lot of money out of the jail. It's something Ararat needs, no doubt about that" (Cowan, 2017).

The most recent Australian census data (ABS, 2016) showed that of those who are employed in Ararat, 7.2 per cent work in 'correctional and detention services' compared to 0.2 per cent across the state of Victoria. The lack of resistance to prison expansion may also be owing to a sense of normality incurred by the long-standing presence of institutions in the town, whereby the concept of the prison is so commonplace that it is unremarkable – and even iconic. The Hopkins Correctional Centre exemplifies a prison situated in a remote part of a rural town. Even in a rural location, the presence of a prison can be further camouflaged by its siting in a space that makes it relatively unnoticeable, disguising its magnitude both in a literal sense and symbolically in terms of the detrimental impacts on imprisoned persons.

With very few exceptions, prisons are often both harmful and violent, and in some rural spaces they operate with increased invisibility, representing 'black sites' that conceal their purpose and obscure the ability to see and know what goes on within (McClanahan and Linnemann, 2018: 513). The rural prison-scape is a 'frequently invisible geography because of the fundamental spatial contours of the rural: rural places can be difficult to access, and the emerging terrains of rural incarceration recognize and make use of that isolation' (McClanahan and Linnemann, 2018: 517). After all, 'what is incarceration if not isolation, and so what better way to underline the isolation of imprisonment than to conduct and enact it within an already isolated material space?' (519). At the same time, notions of the rural idyll and, for example, notions of peace or tranquillity and 'getting back to basics' or 'in one with nature' have also been drawn on with respect to rehabilitative ideals.

One mechanism with the potential to challenge this concealment is the 'will to know' (McClanahan and Linnemann, 2018: 515). However, the relative punitivity of rural communities may evoke a certain degree of unwillingness to inquire about the harms surrounding punishment, including the failings of prisons to ensure community safety in the long term, particularly in the face of immediate economic benefit set in the context of rural decline. Here again is an illustration of complexity and nuance.

Rural prison and post-release challenges

Prisons are largely experienced as harmful spaces, but for people imprisoned in rural locations the harms are often increased. This reality raises questions about the nature of punishment and whether a sentence of incarceration (and associated deprivation of liberty) is the punishment itself, or whether individuals are punished *further* once incarcerated in a rural prison due to its siting – the prison 'for' or 'as' punishment debate. The 'pains of imprisonment' outlined by Gresham Sykes (1958) are undoubtedly amplified when persons are imprisoned in relatively remote areas. Most notably, the deprivation of contact with social supports (family, children, friends, partners) created by the tyranny of distance, which impacts heavily on many of those whose supports reside in urban locations.[3]

The maintenance of social ties is integral to the well-being of incarcerated persons (Bales and Mears, 2008). Rural prisons jeopardise this, whereby visitors may not be able to travel long distances to visit or may not be willing to visit when the duration of travel to reach the prisons may far exceed the time of the visit itself. Public transport options in rural areas, too, are quite limited. Consider the prison network in Victoria, Australia, for example. Of the 15 prisons in the state, nine are located outside of the Greater Melbourne metropolitan area. For eight of the nine non-metro prisons, a courtesy bus is provided on weekends only: in the ninth case, no alternatives to private vehicle access are provided to connect to the nearest town with a train station (11 kilometres away) (Corrections Victoria, 2021). In this context, for those who originate from urban communities, maintaining social and cultural connectedness during incarceration is less likely. This disconnection and isolation have the potential to cause severe emotional distress, which can extend beyond the prison experience to jeopardise post-release (re)integration and desistance efforts.

Studies of post-release, like much criminological inquiry, have focused predominantly on the urban context resulting in a relative lack of insight regarding the unique experience of release into rural settings, and the impacts on (re)integration and recidivism. Although the number of individuals re-entering rural communities from prison is smaller, a rural perspective on re-entry is important given that rural citizens face unique challenges and barriers not experienced by their urban counterparts (Wodahl, 2006). These insights are valuable in guiding effective supports that promote desistance from crime, alleviating barriers to desistance that are particular to rural settings.

Regarding (re)integration, while rural communities may be welcoming of prisons due to their economic appeal, the same level of hospitality is unlikely to extend to those housed within prison walls. Based on increased punitiveness evident in rural locations, it is reasonable to assume that the ability to integrate into the community would be more difficult for persons released to rural locations, particularly for sex offenders and persons experiencing mental illness (Zajac et al, 2014). Some rural communities are especially small and intimate, which may lead to increased awareness that an individual has been previously incarcerated, lending to stigmatisation and labelling of the rural 'ex-prisoner'.

Despite the lack of evidence specifically relating to rural post-release experiences, we can draw on the abundant existing knowledge on the post-prison challenges in the urban context and imagine how these issues are likely to be exacerbated in rural settings based on what *is* known about rural communities regarding social support and welfare provisions. These challenges might best be described as 'access' issues. Let us consider then, in turn, access to: housing; employment options; transport; web-based communications; and legal and support services.

Access to housing

The absence of suitable housing options post-release has consistently found to be linked to recidivism (AHURI, 2004); the accessibility of appropriate safe housing options following incarceration is integral to the ability to move away from offending. Without safe and secure housing, other post-release needs (such as education and employment) are difficult to pursue and maintain. In rural areas, suitable housing options are generally more limited than in urban areas: this includes affordable rental options and government-subsidised public housing, which are often the only suitable options for those released from prison given histories of poverty and disadvantage.

Access to employment

Employment has also consistently been linked to desistance from crime, and conversely unemployment is a known criminogenic risk factor (Raphael and Winter-Ebmer, 2001). Meaningful employment can elicit a sense of pride for those released from prison in the face of shame and stigma, and can serve as a mode of inclusion and connection to prosocial peers, as well as offering obvious economic benefits. For those who commit subsistence-related offences, a lack of access to the most basic needs drives lawbreaking to survive: therefore, stable, long-term employment can reduce the need to offend to meet one's basic needs. However, in some rural areas, scarce job opportunities may render it difficult to acquire post-release employment, particularly work that is meaningful and fulfilling to the individual. The stigma associated with having a criminal record is also a significant barrier to employment, which may be exacerbated in rural locations where the likelihood of 'knowing' someone's history is amplified due to the close-knit nature of some RRR communities.

Access to transport

There exist a series of rural-specific transport challenges associated with, for example, community-based orders. In many jurisdictions, adhering to bail, probation and parole conditions or attending court may warrant travel, a simpler proposition in urbanised settings replete with public transport options, but difficult in rural places – and accentuated by, say, the lack of access to a vehicle or absence of a driving licence. Challenges in accessing transportation can greatly jeopardise the chances of fulfilling parole or order obligations, therefore increasing the risks of reincarceration for breaches based on non-attendance and lack of engagement (Zajac et al, 2014). Transportation is also critical to acquiring housing post-release (attending open houses, for example), securing employment and undertaking education, all of which support desistance from crime.

Access to communications

Social and geographical isolation of rural locations results in differences in internet access and affordability compared with metropolitan settings (Collins and Wellman, 2010). 'Broadband technology that facilitates internet connectivity is poorer in rural and regional communities' (Smith, 2020: 76) leading, essentially, to a rural–urban digital divide. Rural communities often rely on satellite or fixed wireless technology, impeding access to online justice infrastructure, which can lead to breaches of justice obligations (such as non-reporting while on parole). In Australia, there is disproportionate representation of Aboriginal and Torres Strait Islander persons incarcerated for justice-related offending, which includes breaches of order obligations (Australian Law Reform Commission, 2017). In the context of the COVID-19 pandemic, justice processes have been required to transition online in some countries to maintain physical distancing, hence the inaccessibility of online communications is increasingly disadvantageous (for example Baldwin et al, 2020).

Access to legal and support services

In RRR communities globally, there is often a relative shortage of services and supports across many domains of social welfare – mental health support, drug and alcohol counselling, disability services – particularly in the most remote areas. For those released from prison, adequate support is essential to post-release well-being, integration, survival and desistance from crime. The lack of healthcare options in rural locations may limit one's ability to receive support and treatment for mental health needs, which, for some, are directly related to offending behaviour. In many RRR communities, there are reduced opportunities to access adequate legal support as needed (for example Hale et al, 2021). Urban-based organisations may visit RRR communities on a circuit, and therefore access becomes infrequent and disjointed.

In urban locations, navigating the support system is challenging owing to its complex and fragmented nature, something which individuals released from prison find particularly difficult to navigate at the point of release, a time characterised by uncertainty and fear. These challenges are likely to be amplified for those in rural locations who may be required to travel to central business districts on different days of the week to access different services. These challenges can result in individuals not accessing the supports they need to pursue desistance pathways within RRR communities because it becomes too burdensome.

Complexities and nuance surrounding rural punishment

The complexities and nuances surrounding rural punishment (including prisons) are starkly apparent. Although this chapter has referred to 'rural punishment' and 'rural prisons', to assume there exists a monolithic approach to either would be inaccurate. It is important to acknowledge that the design and operation of prisons varies markedly from one place to another, including across rural spaces. The negotiation and navigation of punishment and imprisonment in rural locations is nonetheless unique, relative to urban settings, and warrants further scholarly exploration.

The strong support for prison development in some rural communities, from a critical perspective, may be perceived as contributing to the maintenance of a mass incarceration trajectory, oft coupled with numerous widespread, detrimental impacts. After all, prisons can be traumatising spaces, particularly so for women with histories of complex trauma and victimisation that are exacerbated in the penal space (Hale, 2020). Prisons, indeed, can provide the mechanism for the perpetration of state-sanctioned violence through, for example, solitary isolation, strip-searching or conditions that facilitate high rates of male prison rape (Booyens et al, 2004). The injurious impacts of rural prison siting and development are not just felt at the individual level but may also extend to the environment (Greenfield, 2018). Take, for example, prison overcrowding, which produces an excess of waste dumped into nearby waterways, or the building of prisons in environmentally sensitive areas. Questions may therefore abound regarding whether these harms are known by rural communities, and if they are why there then is persistent support for prison development.

This chapter has discussed probable drivers of punitive attitudes and support for prisons in rural spaces. What has become apparent is that the stance which many criminologists (particularly critical) and other scholars might take against imprisonment as a response to crime – that prisons are ineffectual and harmful in many aspects – is undoubtedly not one which is shared unanimously by rural citizens. Care ought to be taken not to reduce this to simply an 'out of sight, out of mind' explanation in making sense of the phenomenon of geographically remote prison siting. While prisons may well be physically out of sight, the realities of the treatment of prisoners themselves are likely to be front of mind for those rural citizens who consider imprisonment an appropriate, deserved – perhaps even essential – form of punishment.

Indeed, much of what we might understand at a community level of what is to be done about the question of law and order is divided by political ideology. At an individual level, how one sees crime causation directly informs one's support for particular ameliorative solutions. In other words, if one was to view crime as originating as a rational choice made by a rational individual, absent of regard for wider social forces, preferences for punishment would be likely to be highly individualistic and punitive – in other words, supportive of imprisonment – as noted in rural areas. Legitimate differences in political ideology must therefore also be acknowledged when considering the place of prisons in rural spaces and reformative efforts more broadly.

Somewhat ironically, in the context of rural economic decline and the subsequent role of wider social forces such as poverty and inequality in crime causation, as well as the persuasive economic incentives of prison development, the human impacts of imprisonment are often disregarded. As Yanarella and Blankenship (2008: 122) note, 'the "success" of this economic development strategy hinges on the suffering of one's fellow citizens ... the corrections industry is a component of an economy built on human misery'. While this perspective may be welcomed by many criminologists, it is important to acknowledge the realities of life for rural citizens who, in the face of rural decline, may support prison development. If prisons in rural communities are seen to (or do) provide access to one's basic needs – sustenance, housing, healthcare – through the provision of stable, well-paying employment, then such support can be understood very well.

This is in no way to suggest that prison development in rural areas is a positive development or a remedy for social problems. Of course, economic development through other, less injurious, ventures, alongside investment in social welfare, would be far more beneficial in meeting the needs of rural communities. It is to say, though, that the phenomenon of rural punishment and prison siting is abounding in complexity and nuance, and scholars ought to be sensitive to the local context.

Conclusion

Prisons are more often sited in rural locations because of both real and perceived economic benefits. However, the promised economic benefits of prison development are not always felt by host communities. This is both concerning and saddening – prison development in rural areas often preys on the relative economic deprivation of rural communities in the context of rural decline, the very same disadvantage with the potential to propel individuals into the criminal justice system.

To site more prisons in urban centres does not alleviate this issue either. Prisons are not the remedy for societal problems. Building more prisons, regardless of location, will not prove to reduce levels of crime; if anything, incarceration is a criminogenic experience, often fuelling further offending through the amplification of disadvantage and exacerbation of trauma. Notwithstanding this, political decision-making in majoritarian electoral systems is highly influenced by public sentiments – a crucial factor in the development and implementation of criminal justice policies.

Notes

[1] Importantly, despite the focus on prisons in this chapter, prisons are by no means the only location whereby a person might be held as their liberty is removed: a person can also be held in custody at a police station, remand centre, juvenile detention centre, immigration detention centre, military prison or secure facilities in psychiatric hospitals (White and Perrone, 2005: 207).

[2] There are arguments that prisons can offer long-term protection, if they capture the individual's primary criminal years. That is, old men do not commit as much crime proportionally to young men.

[3] This may not be relevant to those persons who come from rural communities and whose social connections, therefore, may be located nearby to rural prisons, particularly so for Indigenous persons.

References

ABS (Australian Bureau of Statistics) (2016) '2016 Census QuickStats'. Available from: https://quickstats.censusdata.abs.gov.au/census_services/getproduct/census/2016/quickstat/SSC20052 [Accessed 26 May 2021].

AHURI (Australian Housing and Urban Research Institute) (2004) 'The role of housing in preventing re-offending', *AHURI Research and Policy Bulletin*, 36. Available from: https://www.ahuri.edu.au/sites/default/files/migration/documents/AHURI_RAP_Issue_36_The_role_of_housing_i n_preventing_re-offending.pdf [Accessed 27 May 2021].

Alexander, M. (2010) *The New Jim Crow: Mass Incarceration in the Age of Colorblindness*, New York: New Press.

Armborst, A. (2017) 'How fear of crime affects punitive attitudes', *European Journal on Criminal Policy and Research*, 23(3): 461–81.

Australian Law Reform Commission (2017) 'Offences that lead to a sentence of imprisonment', *Pathways to Justice: An Inquiry into the Incarceration Rate of Aboriginal and Torres Strait Islander Peoples* (ALRC Report 133), Sydney: Commonwealth of Australia, pp 111–16. Available from: https://www.alrc.gov.au/wp-content/uploads/2019/08/final_report_133_amend ed1.pdf [Accessed 26 May 2021].

Baldwin, J.M., Eassey, J.M. and Brooke, E.J. (2020) 'Court operations during the COVID-19 pandemic', *American Journal of Criminal Justice*, 45(4): 743–58.

Bales, W.D. and Mears, D.P. (2008) 'Inmate social ties and the transition to society: does visitation reduce recidivism?', *Journal of Research in Crime and Delinquency*, 45(3): 287–321.

Been, V. (1993) 'What's fairness got to do with it? Environmental justice and the siting of locally undesirable land uses', *Cornell Law Review*, 78(6): 1001–85.

Binder, G. (2002) 'Punishment theory: moral or political?', *Buffalo Criminal Law Review*, 5(2): 321–72.

Bonds, A. (2009) 'Discipline and devolution: constructions of poverty, race, and criminality in the politics of rural prison development', *Antipode*, 41(3): 416–38.

Booyens, K., Hesselink-Louw, A. and Mashabela, P. (2004) 'Male rape in prison: an overview', *Acta Criminologica*, 17(3): 1–13.

Brown, S.D. and Piscitelli, A. (2016) 'A "criminal immigrant" mindset and punitiveness: the Canadian case', *International Journal of Criminology and Sociological Theory*, 9(2): 1–18. Available from: https://ijcst.journals.yorku. ca/index.php/ijcst/article/view/40261/36358 [Accessed 8 March 2022].

Collins, J.L. and Wellman, B. (2010) 'Small town in the internet society: Chapleau is no longer an island', *American Behavioral Scientist*, 53(9): 1344–66.

Corrections Victoria (2021) 'Hopkins Correctional Centre', Corrections, Prison & Parole (Victoria). Available from: https://www.corrections.vic. gov.au/prisons/hopkins-correctional-centre [Accessed 26 May 2021].

Cowan, J. (2017) 'What is it like to live next to a prison?', ABC News (Australia), 20 February. Available from: https://www.abc.net.au/news/2017-02-20/what-is-it-like-to-live-next-to-ararat-prison/8280332 [Accessed 27 May 2021].

Currie, E. (2010) 'Plain left realism: an appreciation, and some thoughts for the future', *Crime, Law and Social Change*, 54(2): 111–24.

Davis, A.Y. (2003) *Are Prisons Obsolete?*, New York: Seven Stories Press.

Donnermeyer, J.F. and DeKeseredy, W.S. (2014) *Rural Criminology*, New York: Routledge.

Eason, J.M. (2008) 'Big house on the prairie: investigating the growth and impact of rural prison siting', PhD thesis, University of Chicago, Chicago.

Eason, J.M. (2017) 'Prisons as panacea or pariah? The countervailing consequences of the prison boom on the political economy of rural towns', *Social Sciences*, 6(7): art 7. Available from: https://www.mdpi.com/2076-0760/6/1/7 [Accessed 8 March 2022].

Eason, J.M. (2019) 'Prisons and the rural ghetto', Dissent. Available from: https://www.dissentmagazine.org/article/prisons-and-the-rural-ghetto [Accessed 26 May 2021].

Edwards, J. (2017) 'Secure unit for Victorian criminals deemed unfit for release to be built at Ararat', ABC News (Australia), 13 February. Available from: https://www.abc.net.au/news/2017-02-13/secure-unit-for-criminals-unfit-to-be-to-be-built-at-ararat/8266248 [Accessed 28 May 2021].

Foucault, M. (1977) *Discipline and Punish: The Birth of the Prison*, New York: Vintage.

Garland, D. (2013) 'The 2012 Sutherland Address: penality and the penal state', *Criminology*, 51(3): 475–517.

Gelb, K. (2011) 'Alternatives to imprisonment: community views in Victoria', Melbourne: Sentencing Advisory Council. Available from: https://www.sentencingcouncil.vic.gov.au/publications/alternatives-imprisonment-community-views-victoria [Accessed 26 May 2021].

Green, D.A. (2008) *When Children Kill Children: Penal Populism and Political Culture*, New York: Oxford University Press.

Greenfield, N. (2018) 'The connection between mass incarceration and environmental justice', NRDC (Natural Resources Defense Council), 19 January. Available from: https://www.nrdc.org/onearth/connection-between-mass-incarceration-and-environmental-justice [Accessed 28 May 2021].

Hale, R. (2020) 'Good intentions: women's narratives of post-release anticipatory desistance in the context of historical and contemporary disadvantage and trauma', *Feminist Criminology*, 15(5): 519–44.

Hale, R., Stewart-North, M. and Harkness, A. (2021) 'Post-disaster access to justice: the road ahead for Australian rural communities', in A. Harkness and R. White (eds) *Crossroads of Rural Crime: Representations and Realities of Transgression in the Australian Countryside*, Bingley: Emerald, pp 167–79.

Hogg, R. (2016) 'Penology from city to country: rurality and penalty in Australia', in A. Harkness, B. Harris and D. Baker (eds) *Locating Crime in Context and Place: Perspectives on Regional, Rural and Remote* Australia, Sydney: Federation Press, pp 129–39.

Huling, T. (2002) 'Building a prison economy in rural America', in M. Mauer and M. Chesney-Lind (eds) *Invisible Punishment: The Collateral Consequences of Mass Imprisonment*, New York: New Press, pp 197–213.

Jacobs, D. and Helms, R.E. (1996) 'Toward a political model of incarceration: a time-series examination of multiple explanations for prison admission rates', *American Journal of Sociology*, 102(?): 323–57.

Jacobs, D. and Wood, K. (1999) 'Interracial conflict and interracial homicide: do political and economic rivalries explain White killings of Blacks or Black killings of Whites?', *American Journal of Sociology*, 105(1): 157–90.

Jones, C. and Weatherburn, D. (2010) 'Public confidence in the NSW criminal justice system: a survey of the NSW public', *Australian and New Zealand Journal of Criminology*, 43(3): 506–25.

Karstedt, S. (2015) 'Trust in transition: legitimacy of criminal justice in transitional societies', in G. Meško and J. Tankebe (eds) *Trust and Legitimacy in Criminal Justice: European Perspectives*, Cham: Springer, pp 3–32.

Kennedy, J. (2000) 'Monstrous offenders and the search for solidarity through modern punishment', *Hastings Law Journal*, 51(5): 829–908.

Koritansky, P. (2005) 'Two theories of retributive punishment: Immanuel Kant and Thomas Aquinas', *History of Philosophy Quarterly*, 22(4): 319–38.

Loader, I. and Sparks, R. (2016) 'Ideologies and crime: political ideas and the dynamics of crime control', *Global Crime*, 17(3/4): 314–30.

Martinson, R. (1974) 'What works? Questions and answers about prison reform', *The Public Interest*, 35: 22–54.

McClanahan, B. and Linnemann, T. (2018) 'Darkness on the edge of town: visual criminology and the "black sites" of the rural', *Deviant Behavior*, 39(4): 512–24.

Moore, J.M. (2014) 'Is the empire coming home? Liberalism, exclusion and the punitiveness of the British state', *Papers from the British Criminology Conference*, 14: 31–48. Available from: http://britsoccrim.org/new/volume14/pbcc_2014_moore.pdf [Accessed 28 May 2021].

Mulrooney, K. and Wise, J. (2019) 'Punitive attitudes across geographical areas: exploring the rural/urban divide in Canada', *International Journal of Rural Criminology*, 5(1): 19–46.

O'Neill, D., Sands, V. and Hodge, G. (2020) 'P3s and social infrastructure: three decades of prison reform in Victoria, Australia', *Public Works Management & Policy*, 25(3): 214–30.

Pratt, J., Brown, D., Brown, M., Hallsworth, S. and Morrison, W. (2005) *The New Punitiveness: Trends, Theories, Perspectives*, Cullompton: Willan.

Prison Policy Initiative (2021) 'Prison Gerrymandering Project', Prison Policy Initiative. Available from: https://www.prisonersofthecensus.org/ [Accessed 28 May 2021].

Raphael, S. and Winter-Ebmer, R. (2001) 'Identifying the effect of unemployment on crime', *Journal of Law and Economics*, 44(1): 259–83.

Reiman, J. (2007) *The Rich Get Richer and the Poor Get Prison: Ideology, Class, and Criminal Justice* (8th edn), Boston, MA: Allyn and Bacon.

Sakoda, R.T. and Simes, J.T. (2021) 'Solitary confinement and the US prison boom', *Criminal Justice Police Review*, 32(1): 66–102.

Smith, N. (2020) 'Social media, rural communities and crime prevention', in A. Harkness (ed) *Rural Crime Prevention: Theory, Tactics and Techniques*, Abingdon: Routledge, pp 73–83.

Sykes, G.M. (1958) *The Society of Captives: A Study of a Maximum Security Prison*, Princeton, NJ: Princeton University Press.

Thomas, N., van de Ven, K. and Mulrooney, K.J.D. (2020) 'The impact of rurality on opioid-related harms: a systematic review of qualitative research', *International Journal of Drug Policy*, 85: art 102607. Available from: https://doi.org/10.1016/j.drugpo.2019.11.015 [Accessed 8 March 2022].

Tootle, D.M. (2004) 'The role of prisons in rural development: do they contribute to local economies?', Prison Legal News, 1 April. Available from: https://www.prisonlegalnews.org/news/publications/prisons-rural-development-economic-study-deborah-m-tootle-2004/ [Accessed 26 May 2021].

Tubex, H., Brown, D., Freiberg, A., Gelb, K. and Sarre, R. (2015) 'Penal diversity within Australia', *Punishment and Society*, 17(3): 345–73.

Vera (2021) 'Reimagining prison', Vera Institute of Justice. Available from: https://www.vera.org/projects/reimagining-prison [Accessed 2 June 2021].

Wacquant, L. (2009) *Punishing the Poor: The Neoliberal Government of Social Insecurity*, Durham, NC: Duke University Press.

Weisheit, R., Falcone, D.N. and Wells, L.E. (2006) *Crime and Policing in Rural and Small-Town America* (3rd edn), Long Grove, IL: Waveland Press.

White, R. and Perrone, S. (2005) *Crime and Social Control* (2nd edn), Oxford: Oxford University Press.

Wodahl, E.J. (2006) 'The challenge of prisoner reentry from a rural perspective', *Western Criminology Review*, 7(2): 32–47.

Yanarella, E.J. and Blankenship, S. (2008) 'Big house on the rural landscape: prison recruitment as a policy tool of local economic development', *Journal of Appalachian Studies*, 12(2): 110–39.

Zajac, G., Hutchison, R. and Meyer, C.A. (2014) 'An examination of rural prisoner reentry challenges', Center for Rural Pennsylvania, March. Available from: https://www.rural.palegislature.us/download.cfm?file= Resources/PDFs/research-report/rural_prisoner_reentry_2014.pdf [Accessed 27 May 2021].

11

The Future for Rural Criminology: Transcendence and Transformation of Borders

Alistair Harkness, Matt Bowden and Joseph F. Donnermeyer

Introduction

A chance encounter in 1851 occurred in Seneca Falls, New York. Introduced on a street corner to one another by mutual friend Amelia Bloomer, Elizabeth Cady Stanton and Susan B. Anthony formed a lifelong friendship, the suffrage movement emanated and women's right to vote went on to be legislated around the world. Another example of happenstance: choosing to attend a church fete on a hot day in Liverpool in 1957, Paul McCartney happened to hear a local high school band, The Quarrymen, perform. A mutual friend introduced him to John Lennon, who ultimately invited Paul to join the band which later transformed into The Beatles.

Similarly, in academia, as with so many other facets of life, unplanned encounters can have quite profound transformative outcomes. Let's consider the journeys into rural criminology of the authors of this chapter. Alistair Harkness transitioned back into academia in 2011 after a hiatus. A colleague sagely suggested that he find a research niche and, given the university where they worked was in a regional location, a focus on farm crime was chosen largely because of the paucity of focus on this at the time. Fast-forward to 2015 when the Crime, Justice and Social Democracy conference was convened in Brisbane, and attended by Joe Donnermeyer who travelled there from Columbus, Ohio, as a keynote speaker. "Let's have lunch!" he declared within no more than a few minutes of meeting, and thus began an international collaborative friendship.

The following year, Alistair and Joe met in person again at the 2016 conference of the American Society of Criminology in New Orleans. It was at this conference that Matt Bowden became entwined in the field, having been encouraged by colleagues in Europe – who knew he was travelling there from Dublin – to make the acquaintance of Joe. For Matt, with his sociological background, a realignment to rural criminology was driven most notably by a curious doctoral student whom he had agreed to supervise and for whom rural crime was the abiding research focus. And it was at this conference that Alistair and Matt first met, too.

Joe's history may be a bit longer, but it possesses the same interpersonal dynamics. Back in the late 1970s while working at Purdue University, he met G. Howard Phillips from The Ohio State University (OSU) at a conference. Philips had acquired grants to develop rural crime prevention from the Ohio Farm Bureau Federation and the US Department of Agriculture. Joe's interest in rural crime was only just beginning. Subsequently, Joe co-edited a book with him and other colleagues, published in 1982. It was arguably the first book to focus exclusively on rural crime (Carter et al, 1982). By then, Joe had moved to OSU to work with Phillips but began to drift away from rural crime studies after Phillips retired, nearly to the point of no return, while pursuing other areas of scholarly interest. However, he came back to rural crime under the influence of Ralph Weisheit and colleagues at Illinois State University, who wrote what was then the most advanced academic treatment of various rural crime topics (Weisheit et al, 1996). Soon after, Joe enjoyed a rich writing partnership with Elaine Barclay and Pat Jobes during his many frequent visits to the University of New England in New South Wales, Australia; and a long-lasting and continuing relationship with Walter S. DeKeseredy, Director of the Center for Violence Research at West Virginia University. Without Ralph's influence, Joe would not have been around to meet Elaine, Pat, Walter, Alistair, Matt and dozens of other rural crime scholars.

As is often the case at professional conferences, much of the 'plotting and planning' and advancement of ideas occurs at informal occasions, over meals or drinks. Ideas for books, papers, future roundtables and so much more were discussed, as well as the future of rural criminology itself. One more meeting of the American Society is worth noting: it was the 2019 conference in San Francisco, where Alistair and Matt met in person again – and this book series was born.

This book is the first in the Bristol University Press Studies in Rural Crime series. The ten preceding chapters have canvassed an array of transformative matters in the field of rural criminology. This chapter will consider the past, present and future of rural criminology, considering its transformation from a niche area of interest in the criminological field, oft overlooked, to what has become a burgeoning subdiscipline in its own right with an enviable growth trajectory. In so doing, it will consider the notion of borders in a globalised world, the role and importance of networks, rural criminology as public criminology, and it will ruminate on what the future might hold.

Transcending and transforming borders in a globalised world

Even in a globalised world, both physical and intangible borders persist. Tertrais (2021) offers a thought-provoking assessment of this persistence, noting that while in the 1990s a perpetually borderless world seemed inevitable, this has been tested more recently by terrorism, migration and pandemics.

Thinking geographically, sometimes these borders can be glaringly obvious, such as with island nations. Some borders are curious: take the Caucasus Mountains, for example, which serve as a barrier between Europe and Asia, and places within such as Chiatura where someone might live on one continent and work on another each day (Bald and Bankrupt, 2019b[1]). Other borders are controversial and contentious, both historically and now – such as the divide between Northern Ireland and the Republic of Ireland, and in Kashmir between India and Pakistan. Borders transform, too, with geographic locations merging or separating: the collapse of the Soviet Union between 1989 and 1991 is an obvious example, as is the emergence of South Sudan from Sudan in 2011. Borders can be solid and nearly impenetrable such as with North Korea, or much more fluid as with countries in the European Union where transit from one nation state to another is no longer subject to border crossings and in many instances the euro serves as a common currency.

Even within nation states, borders exist – between states, provinces, counties, prefectures, departments and so on. Less tangible are the borders, real or perceived, not necessarily between nation states but between 'the urban' and 'the rural'. Places such as Cumbria in England's north-west and the Northern Territory in Australia's top end are examples of predominantly 'rural' bordered places. But borders can also exist, not explicitly as lines on a map, but intangibly. Here we can think of the divide which has emerged in the US in recent years, between the so-called 'blue' (Democrat) east and west coast states and 'red' (Republican) rural states, where attitudes to mask mandates and other responses to COVID-19 are based more on political partisanship than on science and evidence-based policy. Indeed, while the virus respects no borders whatsoever, the distribution and uptake of COVID-19 vaccinations presents another border: between developed and developing countries, and between areas of socio-economic advantage and disadvantage.

The urbanised notion of an idyllic crime-free countryside has been explored and debunked extensively elsewhere (for example Harris and

Harkness, 2016), as has the notion of rural horrors (for example DeKeseredy et al, 2014; Scott and Biron, 2016). For instance, Hayden (2021) offers a fresh appraisal of the stereotypes that exist of rural places and people who continue to dominate popular culture depictions, challenging the assumptions and myths of the 'rural primitive'. In essence, a misguided dichotomy exists between those who perceive rural spaces as crime-free environs – perhaps informed by personal experiences when on holiday – and those who view rural spaces as unrefined backwaters, as less sophisticated, or as sites of horror as portrayed in some aspects of popular culture. Nevertheless, there is a boundary in the minds of many: of the 'here' and of the 'there'; between insiders and outsiders.

Borders, whether physical or metaphorical, are often guarded and protected vigorously. For instance, we can consider the former border between East and West Berlin, in the form of a wall replete with armed guards. And let us not forget the four year-long campaign from 2017 for (and faltering attempts to construct) a physical wall along the length of the US–Mexico border. Metaphorical borders, though, are much more nuanced. Different tones, whether verbal or non-verbal, quickly signify who might be from which side of a border; expressions and mannerisms differ greatly between, say, the office worker and the farm hand.

Academic borders are indeed metaphorical, but nonetheless pervasive. In fact, it can be argued that the hair-splitting differences which define subdisciplinary boundaries are the central driving characteristic of scholarship in many fields of science, like criminology. The so-called right methods, the right theory and the right colleagues can dominate thinking and turn a healthy criminological imagination into a goose-stepping rigidity of the brain. Closing the proverbial gate to others can be misperceived by those who slammed it shut as proof of their superior scientific rigour and standards. It only means, however, that they are a part of the anatomy familiar to proctologists all around the world. As the rural criminological community matures over the next several decades, it needs be mindful of not losing its imagination, and of elitist forms of exclusion. All who study rural crime, regardless of academic background, and all who address rural security and safety issues, including law enforcement, community leaders and citizens, are rural criminologists. Otherwise, rural criminology will resemble so many other subdisciplines within criminology.

The globalised nature of rural crime

Since 2007, more than half of the world's population now reside in urbanised areas: that is, urbanisation is a relatively recent trend, and one that is set to continue. It is projected that more than two thirds of the world's population will reside in urban areas by 2050 (Ritchie and Roser, 2018). Throughout the nineteenth and twentieth centuries, there was in the Western world an exodus from the rural to the urban, initially as a consequence of the Industrial Revolution whereby the thirst for (often cheap) labour saw mass migration from agrarian-based rurality to the rapidly growing cities of the world. More contemporaneously, in places such as Australia there has been net migration to cities (see for example, Hugo, 2002) brought about by rural unemployment combined with the lure and promise of city life. In an Australian context, this has been combined with the mechanisation of agriculture, the decline in rural-based services such as banks, and a lack of appeal in a working rural life. However, the rural population decline has not been universal across regional areas (Lee and Clancey, 2016) with some larger regional centres continuing to grow (Coverdale, 2016). COVID-19 has seen a reversal of trends somewhat in places such as Australia with a retreat to the country, at least for those who can afford it, as city living is no longer essential in the Zoom age and sea-changer / tree-changer lifestyle changes have become desirable.

There is, most certainly, a sense of ebb and flow. In the latter half of the nineteenth century, railways allowed for development and expansion of the rural – an expansion into previously uncharted territories. Ponder two examples: in the US, the railroads connected the Atlantic with the Pacific and, in so doing, opened up the literal middle of America, and in the early part of the twentieth century in Australia, The Ghan railway connected Adelaide with Alice Springs (and very much later in 2004, Darwin). In both cases, trains opened up new territories, although this often came at the expense of first-nations inhabitants of these areas. By the turn of the twenty-first century, with massive demand for iron ore and other minerals, large tracts of remote Australia have again been opened up, this time for resource extraction: the trains are back, as they traverse relentlessly from outback mine to coastal port, and then the commodities onwards to furnaces in China and elsewhere.

We can think of the train in a metaphorical sense too. The enormous paradigm shifts that have occurred in recent decades – though advances in transportation and technology, and changes in economic dogma (particularly from the 1980s onwards) – have led to an overlooking of rural areas and, perhaps, an ignorance of rural matters and rural people. Created here, then, is the hitherto two worlds of 'the rural' and 'the urban': the places that prosper (although let us not forget relative poverty) and those that do not.

Take, for example, the cities of the countries of the former USSR and the provincial parts of these same countries – and other rural settings, too; the places that have prospered since the fall of the Soviet Union and those left behind – the places where the train no longer travels or does not stop; where the weeds have grown over the tracks and where there is little or no infrastructure in place; where people fend for themselves without the nation state casting a second glance. That is, these two worlds have been on quite different trajectories. Similarly, in the US there exists now a notion of 'flyover states' – places, such as West Virginia, where more air travel occurs above a state than to the state (Champion Traveler, 2021).

In some parts of the world, the rural has been all but completely forgotten. In Venezuela, in light of a serious economic and social crisis, resources are directed to the capital Caracas at the expense of places beyond the city – places such as Parmana, where policing, road maintenance, healthcare and public utilities are no longer funded and have essentially been abandoned. 'And the burden of the country's collapse has fallen largely in Venezuela's provinces, where many residents have been effectively cut-off from the central government', a circumstance that has led inevitably to smuggling and cross-border trade for survival (Kurmanaev, 2020).

Rural areas are not overlooked by perpetrators of crime and harm when it comes to accessing and plundering resources – that is, rural offending occurs across borders, yet these matters are oft overlooked by criminologists in developed countries. An example of the intersect between borders, the environment and criminality comes from Moreh in Manipur, on the Indian side of the Myanmar border in India's remote north-east (Bald and Bankrupt, 2019a). Notwithstanding a ban imposed by the Myanmar government in 2014 on the exporting of old-growth teak logs – a popular hardwood in India, China, Europe and elsewhere – illegal logging persists despite the potential for lengthy prison sentences. Loggers get paid more (and often in drugs) than if they were to work as a farm hand (Salopek, 2020). In addition to teak smuggling, Moreh is a bidirectional smuggling hub for drugs, gold and firearms into India from Myanmar and for precursor chemicals for drugs, and wildlife and exotic flora into Myanmar (Mahadevan, 2020).[2]

Consider, too, the example of illegal sand mining in India, to illustrate criminality across rural and urban boundaries. A burgeoning middle class is spurring economic growth in that country, which is in turn is supporting a construction boom. This is having an enormous environmental impact, contributed to by the illegal mining of sand for concrete used in the construction sector (Hawley, 2017). With an insufficient quantity of legally obtainable sand available, supply and demand economics has led to sand being illegally extracted (Menon, 2018). Referred to as 'India's gold', this illegality is the work of organised criminals dubbed the 'sand mafia' and a black market has been created that is destroying riverbeds, canals and beaches (Hawley, 2017). Another by-product of this illegal extractive operation is the corruption of public officials (Walsh, 2017) and underpayment or non-payment of royalties to government for mineral extraction (Gupta, 2010). Lack of data, though, masks the real extent of illegal sand mining in India (Kukreti, 2017). This is a matter with grave consequences for rural communities. As rural crime scholars and practitioners the world over, we need to expand our horizons and take greater interest in issues such as this.

This is why research into these rural spaces is important, if for no other reason than to tell a story about the crimes and harms that affect rural peoples and rural communities. For example, green technologies are praised for their so-called eco-friendly nature and of their potential to slow down and perhaps reverse global warming. But it can present as a green idyll, a glossy stereotype like the one we know as the rural idyll. The lithium, nickel, cobalt and other precious metals needed for green technologies come from mining activities that poison water, destroy forests and threaten the health of the people who live in nearby villages, much as coal mining did and continues to do in rural regions throughout the world as it industrialised over the past 200 years and more. Now, add in untold stories of genocide in rural areas, of cross-border smuggling, of violence against rural women, of victimisation of farm property and violence against farm families. Despite rural criminology's roar, there remains even greater silence. Rural criminological scholarship – from the most qualitative and narrative-based research to the most quantitative explanatory approaches – can tell those stories and place a human face on the ways the rural suffers.

Rural criminology: the past to the present

Metaphorically, borders exist in academia based on geography, wealth and language, as well as between insiders and outsiders. That is, borders exist between the scholars in resource-rich institutions able to employ research assistants and attend conferences, and those in other places with little but good ideas and hard graft. So too do borders exist between a cohort of scholars and practitioners, with the former shy of public scrutiny and engagement, content in a bubble of academic peers.

Criminology, as a whole, has become somewhat of a leviathan. Rural criminology, though, offers something different: an academic space with humble beginnings, but with a bright future with a public criminological outlook. Now a subdiscipline in its own right, it is very much in a growth phase. Those who operate in this space have not Balkanised, as has been the experience in other disciplines and subdisciplines. Indeed, rural criminology offers a glimpse of what is possible to transcend these borders, to break them down and to offer journeys through and beyond them.

Rural crime itself is by no means a new phenomenon – people have been offending against one another regardless of geography, and premodern and predominantly rural, agrarian societies were much more violent and bloody (Eisner, 2014). In terms of the formal study of rural crime, though, there have been various sporadic pieces of research work dating back to the 1930s (Smith and Byrne, 2018) but the concentrated and organised study of rural crime is much more contemporary, and not yet a generation old. There is even a rare statistical study comparing crime rates across manufacturing, mining and agricultural communities of England and Wales published in 1839 (Rawson, 1839).

Along the way, as criminology developed, ironically during a time when the world's population was much more rural than it is today, the focus was almost exclusively on urban crime, accompanied by many facile stereotypes in the criminological literature about the rural, and of differences from the urban that became cemented into the habitus of the discipline. A great deal of the rural neglect during the first eight decades of the twentieth century can be traced to the Chicago School of Sociology. Its penchant for distinguishing changes in urban neighbourhoods and drawing concentric circles to identify borders to differentiate safe places from the not-so-safe places, also served to intellectually shut out the hinterland. This metaphorical border is falling down, but remains strong among many in criminology throughout the world today.

It is impossible to point to a single 'in the beginning' event that started it all, but by the mid-1970s, interest in rural crime began to emerge. In the US, it was the establishment of the National Rural Crime Prevention Center (NRCPC) at The Ohio State University under the leadership of G. Howard Philips. An edited book (Carter et al, 1982) was published, a national conference was held at OSU, and a series of 'farm and home' security pamphlets were written. Although the funding for NRCPC lasted only a few short years, it brought attention to the issue of crime, but mostly among rural sociologists, not criminologists. Through their research, funded by the research arm of the Colleges of Agriculture in the US land-grant system of universities, two clusters of research were undertaken, one on farm crime and the other on the impacts of boomtowns during various energy developments projected of the 1970s and 1980s.

Meanwhile, in both Australia and England, scattered scholarship also began. In Australia, O'Connor and Gray's study (1989) of crime in the small town of Walcha, New South Wales and the edited work of Chappell and Egger (1995) from a national conference on violence that included rural and remote regions, represent two examples of pioneering scholarship there. Chambliss's (1964) analysis of vagrancy laws in England, and both Hopkins's (1985) and Jones's (1979) analysis of poaching helped begin rural criminology's development in the United Kingdom (Smith and Byrne, 2018). Rural crime studies in Canada proceeded at the same pace as Australia, the United Kingdom and the US, with scattered studies of crime and Indigenous peoples (Auger et al, 1992) and rural policing, among others topics (Wood, 1991). Wood (1990) was the first to propose a critical viewpoint for rural criminology, advocating specifically for a left realist perspective.

Rural crime studies from these four countries, often referred to as 'the big four', may have begun rural criminology, but this is not meant as a salutary phrase as much as it is a recognition that a greater and greater international character is necessary to make the discipline grow and mature. Weisheit et al's first edition in 1996 of *Crime and Policing in Rural and Small-Town America* marks the beginning of this expansion, despite the book's title. The reason is that it coalesced a great deal of the extant literature at that time. Soon after, waves of diverse research on homicide, violence, testing social disorganisation theory with rural data, farm victimisation, environmental crime and the impacts of energy development in a rural context began, and many other topics. With every swell came more studies from scholars focused on regions of the world other than the big four (Donnermeyer, 2019).

Recognising that the kinds of crime that happen in rural areas can be influenced by the economic, social and cultural influences, and often dominance, of cities, the nature of cross-border crime, such as smuggling of people, drugs, livestock and other fauna, flora, archaeological artefacts and many other commodities, the continued deleterious effects of energy development projects on rural peoples and communities, plus many more crime and criminal justice issues with a decided rural dimension – all of it means that rural criminology will continue to internationalise as it expands.

Six challenges to forge new frontiers and transform the field

What follows are six key challenges. These are challenges in both senses of the word: first as hurdles to overcome, and second as an invitation to engage. For each, the problem is identified and a response is offered for us, collectively, to forge new frontiers across borders and to transform the field. This chapter advocates for: internationalising rural criminology as public criminology; addressing the isolation of rural criminology through networks; the need for an expansion of the infrastructure of scholarship and information; the crafting of a universal definition of 'rural'; increased weight placed on rural narratives; and the development of rural-adjusted theories.

Rural criminology as internationalised public criminology

The development of rural criminology thus far has been somewhat scattered. For instance, rural criminology in Ireland is in its infancy. In Africa, an emerging group of scholars have made great strides in coalescing a network of colleagues and students around the study of rural crime. Rural criminologists energised by recent developments, though, are emerging throughout the world and getting important work published, in places such as Sweden, Slovenia and elsewhere. A greater number of scholars in countries where rural criminology as a specific field of study is more established (such as the

US and Australia) are increasingly mobilised to publish on matters associated with rural criminology in their countries of origin, such as China.

There is much more to be done in order to break down borders that still exist. Metaphorical borders in our knowledge consumption will always exist. Take international news reporting, for instance. A flood in New Orleans in the US or in southern Germany will make it to the nightly news around the world, and perhaps with quite some prominence. The same cannot be said of the floods elsewhere, such as those in 2021 which killed, injured or displaced 669,000 people in west and central Africa (OCHA, 2021).

So, too, with research studies. Eberhard et al (2021) advise that there are 7,139 living languages globally. These can be concentrated in relatively small geographic areas. Take, for example, Dagestan, a republic in the North Caucasus mountains, where there are more than 40 languages spoken in a population of three million people in a country of 50,300 square kilometres (19,400 square miles) (Dobrushina et al , 2017). Residents of one village might not understand those of the next village – we live in a globalised world and yet there are many instances where it is still small, still local.

As with many other disciplines, across academia broadly and in the social sciences specifically, the vast bulk of dialogue both written and verbal is provided in English alone. A notable exception was a colloquium on Safety, Resilience and Community: Challenges and Opportunities Beyond the City, which was convened by Vania Ceccato and colleagues in September 2020 with sessions offered in English or Swedish. But such examples are few and far between. What is needed is a concerted effort to break down the barriers than limit or prohibit the excellent work that is being carried out in non-English speaking parts of the world: to ignore this work is akin to being blindfolded.

Rural criminology literature, especially in book form, has hitherto been in English and emanating predominantly from the US (for example Weisheit et al, 1994; Donnermeyer and DeKeseredy, 2014; DeKeseredy, 2021), the UK (for example Mawby and Yarwood, 2016) and Australia (Hogg and Carrington, 2006; Barclay et al, 2007; Harkness et al, 2016; Harkness and White, 2021). Herein lies an issue, as these countries dominate the discourse and the theoretical development of the field. There has been recently an expansion beyond these countries, such as Ceccato's (2016) analysis of rural crime and safety in Sweden, but many voices on crime and criminology beyond the urban places of these three countries have largely been excluded from the traditional criminology.

To address this, greater effort must be made to incorporate non-English perspectives – perhaps though the array of growing networks. One example could be the regular inclusion of online roundtables, panels and so on that are offered in a language other than English and which can then be subtitled.

The technology exists; it can happen, but it will necessitate engaged scholars taking a leadership role.

Addressing isolation through networks

A sense of isolation can develop for rural criminologists, either because of geographic location or because their research interests do not coincide with others within their institution. Take, for example, the case of a young scholar whose first job was at a university in the Appalachian region of Ohio, and finding that other staff had dismissed rural scholarship as unimportant because they considered it not of the mainstream and not valuable for the advancement of one's criminological career. Yet, the rural population surrounding the university town was deep-set with poverty, organised drug trafficking and drug abuse, and various forms of interpersonal violence. The police departments were small, under-resourced and overburdened, but rather than engage with scholars that might do something good for them, the advice was to focus on databases from big cities or national in scope. Fortunately, he resisted, but the barriers are great and difficult to resist without a supportive network.

Since 2011, there has been much expansion of rural criminology though various networks, with a particular emphasis on international approaches. In terms of books, more recent volumes have adopted an international approach, such as Donnermeyer's (2016) international handbook and Harkness's (2020) edited collecting assessing rural crime prevention. The growth of an internationalised network of rural criminology continues apace, and six landmark developments are significant:

1. the emergence of the *International Journal of Rural Criminology* (IJRC) in 2011;
2. the publication in 2016 of the *Routledge Handbook of Rural Criminology* (Donnermeyer, 2016) and the subsequent creation of the Routledge Studies in Rural Criminology series of longer length monographs;
3. the establishment of the Division of Rural Criminology in the American Society of Criminology in November 2018;
4. the creation of the International Society for the Study of Rural Crime (ISSRC) in March 2019;
5. the launch of the Centre for Rural Criminology (at the University of New England, Armidale, New South Wales) in September 2019; and
6. the creation in May 2020 of the European Society of Criminology's rural crime working group.

Another key development is this book series itself. This first book in the series takes its impetus from all these relatively new energies surrounding the rural as a focus and locus of criminological theory and empirical research – and will serve, it is hoped, as a watershed in the study of rural crime and as a setting-off point for new and different trajectories from scholars and practitioners alike around the globe.

The IJRC, between 2011 and 2021, has published ten issues and 64 articles: 126,000 item views and downloads have come from 157 different countries. The bulk of downloads come from North America (53.0 per cent), followed by Europe (26.9 per cent), Australasia (6.6 per cent), Asia (6.3 per cent), sub-Saharan Africa (5.6 per cent) and the rest of the world (1.6 per cent).

The ISSRC is a stand-out example of the future direction of the field. Happenstance, again! It was casual conversations at a workshop on rural crime held in Churchill in Victoria, Australia, in February 2019 that led to the Society being established a month later, with aims to:

- unite cross-disciplinary international scholars with research interests in rural crime and rural society;
- facilitate collegial alliances and collaborations between researchers and practitioners;
- allow for the sharing of cutting-edge research for engagement and impact;
- promote and organise events;
- provide opportunities for postgraduate and early career researchers to disseminate their work;
- produce valuable evidence-based information that enhance the well-being of rural communities; and
- heighten international scholarly, community and industry awareness of the study of rural crime. (ISSRC, 2021)

There now exists an infrastructure for rural criminology via ISSRC and other networks to draw together a growing global network aided and abetted by technology. Online video conferencing platforms have made 'meetings of the minds' much more readily possible, crucial as the world responded to COVID-19 by pivoting to online meetings when in-person professional meetings were no longer possible. In essence and to an extent, technology has democratised academic conferences. A caveat to this claim, of course, is the limited, tenuous or non-existent access to broadband services in various geographic locations. ISSRC is an exemplar – members have been meeting four times a year since 2019, a series of 90-minute roundtables have been offered, yet no member has met in person.

Expanding the infrastructure of information

For rural criminology to move forward in the third decade of the twenty-first century and beyond, it will be necessary to develop a strong infrastructure of scholarship. One aspect of this infrastructure is to recognise, as previously mentioned, that rural criminologists come in many shapes and sizes, from professors to the police. Anyone who addresses issues associated with rural crime and criminal justice is a rural criminologist. Inclusion creates strong networks, and strong networks enhance intellectual dialogue about theory, research and crime prevention. These networks must have a name and a place for rural criminologists from around the world to meet, and they tie together the scatterings of rural criminologists in various regions and allow them to engage in discussions about rural crime and rural security.

Beyond the networks themselves, there is a great need to continue to develop products that address the rural. Much progress here includes this Research in Rural Crime series for Bristol University Press, and a Routledge series on Rural Criminology. With distinctive editorial policies, they provide complementary opportunities for those who write about rural crime. The revised version of the *International Journal of Rural Criminology* also provides an outlet for rural scholars, along with podcasts, online roundtables and other electronic get-togethers for the rural criminological community. In a sense, a unified cohort of rural criminologists would not have been possible before the advent of social media and video conferencing because these media allow for long distance, face-to-face communication and information exchange without the expense of travelling long distances to a conference. The boundary-blurring power of social media has afforded those who are interested in rural crime studies to be inspired by each other.

There is one final action that must be undertaken, and is in the preliminary planning stage already. This one would also be impossible without the wonders of computers, word processing and the ability to save large caches of information electronically. The next step is to create a curated library of rural crime studies, saved as PDFs or other forms for the electronic storage of documents. Every rural criminologist has a private library of journal articles, book chapters, books, government reports and other kinds of publications. It is time to open the doors of our private libraries to others by creating a communal library, which the next generation of scholars may easily access and use for the development of their own rural-adjusted theory, rural-focused research and rural-customised safety and security programmes.

Crafting a universal definition of 'rural'

With billions of people who live in what is probably millions of small towns, villages and the open countryside around the world, and with the very different ways that countries count up their populations as either living in urban environs or in rural places, it is impossible to develop a single comprehensive, or even a small set of definitions, of what is meant by rural. There is only one universal trait, and it is population size. However, this assertion only begs the question for it is impossible to designate an exact number that differentiates what is rural from what is urban.

Further, it is unwise to attempt definitions that are anything other than single dimensional, that is, other than population size. That is because all other cultural, social and economic dimensions of specific rural localities vary from place to place. They may be features highly correlated with rural localities, but they are not intrinsic to what is meant by rural, for to define rural beyond population size would exclude many localities that display a different set of characteristics. It should be beholden on researchers to describe the places where their research is conducted, and not assume features that may not exist there. To travel down a road of assumptions about the rural may lead scholars to a sign that says 'Next right, Chicago School of Sociology', and we will be right back to the rural stereotypes of yesterday. Again, the only intrinsic and essential property of rural is small population size, even though a universal numeric dividing line to sort places as either rural or urban is impossible to determine.

Relevance and importance of rural narratives

Essential, too, is a conscious recognition of the relevance and importance of rural narratives. As chapters in this volume attest, we cannot assume that the rural is the locus for a simple way of life: rural social life is penetrated by global processes and integrated into divisions of labour. As the chapters by Bowden and Pytlarz (4), Windle (6), Wooff (8) and Stenbacka (9) have discussed, rural practices and connections with the state are reshaped by institutional reform and by the 'liquefaction' of the old solid institutions; and has been respatialised in these respects as they become subdivided into units of governance. Critical here, as Windle (Chapter 6) argues, is the left realist principle of listening to the rural voice: of taking account of what rural people say impacts their lives in relation to crime and security. This, then, ought to be incorporated into our research designs, into policy development, into practical solutions and theorising about the rural.

Crime, justice and security are not just abstract processes but are incorporated into everyday discourse and practice. In their article on crime–talk in the countryside, Pytlarz and Bowden (2019) argue that national- and global-level media representations about crime, together with the politicisation of rural crime, produces a discourse which is empirically observable through how local people talk about crime. We can infer through engaging with rural people's 'talk', the underlying structure that they have internalised. Bourdieu's (Bourdieu and Nice, 1977; Bourdieu, 1991) habitus which captures how actors internalise external reality has analytic merit for us here. Habitus can be accessed through narrative approaches, accessing as it were, the 'narrative habitus' (Fleetwood, 2016) by engaging with rural people's stories; and in the case of rural criminology, about how they experience and bear witness to social and technological change, and how their experiences of crime and (in)security intersect with that process. Similarly, as DeKeseredy (Chapter 5) has articulated how rural women experience the sharp end of patriarchal power, we need to engage with the narratives of the lived experiences of victims of such violence.

Development of rural-adjusted theories

Criminological theory is a set of postulates or assumptions that attempts to bring understanding to an issue, such as why people commit crime or who is more likely to be the victim of a crime. Like all sciences, theory in criminology is subject to peer review. That is, nothing is a theory until it is written up and shared with other scholars who are then presented an opportunity to comment on the theory, perhaps rejecting it, or at the very least, suggesting revisions.

Even though much of this chapter has praised the development of rural criminology over the past couple of decades, it remains true that rural-adjusted theories remain relatively underdeveloped, and that is especially true for theories of the middle range. By middle range is meant theories that focus on a subset of phenomena. For example, DeKeseredy (2021) and colleagues (see Chapter 5) proposed a middle-range theory called 'male-peer support' to explain how patriarchal norms, as learned and reinforced through like-minded men at specific rural places, contribute to violence against women there. Likewise, Matthew Lee and colleagues published a series of articles in various criminological journals testing the assumption behind a theory known as 'civic community' (see, for example, Lee, 2008). It is similar to the systemic version of social disorganisation theory, but varies from it by proposing various relationships, tested statistically, between operationalised measures of 'civility' (such as the percentage of the population who belong to a faith group) and measures of crime (such as the rate of assault) within rural communities.

Mostly, so far, rural criminology has either ignored theory or adopted and applied various criminological theories uncritically. Attempts to rewrite theory, or to create whole new theories for rural contexts, has happened infrequently. Yet, there is no area of rural criminology that could potentially expand its intellectual vigour, or potentially impede its development, than a lack of theory. Furthermore, theory development in rural criminology must take seriously the fundamentally simple definition of rural places as localities with a smaller population. It is the cultural, social and economic contexts, that is, their local social structure, that is the stuff from which rural-adjusted theory can be developed. Therefore, to assume anything more than population size about rural communities retards theory development with assumptions that are not yet subjected to empirical testing, shared with colleagues and, also, that can withstand their criticisms and commentaries.

Conclusion

The various networks that make up rural criminology constitute an assemblage of an eclectic grouping of scholars, students and practitioners alike, with a wide array of ideological perspectives but unified in the key aim of developing new theoretical perspectives and empirical data leading to reformed policy and practice. 'The rural' has hitherto been left out, isolated or left on the fringe in academic discourse. But the rural can be considered in a variety of ways – socially, culturally, politically, economically. And there exists a need for research focused on improving the health, safety and well-being of those that reside in non-urban environments and settings. Rural criminology can provide a unified, engaged, open and collaborative approach,

Notes

[1] Fascinating first-hand insights into borders and the people who live within and across them are offered by the YouTuber vlogger Bald and Bankrupt, who has inspired some of the examples offered in this chapter. Visit his channel at https://www.youtube.com/channel/UCxDZs_ltFFvn0FDHT6kmoXA

[2] Noteworthy is Mahadevan's (2020) research report, 'Crossing the line', which offers an excellent analysis of this town and the illicit trades it supports, and the geopolitical contexts in which smuggling here thrives.

References

Auger, D.J., Doob, A.N., Auger, R.P. and Driben, P. (1992) 'Crime and control in three Nishnawbe-Aski nation communities: an exploratory investigation', *Canadian Journal of Criminology*, 34(3/4): 317–38.

Bald and Bankrupt (2019a) 'Inside India's smuggling town', 1 February [video]. Available from: https://www.youtube.com/watch?v=zK95gclG GCM [Accessed 23 September 2021].

Bald and Bankrupt (2019b) 'Slavic girl meets Georgian man', 5 July [video]. Available from: https://www.youtube.com/watch?v=BC7Oe0jB3dA [Accessed 23 September 2021].

Barclay, E., Donnermeyer, J.F., Scott, J. and Hogg, R. (eds) (2007) *Crime in Rural Australia*, Sydney: Federation Press.

Bourdieu, P. (1991) *Language and Symbolic Power*, Cambridge: Polity Press.

Bourdieu, P. and Nice, R. (1977) *Outline of a theory of practice*, trans R. Nice, Cambridge: Cambridge University Press.

Carter, T.J., Phillips, G.H., Donnermeyer, J.F. and Wurschmidt, T.N. (1982) *Rural Crime: Integrating Research and Prevention*, Montclair, NJ: Allanheld, Osmun.

Ceccato, V. (2016) *Rural Crime and Community Safety*, Abingdon: Routledge.

Chambliss, W.J. (1964) 'A sociological analysis of the law of vagrancy', *Social Problems*, 12(1): 67–77.

Champion Traveler (2021) 'Flyover states: flight data shows which states Americans thin are boring', *Champion Traveler*. Available from: https://championtraveler.com/news/flyover-states-flight-data-shows-which-states-americans-think-are-boring/ [Accessed 11 September 2021].

Chappell, D. and Egger, S. (1995) *Australian Violence: Contemporary Perspectives II*, Archive no. 160. Canberra: Australian Institute of Criminology. Available from: https://www.aic.gov.au/publications/archive/archive-160 [Accessed 28 September 2021].

Coverdale, R. (2016) 'Accessing justice in regional Australia: evolving perspectives and contexts', in A. Harkness, B. Harris and D. Baker (eds) *Locating Crime in Context and Place: Perspectives on Regional, Rural and Remote Australia*, Sydney: Federation Press, pp 108–19.

DeKeseredy, W.S. (2021) *Woman Abuse in Rural Places*, Abingdon: Routledge.

DeKeseredy, W.S., Muzzatti, S.L. and Donnermeyer, J.F. (2014) 'Mad men in bib overalls: media's horrification and pornification of rural culture', *Critical Criminology*, 22(2): 179–97.

Dobrushina, N., Staferova, D. and Belokon, A. (eds) (2017) 'Atlas of multilingualism in Dagestan online', *Linguistic Convergence Laboratory, HSE*. Available from: https://multidagestan.com/about [Accessed 23 September 2021].

Donnermeyer, J.F. (ed) (2016) *The Routledge International Handbook of Rural Criminology*, Abingdon: Routledge.

Donnermeyer, J.F. (2019) 'The international emergence of rural criminology: implications for the development and revision of criminological theory for rural contexts', *International Journal of Rural Criminology*, 5(1): 1–18.

Donnermeyer, J.F. and DeKeseredy, W. (2014) *Rural Criminology*, Abingdon: Routledge.

Eberhard, D.M., Simons, G.F. and Fennig, C.D. (eds) (2021) *Ethnologue: Languages of the World* (24th edn), Dallas, TX: SIL International. Available from: https://web.archive.org/web/20210923155454/https://www.ethnologue.com/ [Accessed 23 September 2021].

Eisner, M. (2014) 'From swords to words: does macro-level change in self-control predict long-term variation in levels of homicide?', *Crime and Justice*, 43: 65–134.

Fleetwood, J. (2016) 'Narrative habitus: thinking through structure/agency in the narratives of offenders', *Crime, Media, Culture*, 12(2): 173–92.

Gupta, S. (2010) ' "They don't want the lokayukta to proceed because these mining permits were given during the tenures of JD-S, Congress and BJP"', *Indian Express*, 20 July. Available from: http://archive.indianexpress. com/news/they-dont-want-the-lokayukta-to-proceed-because-these-min ing-permits-were-given-during-the-tenures-of-jds-congress-and-bjp/649 077/0 [Accessed 10 September 2021].

Harkness, A. (ed) (2020) *Rural Crime Prevention: Theory, Tactics and Techniques*, Abingdon: Routledge.

Harkness, A. and White, R. (eds) (2021) *Crossroads of Rural Crime: Representations and Realities of Transgression in the Australian Countryside*, Bingley: Emerald.

Harkness, A., Harris, B. and Baker, D. (eds) (2016) *Locating Crime in Context and Place: Perspectives on Regional, Rural and Remote Australia*, Sydney: Federation Press.

Harris, B. and Harkness, A. (2016) 'Locating regional, rural and remote crime in theoretical and contemporary context', in A. Harkness, B. Harris and D. Baker (eds) *Locating Crime in Context and Place: Perspectives on Regional, Rural and Remote Australia*, Sydney: Federation Press, pp 1–12.

Hawley, S. (2017) 'The "sand mafia" fuelling India's $120 billion building boom', *ABC News* (Australia), 28 March. Available from: https://www. abc.net.au/news/2017-03-28/the-great-sand-heist-fuelling-india-120-bill ion-building/8390984 [Accessed 10 September 2021].

Hayden, K.E. (2021) *The Rural Primitive in American Popular Culture: All Too Familiar*, Lanham, MD: Lexington Books.

Hogg, R. and Carrington, L. (2006) *Policing the Rural Crisis*, Sydney: Federation Press.

Hopkins, H. (1985) *The Long Affray: The Poaching Wars 1760–1914*, London: Secker & Warburg.

Hugo, G. (2002) 'Changing patterns of population distribution in Australia', joint special issue, *Journal of Population Research and NZ Population Review*, September. Available from: https://www.accc.gov.au/system/files/Fn%20 118%20-%20Hugo%2C%20Changing%20patterns%20of%20populat ion%20and%20distribution.pdf [Accessed 9 March 2022].

ISSRC (International Society for the Study of Rural Crime) (2021) 'About ISSRC'. Available from: https://issrc.net/about/issrc/ [Accessed 24 September 2021].

Jones, D.J.V. (1979) 'The poacher: a study in Victorian crime and protest', *Historical Journal*, 22(4): 825–60.

Kukreti, I. (2017) 'How will India address illegal sand mining without any data?', *Down to Earth*, 30 September. Available from: https://www.down toearth.org.in/news/mining/flouted-with-impunity-58736 [Accessed 10 September 2021].

Kurmanaev, A. (2020) 'Rural Venezuela crumbles as president shores up the capital and his power', *New York Times*, 13 January. Available from: https://www.nytimes.com/2020/01/13/world/americas/Venezuela-collapse-Maduro.html [Accessed 10 September 2021].

Lee, M. and Clancey, G. (2016) 'Placing crime: the failings of urban-centric environmental criminology', in A. Harkness, B. Harris and D. Baker (eds), *Locating Crime in Context and Place: Perspectives on Regional, Rural and Remote Australia*, Sydney: Federation Press, pp 25–34.

Lee, M.R. (2008) 'Civic community in the hinterland: toward a theory of rural social structure and violence', *Criminology*, 46(2): 447–78.

Mahadevan, P. (2020) 'Crossing the line: geopolitics and criminality at the India–Myanmar border', Geneva: Global Initiative Against Transnational Organized Crime. Available from: https://globalinitiative.net/wp-content/uploads/2020/11/Crossing-the-line-Geopolitics-and-criminality-at-the-India-Myanmar-border.pdf [Accessed 11 September 2021].

Mawby, R.I. and Yarwood, R. (2016) *Rural Policing and Policing the Rural: A Constable Countryside?* Abingdon: Routledge.

Menon, N. (2018) 'Illegal sand mining: India's biggest environmental challenge?', *The Weather Channel*, 26 October. Available from https://weather.com/en-IN/india/news/news/2018-10-26-illegal-sand-mining-indias-biggest-environmental-challenge [Accessed 10 September 2021].

O'Connor, M. and Gray, D.E. (1989) *Crime in a Rural Community*, Sydney: Federation Press.

OCHA (UN Office for the Coordination of Humanitarian Affairs) (2021) 'West and Central Africa: flooding situation (as of 30 August 2021)', *Reliefweb*, 31 August. Available from: https://reliefweb.int/report/democratic-republic-congo/west-and-central-africa-flooding-situation-30-august-2021 [Accessed 23 September 2021].

Pytlarz, A. and Bowden, M. (2019) '"Crime-talk", security and fear in the countryside: a preliminary study of a rural Irish town and its hinterland', *International Journal of Rural Criminology*, 4(2): 138–72.

Rawson, R.W. (1839) 'An inquiry into the statistics of crime in England and Wales', *Journal of the Statistical Society of London*, 2(5): 316–44.

Ritchie, H. and Roser, M. (2018) 'Urbanization', *Our World in Data*. Available from: https://ourworldindata.org/urbanization#number-of-people-living-in-urban-areas [Accessed 10 September 2021].

Salopek, P. (2020) 'After a century of logging, Myanmar struggles to preserve its teak groves', *National Geographic*, 5 August. Available from: https://www.nationalgeographic.com/history/article/after-century-logging-myanmar-struggles-preserve-teak-groves [Accessed 11 September 2021].

Scott, J. and Biron, D. (2016) 'An interpretive approach to understanding crime in rural Australia', in A. Harkness, B. Harris and D. Baker (eds) *Locating Crime in Context and Place: Perspectives on Regional, Rural and Remote Australia*, Sydney: Federation Press, pp 14–24.

Smith, K. and Byrne, R. (2018) 'Reimagining rural crime in England: a historical perspective', *International Journal of Rural Criminology*, 4(1): 66–85.

Tertrais, B. (2021) 'The persistence of borders in a globalized world', *World Politics Review*, 22 June. Available from: https://www.worldpoliticsreview.com/articles/29749/the-persistence-of-borders-in-a-globalized-world [Accessed 9 September 2021].

Walsh, B. (2017) 'Corruption, sand mafias and water security on India', *Future Directions International*, 15 March. Available from: https://web.archive.org/web/20180921041925/http://www.futuredirections.org.au/publication/corruption-sand-mafias-water-security-india/ [Accessed 10 September 2021].

Weisheit, R.A, Falcone, D.N. and Wells, L.E. (1994) *Rural Crime and Rural Policing*, Long Grove, IL: Waveland Press.

Weisheit, R.A., Falcone, D.N. and Wells, L.E. (1996) *Crime and Policing in Rural and Small-Town America*, Long Grove, IL: Waveland Press.

Wood, D.S. (1990) 'A critique of the urban focus in criminology: the need for a realist view of rural working class crime', unpublished manuscript, School of Criminology, Simon Fraser University, Burnaby, BC.

Wood, D.S. (1991) 'Violent crime and characteristics of twelve Inuit communities in Baffin Region, NW', doctoral dissertation, School of Criminology, Simon Fraser University, Burnaby, BC. Available from: https://summit.sfu.ca/item/7361 [Accessed 9 March 2022].

Index

CPSIA information can be obtained
at www.ICGtesting.com
Printed in the USA
BVHW092046250722
642968BV00002B/30

9 781529 217759